"A hilarious, albeit accurate portrayal of life as a young wildland firefighter. As wildland firefighters, we have all lived these stories in some way or another; to read this book took me back in time and evoked the unforgettable smell of smoke as if it were yesterday."
~ **Emily Webb, former wildland firefighter**

"This is one of the few books – if not the only one – to accurately portray the realities of being a wildland firefighter. Ben Walters tells the story for many of the young men and women who live this life, and he does it with humor, sadness, and vivid storytelling that captures the days and nights on the fireline. *FIRE CREW: Stories from the Fireline* offers insight into why people do this hard, dirty and dangerous work."
~ **Marc Rounsavile, Area Commander Team 4, retired**

"Walters' narrative offers a unique insight into the archetypal character of the American wildland firefighter."
~ **Steve Jackson**

"Light, humorous and easy to read, this book brings back memories of a fun time to be working in fire. It's extremely accurate - I know because I was there!"
~ **Bob Mallett, Deputy Fire Management Officer, Idaho Falls District**

BEN WALTERS

FIRE CREW
Stories from the Fireline

FIRE CREW: Stories from the Fireline
COPYRIGHT © 2011 Ben Walters

ALL RIGHTS RESERVED

Contact Ben Walters at jbtaktez@msn.com

ISBN-10 061555248X
ISBN-13 9780615552484

Privacy Notice

_____

Some – but not all – names have been changed to
respect privacy (or, in some cases, to protect the guilty).
Organizations, places, situations and descriptions are
otherwise all authentic.

For Sam and Will

Preface

THIS STORY BEGINS IN THE WINTER OF 1993 and ends somewhere around the first part of the 21st century. The narrative is as close as possible to true, based on my memory and my extensive notes from those years. There were so many strange, crazy, and fun times during those fire seasons that it would be a shame not to put it down in writing while I am still young enough to remember so much of it.

I would probably be described by some who worked with me during those years as the quintessential class clown. Once I became comfortable with the people on a fire crew, I was pretty jovial – and loose enough that I would never make it beyond the first tiers of management, regardless of my qualifications and experience. Those with whom I developed a closer relationship during those ten seasons knew me as more introspective than your average buffoon, and able to work hard once in a while. I still count those people as good friends, though we seldom have the opportunity to visit now.

During my fire crew years, I never missed the chance at a good time or a good laugh, whether on the job or off duty – and on fire crews in those days, there wasn't always a clear line between the two. Sometimes life seemed a strange sort of sitcom: real people doing and saying almost unreal things, and unreal situations that really did happen. I was fortunate to witness people at their finest, and sometimes at their not-so-finest, and I became friends with some with whom I'd thought I had nothing in common. Many years and many jobs later, I believe I have finally reached a proper perspective for those days, and I miss them.

If you were a character in one of life's human interest stories that played out somewhere, during some summer, in the United States, in yellow and green or black and gray, I have one remark for you – *It was fun, wasn't it?*

No Happy Hour

ONE OF THE COOLEST THINGS about returning from a firefighting detail is pulling into the home station or yard in your muddy, dusty, scratched-up fire engine. As you make that turn into the parking lot, you are aware of, or at least you are imagining, firefighters from other crews and even office people welcoming you home like a bloodied soldier returning from battle. You ceremoniously pull your rig into the designated parking area, creakily step down from the cab, and do your best to strut your greasy, dirty self into the dispatch office to turn in your time reports and other paperwork. This is, after all, a government job, and with a government job comes lots of paperwork.

This was the scene on July 11, 1999 in Idaho Falls, Idaho, at the Interagency Fire Center. Kelly Hayes and I had just returned from a fire as part of a two-week work detail with a BLM district south of us. What happened to us on that fire was exciting – but that would be an understatement. I had sweated so much and gotten so dirty that my yellow and green Nomex fire clothes were now black and gray, and stiff enough to nearly stand up on their own. I had perpetual crusty things in the corners of my raw eyes that I had long since quit trying to remove. My feet felt like I had walked barefoot over burning glass shards, and my quads, calves, and back muscles were badly knotted up. Ah, but this is typical stuff on what would turn out to be another non-typical day in the fire world.

My work goals that day were to turn in my reports from the detail, re-stock the fire engine with the supplies necessary for initial attack duty, and make the forty-five-mile drive north back to our duty station in Dubois, Idaho. I figured that with all these necessary duties, plus a little jawing and bragging, Kelly and I would be back in Dubois with the rest of the station crew sometime around 5:30 that afternoon. If no fires were burning in the district, we would be off duty at 6:00, opening our first beer at about 6:01, and then in freight-train party mode by 7:00. We had worked hard for the last two weeks, and we were all ready to loosen up.

Then I heard the page. "Ben Walters, please report to dispatch. Ben Walters, report to dispatch."

This could mean only one thing. Fire.

I interrupted my academic discourse with our warehouse manager Avery, and stepped out of the supply building to hustle over to dispatch. I had only my left foot out the door when I saw the smoke column. Holy shit. There would be no happy hour for me in Dubois today.

So You Wanna Be A Firefighter

GROWING UP, I WAS TOLD REPEATEDLY and believed wholeheartedly that you could be anything you wanted to be if you just worked hard enough. I worked pretty hard in those days, at least at the things I wanted to do. I had both toughness and perseverance. In high school, I made very good grades and lifted weights or jogged almost every day. I was a co-captain of the state champion Skyline Grizzly football team. I dated one of the popular senior girls. I drove a brand new, black Chevy four-by-four pickup. With these credentials, and with an overly optimistic attitude about my abilities, I decided to pursue college football and pre-medicine. But I had an unclear vision.

With high school ending in June, and college at the University of Chicago not starting until September, I needed something to do over the summer. Until that summer, I had been bagging groceries at Albertson's, but had pretty much outgrown that and felt like I could make some more money and do something more interesting. This is where the fire crew came in.

My favorite movie then, as now, is *A River Runs through It*. My personality and experiences, I thought, were something of a cross between the two brothers, Norman and Paul Maclean, but more so like Norman, the author of the book the movie was based upon. Norman Maclean had fought forest fires and had also authored a book about that. I wanted to fight forest fires, too, but I had no idea how to go about getting a

3

job; my only familiarity with wildland fire was watching the TV news on the Yellowstone National Park fires of 1988. That type of work looked like just the thing for me!

In late January or early February, my best friend Jake almost offhandedly told me that the Bureau of Land Management (BLM) was hiring new wildland firefighters. They were doing the hiring through the job service, and his mother was a supervisor at the local job service office. I had never heard of the BLM. I thought only the U.S. Forest Service fought wildland (forest and range) fires. Nevertheless, I sprang into action.

The BLM is a federal government agency under the Department of the Interior, the head of which is the Secretary of the Interior – an appointee on the President's cabinet. The BLM is further divided into districts or field offices around the United States; these offices are charged with caring for federal lands and the natural resources located on those lands. These BLM districts and offices are also responsible for preventing and suppressing fires that are on these lands or threatening the resources. Most BLM land could be classified as rangeland; it includes a lot of sagebrush and wide open spaces.

The U.S. Forest Service (USFS), on the other hand, operates under the U.S. Department of Agriculture. Like the BLM, the USFS is in charge of managing natural resources, but in this case, on national forest land – including preventing and suppressing wildland fires on national forests and grasslands. The agencies are very similar in their management of wildland fires, and in fact, on most larger fires the agencies will work cooperatively, because range fires turn into forest fires and vice versa. Sometimes state firefighters or other federal firefighters help out – the National Park Service, Fish & Wildlife Service, and Bureau of Indian Affairs also have firefighters and fire management programs. The premier agencies for wildfire control in the United States, though, are the Bureau of Land Management and the U.S. Forest Service.

In the winter, I applied for a job as a BLM range technician's aide, aka wildland firefighter. Applications are taken early in the year so managers can have crews in place and ready to be trained before the fire season begins in the spring. I remember the application as being many pages, though in my case many of the pages were just left blank because I did not have much job experience.

In reality, most 18-year-old kids' applications are probably like this, unless you have done something stupid *and* gotten caught for it by that time in your life. In that case, you noted your "minor-in-possession of alcohol" citation, and that would preclude you from consideration by the managers, who didn't need any 18-year-old blockheads on a fire crew. Otherwise, I was told, Gary, the local fire control officer (FCO) liked to hire newbies (rookies) with no preconceived notion of firefighting but a good work ethic. This way he had a blank slate to work with instead of some dipstick who inevitably got himself or someone else hurt.

So, armed with my blank slate mentality and the good word of Laura, my friend's job-service mom, I went to my first job interview in March. I met Randy, the assistant fire control officer (AFCO) at the district BLM office. The first thing I noticed about the small office was the decidedly Spartan furnishings and décor of what passed for a reception area: minimum wage postings, sexual harassment postings, equal employment opportunity postings, metal chairs, metal tables, and an outdated auto parts catalogue. There was an ancient, dirty coffeemaker there, with some plain, tan, ceramic government coffee cups, also dirty. The second thing I noticed was the somewhat sweet/musty smell. The sweet smell comes from the chemically treated fire-resistant clothing that I would later learn was called "Nomex." The musty smell was probably from a combination of past fire-season sweat and nerves, the collection of old furnishings, and government cleaning policies (or lack thereof).

I was greeted by Kara, who made me forget my nerves for a bit, because of an instant crush. She was a fire dispatcher at the time, a petite thirty-something babe with medium-length blonde hair and a luscious accent with which she enunciated all her words and letters like the lead singer for REO Speedwagon. Kara drew out her r's when she spoke. She touched the back of a metal chair and said "Wait herrrre a second, I'll let RRRRandy know you've arrrrived."

I waited five minutes or so and the nerves came back. This was my first interview for what I considered to be a real job, and I wasn't really sure what I was supposed to say or what kinds of questions I would be asked. After a few minutes, Kara introduced me to Randy, the AFCO. He stands about six-foot-three and at the time weighed about 220 without an ounce of fat. He sported a mustache like Wild Bill Hickok's, collar-length brown hair, and an iron grip when he shook my hand. At the time, Randy was 28 years old, and though he looked like he could whup some ass, he was super cool to me. Although I didn't know it at the time, Randy had also been a high school teacher and athletic coach, so he knew how to neutralize the punk in an 18-year-old.

Randy told me that fighting fire was hot, hard, dirty, and dangerous work. Sleep would sometimes be a luxury, sore feet and dirt in your teeth would be normal, and you might be gone away from home for weeks at a time. But, he said, glancing to his right at the black and white analog government clock on the wall, that clock keeps on ticking and *cha-ching*. He said it would be a lot like being in the military all summer long. Then he glanced down at my application and said, "You put down Carl Pearson as a reference?"

That just may have sealed the deal for me. Coach Pearson was my football coach, and he was a legend in southeast Idaho. I know I wasn't nearly the best football player Pearson had ever coached, but I also knew he recognized my quiet leadership and work ethic. I knew he would give me a good reference, and now I realized how important that reference could be.

When the interview was finished, Randy and I shook hands, and he said he would be in touch. I knew, though, that there were a boatload of applications for relatively few positions, so I was far from confident when I walked back out of the musty office to my truck. I relived the interview over and over in my mind for the next couple of weeks. I called Randy once or twice and asked if they had made any decisions. I got no concrete answers, but I did receive a letter in the mail around the first of April. The letter began, "Congratulations on your tentative selection for employment with the Bureau of Land Management as

a Range Technician Aide/Wildland Firefighter."
Victory!

I accepted the job with absolutely no reservations. In addition to the acceptance section of the letter, I had to fill out some tax information and emergency contacts. The final part of the letter instructed me to purchase a good pair of boots with at least ten-inch leather tops, and to prepare for the physical fitness test to be administered on the first day – a 1.5-mile run that had to be completed in 12 minutes or less.

I mailed my response the next day and figured I'd better start preparing for the first day of work, which, according to the letter, would be Monday, June 7. Here's what I knew about wildland firefighting so far: grass and sagebrush and trees and stuff catch on fire and the fire makes the air smoky, and the firefighters put it out.

I asked my dad what he knew about firefighting and he said, "Oh, that sounds like *high adventure*." My brother's girlfriend said she had a couple of friends who worked on fires in the summertime with the Forest Service. She said they were always having to pull out their fire shelters and hide from the fire. This is complete bullcrap, but I didn't know it at the time. I didn't even know what a fire shelter was. This was the only information I acquired about firefighting; there wasn't much in the way of internet then.

I started preparing for the physical fitness test. I was pretty fit in those days; I had done lots of jogging and was a pretty muscular 5-foot-10 and about 175 pounds. I figured the test run would be no problem.

So, with all my young man cockiness, I laced up my boots, stepped out into a cool April afternoon, and took off down the road to get a baseline time for the 1.5-mile run. I really thought I would have no problem getting it under 12 minutes the first time.

Well, about a quarter-mile into it, I feel like I'm breathing through a straw, my thighs are burning up, and in my mind I can see a fire racing through the timber at me as I try to put this fire shelter thing over me while I run. I'm thinking, *I am screwed.* There is no way I'm running this hard for a mile and a half. Discouraged, I stopped running and started walking. This is the *first* time I had *ever* quit in the middle of a run on account of its being too hard. Hands on hips, I dejectedly walked back down the road to the house. I knew I had my work cut out for me, but at the moment I just needed some water.

In the weeks that followed, I continued to train for the run. I had done some research, talked to some people, and developed a regimen that seemed to be working. I would run hard for a certain distance, stop and walk for awhile, and then take up running again until I had completed a mile and a half. By the end of May, which was also the end of my senior year in high school, I was able to complete the run in just under 12 minutes. I always like to give myself a little leeway in these situations, though, and the small bit of time I had under 12 minutes was not really much comfort. I'd definitely have to bring my "A" game on that first day.

But I got sidetracked with the rest of life – friends, girlfriends, and saying goodbye to high school. I partied like a rock star. I'm pretty sure this is why I got sicker than hell around the first of June. And I do mean sick.

What nailed me was tonsillitis. My throat wasn't just sore – it felt like the devil had tossed fire down my gullet. Swallowing was an *event*. My head ached, I always felt like I was in a dreamy state, my muscles ached, and I couldn't keep anything down. I would be sitting on the toilet and puking in a garbage can at the same time. By the Friday before the Monday start date, I wasn't feeling even a little better, even though I was on antibiotics.

I spent the weekend just watching TV and lying low. The only thing I was worried about was that run, but it could mean the difference between having this job and working at Albertson's again that summer. Failure was not an option.

So Monday rolled up and I shut off the alarm clock. For sure I could do this measly run, right. That's all I was thinking in the BLM room as they did a roll call. I was sitting there with an ice ball in my stomach, and still screwed-up sick.

At 11:00 a.m. we were dismissed from the classroom and told to regroup in a half hour on the running track at Ravsten stadium in our P.T. clothes. God I was nervous. As I changed into my clothes in the locker room under the stadium bleachers, there was the usual nervous chatter among the job applicants. Firefighters had to pass this test before every fire season in order to qualify, so some had already done it many times before and were spewing forth comments ranging from advice to braggadocio. I just wanted to get it over with.

Out on the track, everybody milled around waiting for Randy and one of the other AFCOs to get us started. Most of the runners were hard-bodied and above average in height, with long hair and a general bad-ass look. Even the girls looked like they could whup you, and they were all good-looking. Most of the guys had cowboy mustaches or goatees. All wore mirrored shades, and none betrayed anything less than full confidence. I milled around with the group, did some fake stretching, and felt weak and small. Maybe it wouldn't have been so intimidating if I weren't still feeling so wretched.

Soon enough, we all gathered on the starting line and prepared to qualify. Two people in particular stood out – James Stoddard and Randy Meyers. The former looked tougher than any guy I had ever seen in person, about 6-foot-4, a muscular 230 or so pounds, with long hair that I found out later had been braided by his Shoshone Indian wife. The latter was also ripped, a black guy about my height. Maybe because of how he was bouncing as he got ready to run, I figured he was going to be one fast muthah.

Stoddard was a *big* guy, with a dusting of gray in his long black braid. He was 35 when I met him, but acted like he was 21, i.e., intelligence not commensurate with age. He wore custom fire boots that went clean up to his knees, and maybe those were why he walked with a stride so long it could be best described as a lope. He was always making "I'm gonna … " proclamations, but never did a damn thing, never got off his ass to improve his life. He did try to do the right thing as a firefighter always, though, almost to a fault – he lived the job, or at least acted like it. He smoked cigarettes like a chimney, but looked down on anyone who drank alcohol. In 1995, he had been promoted to engine foreman, but the final straw in his employment at that position came when he filled a diesel engine on his fire truck with unleaded gas and burnt the bastard up. The last thing I heard was that he

11

had been fired from a helitack crew for rappelling out of the helicopter while it was in a straight line of flight – he just hooked up his lines and jumped out of the damn thing. Then he went home, got drunk, beat up his wife, beat up the neighbor's wife, and got sent to prison. Seriously.

At the gun we all took off. I completely forgot about my own situation, however, when I saw Randy and James tear off at sprint speed, right up there with how I would run a 40-yard dash. At first I thought my perception of their toughness was right on the money, but then something told me they really didn't know what they were doing. Even *I* knew to pace myself for this miserable run. At about 200 meters, a quarter of a lap or so, my suspicions came true, and both of them quit. Done, gassed, wasted. Holy crap, what a couple of wussies. I think this actually helped inspire me. Not that I like to witness total and complete failure, but I was puking sick before this run even *began*, and I knew *I* wouldn't quit.

Coming around the stretch and heading north, the cool summer breeze was at our backs, but when we rounded the bend and went south, that breeze turned into a headwind. Not good. I sounded like a freight train with every breath, but I knew after four laps or so that I was going to make it with plenty of time to spare. On the sixth and final lap I actually sped up because it felt so good to know I was going to be successful. I passed the run in eleven minutes and four seconds, still pretty slow compared with the rest of them, but I *passed*. Then I gagged and puked right onto the adjacent football field. I was too relieved to care.

The balance of that first day, after a one-hour lunch break, was spent checking out fire gear and getting to know your engine foreman and crew members. It had gotten really warm and muggy on that June day, and all the clouds had disappeared. This weather, in addition to the tonsillitis, made it a struggle for me to even pay attention.

At all BLM districts where I have worked, there is a warehouse supervisor on the grounds. Most are former firefighters who had injuries, or some other reason that caused them to choose to remain in the yard. Ours was no different in that respect, but Avery Ross was original in other ways. He was about 5-foot-5 and hid behind a huge red beard and sunglasses. I worked with Avery for about seven years and I never heard him say more than probably a couple dozen words, and I never did see him without sunglasses. He seemed to harbor a particular disdain for rookies, evident when it was my turn to check out my gear.

The list of basic firefighting gear checked out at the beginning of each season included shirts and pants, gloves, water bottles, packs, fire shelters, and other essential items for the field. They were in list form like "Shirt-Yellow, Nomex, fire resistant, long sleeve." It was always a game to apply this style to anything else you could – "Dumbass-large, human, stupid" or "Beer-Bud light, cold, 12-ounce."

As a male rookie under Avery's watch, you were issued the crummiest gear he could find, even if there was enough decent gear for everybody. Though I was new, I could certainly recognize that I was an unwilling traveler on someone's little power trip right then. I think I even got the crummiest of the crummy, probably because I looked and felt sick and weak that day, and he knew I wouldn't raise hell with him.

The main office had a small locker room where we could change into our "greens," as we called them, green Nomex fire-resistant fire pants. The tag on mine indicated they were the correct size, but God they were uncomfortable. My butt hung out, my crotch was crushed, and my thighs felt so constricted that I knew if I bent down to pick something up I would probably split the back seam of the pants. I went back to get a larger size from Avery, but he just growled like a dog, then stared at me and made a funny duck-call sound as he gritted his teeth. I stared back as long as I had patience at the sunglasses and beard, and then just figured "screw it" and realized I was going to have to make do with these pants. Little did I know that in a month these pants would be way too big for me; Avery had been around for a while.

Then it was off to get acquainted with our crew and fire engine. As it happened, my foreman, assistant foreman, and fire engine were all in New Mexico on a detail – an out-of-area firefighting trip. This left me with no supervisor and no clear instructions for what I was supposed to do now. Everybody had somewhere to go and something to do for the next two hours; everybody except me and my two other crew members – you guessed it – James Stoddard and Randy Meyers, the two track athletes, who would be given more chances to pass the run they'd failed on their first try.

Wandering around made me feel worthless and sticking out like a sore thumb, so I made my way over to where others – the crew of Engine 351 – were getting a briefing and show-and-tell of their machine by its foreman, Brad Nash. I was the quintessential blank slate, so even just following Brad around as he explained the basics taught me a lot that afternoon.

Brad Nash was a real rock star in this business. He was about 5-foot-10 and maybe 150 pounds, a full-blood Shoshone-Bannock Indian, and in super physical shape. He was always calm and composed, his hair was never even messy, but sometimes he came across as just a little too perfect in a non-perfect world. It seemed like he believed that everyone ought to have his ability and encyclopedic knowledge of the fire world. At the same time, though, he tried hard to help everyone gain that knowledge, and he'd teach people whenever he could. Nash used to look at me the way I'd look at a certain type of monkey at the zoo that I'd never seen before – with a mixture of curiosity and disdain.

The bread-and-butter of a BLM engine crew is its fire engine. Each unit is self-contained; it has everything you need to conduct fire operations either stored in it or mounted on it. Without it, you are not worth much in this part of the business, and if it's broken down, you run the risk of being assigned some uninviting task like cleaning campground shitters while everyone else is out killing fires. Therefore, you are taught and reminded often to take good care of it.

The BLM Type 4 or heavy engine is the real workhorse of wildland fire engines. The typical configuration is a baffled 750-gallon water tank attached to a 26,000-pound GVWR (gross-vehicle weight rated) truck. They are four-wheel drive, and have air brakes, so they require that the operator hold a commercial driver's license. The automatic transmissions are geared low and the engine is governed, so you never can get going more than about 65 mph down the highway, but boy can they crawl and climb over some serious terrain. When assigned to heavy engines, I always had International trucks, but I have seen Freightliners and Ford F-650s. They had light bars, ID numbers, and Motorola radio systems. Unlike the light engines, the steering wheel on these things is about as big around as a tractor tire, and keeping a heavy engine in the proper lane on the highway is like herding cats because of the high profile and short wheel base.

A heavy engine crew is made up of at least three crew members, but sometimes as many as six. The leader is the engine foreman, followed by the assistant foreman, and several other firefighters who may or may not have any fire experience. The cab of the engine can seat only three people, with the foreman or assistant foreman driving, so if there are any more than this on the crew, you have to employ a chase truck, which is simply a four-door, four-wheel-drive pickup that follows the engine.

Our engine was theoretically capable of being out on fires for two weeks at a time, needing only fuel and water re-supplied. The engine and its crew would be able to conduct any standard firefighting procedures, either as an initial attack vehicle by itself, or as part of a strike team or task force for extended attack and mop-up projects. The crew was trained and the equipment was available to conduct direct attack and knock down flames with water (pump and roll), backburn with fusees and drip torches (fight fire with fire), protect the outside of buildings and other structures with hoses and a water/foam mixture (structure protection), or park the engine and conduct handline construction with the crew members becoming essentially small hotshot squads.

Did I learn this all on the first day? Heck no. I was only trying to survive without puking again or passing out. By mid-afternoon I just felt like I was dreaming. It was so hot on the black asphalt of that BLM yard. I nearly collapsed with joy when Gary excused us for the day at 6 p.m., with instructions to report to the Bonneville High School commons at 9:00 the next morning for the first day of basic fire school.

That night I went home absolutely exhausted. Sitting on the couch that evening, I felt a mixture of relief, pride, confusion, and trepidation about what I had gotten myself into. I knew I would report to fire school tomorrow, and I wouldn't quit, but this first day had not really enlightened me much. The next day was the first day of basic fire school. The teachers were excellent, but because I was so sick, I really remember only two bits of information from the first two hours. The first was the concept universal to all firefighting – the fire triangle. The fire triangle consists of the three legs of heat, fuel, and oxygen. Break any one of these legs and the fire triangle collapses and the fire goes out. The other thing, courtesy of the foreman of Engine 342, was that you could store your chewing tobacco in the outside pocket of your red bag.

At 10:30 that morning, prior to an allotted 5-minute break, Gary Eames, our awesome FCO, requested to speak with three people – James Stoddard, Randy Meyers, and Ben Walters. As the rest of the group of students went off for a piss break or smoke break, I was being given an order that would amount to one of those profound moments in life. I was to pack my red bag and prepare to depart from Idaho Falls tomorrow morning at 6:00 to join my foreman, assistant foreman, and Engine 341 in Las Cruces, New Mexico. I went to a pay phone in the foyer of the school and called my mom to tell her the news.

Coming back into a lecture-format class and paying attention after hearing news like that? Well, I tried my best, and was still trying my best when Gary motioned me aside and told me that he had spoken with my mother and that she had informed him I was sick as hell. He cocked his head, stared at me, and with a fatherly tone said he would understand if I couldn't make it on this trip. Nope. I'm going. My most wonderful mother picked me up on my lunch break and took me to the doctor. My throat was really messed up and I felt like I always had to swallow. The doc looked into my mouth and just said, "Ooooh." He prescribed me a stronger antibiotic called Augmentin, and I returned to finish an afternoon at fire school that I never could remember.

How to Pack a Red Bag

Wednesday, June 9, 1993, 6:00 a.m. – I am standing on the passenger side of my pickup transferring my red bag and other gear to the grey F-350 crew cab that will take us to New Mexico. Morning had come early and I had gone to bed late and slept little the night before. The reasons for this were almost exclusively fear of the unknown – and fear of missing home, my girlfriend Stephanie, and my dog, none of which I had been away from for more than a day or two.

Stephanie told her parents she would be spending the night at her friend Molly's house, then sneaked through my bedroom window at midnight after her shift at Subway. We stared at the ceiling, and sometimes each other, and wondered what the next two weeks would bring. Mind you, two weeks is a long time for 18-year-olds in love. I wondered if I was tough enough for this.

That evening my mom had taken me to the store to prepare my red bag for two weeks. I still really had no flippin' idea what the hell was going on in the fire world. Either they had told us and I was too sick to pay attention, or they expected we would know this, but I didn't know.

The government will pay for your food on a firefighting trip. But in our good-hearted ignorance, Mom and I tried to buy food and supplies for me for two weeks, supplies that would all fit in my red bag. We purchased cans and cans of pork and beans, Ramen noodles, beanie weenies, tomato soup, powdered this and powdered that, bags of jerky, 6-packs of Pepsi, and because food was probably a bit higher on the priority scale than hygiene, we bought only sample/travel sized shampoo, toothpaste, soap, and deodorant. Extra clothes were kept to a minimum as well - a shirt or two, a pair of underwear or two, three or four pairs of socks.

The next morning, there was still an early summer dew on the grass and shadows on the west side of buildings and trees when we turned right onto Anderson Street and meshed with the light traffic heading south on Interstate 15. Randy Hanson drove, and Trent Allen, an old teacher still doing summers on the fire crew, rode shotgun. The rest of us crammed into the back bench seat. Because I was the youngest and still pretty timid at that point, I was selected to ride in the middle seat, with Meyers on my left and Stoddard on my right. This was going to be a long ride.

None of us spoke to each other in the back seat and were only aware of each other's presence with the subtle elbow jab and sidelong glance. Stoddard said fawning stupid stuff to Randy from time to time, like "the grass on those hills is browning nicely," and "Hey Randy, do we still get steaks and shakes after every fire?"

Just north of Provo, Utah, the air in the cab was replaced with choking gaseous fumes, and Randy began to laugh. It was the worst odor I had ever smelled, and being already sick, I nearly puked. No one rolled down their windows.

Who were these people, and what the hell was I doing here? We spent the first night in a motel room in

Durango, Colorado. Thankfully, I was given my own room, so I could call Stephanie and my mom and whine about missing them and that these people were mean. Dinner that night was courtesy of the government credit card, but I couldn't yet eat much.

Music on the truck radio made me melancholy and homesick that whole day. Songs and smells, good or bad, define moments in time for many people, and they'll instantly bring me back to those times if I let them. There is a point, when you are driving to the southwest along this route, where you cross from the steep canyons of some red rock country out onto a beautiful plateau with a mosaic of aspen groves, mini-cliffs, and tall grass fields. We crossed there sometime on the first evening, right before the sun went down. I was battling the blues and looking for anything to grasp onto.

We arrived at the local BLM office the afternoon of June 12 and pulled the truck around to the rear of the building into the fire yard, where they keep all their fire engines and field vehicles. We had been in the air-conditioned cab since morning and had not yet experienced the ambient air of southern New Mexico. I nearly dropped to the ground when the doors of the pickup were opened and the cool air vanished into memory. I felt as if I had landed on the face of the Sun. Never in my life had I experienced heat like this. And I was supposed to do hard work in this?! While sick?! *Oh shit, what have I done?*

The five of us walked through the metal door into the relatively cool warehouse, and were introduced to the fire management officer (FMO), Ken Porter. Almost immediately, the phone rang in the adjacent fire office and I heard a woman's voice answering it. Moments later, a square-shaped Hispanic woman emerged from the office and began running around the warehouse breathlessly exclaiming, "Fire, there's a fire, oh God, there's a fire, what do we do, there's a fire!"

Ken motioned with his thumb toward the woman and informally introduced us to Penny, foreman for one of the two full-time fire engine crews based out of this office. Penny was panicking about the fire, and Randy coolly said, "Why don't we go put it out?"

At the conclusion of this scene, Penny was breathing into a paper lunch bag to calm her hyperventilation before she and her crew could respond to the one-acre smoldering grass fire. In all fairness, this was her first fire as engine foreman, and also the first fire she had responded to this season. It was sure a strange thing to witness, though. I hoped I wouldn't act like that.

Once again, we were put up in a motel for the night and offered supper on the government dime. I was pleased because I hadn't had to use any of the food from my red bag yet, but displeased because I didn't get my own room this time. I got stuck with Meyers, a wannabe Mississippi gangsta who insisted on having the bed by the air conditioner. We did not talk.

Friday, June 11, 1993, 7:30 a.m. – There is a persistent and worried banging on our motel room door and Trent Allen is outside clucking like a nervous hen. "Wake up, we've been dispatched to a fire."

Meyers pooches out his lower lip and scampers into the shower. I stand there in the doorway and ask Allen what I should do. "Get in the goddamn truck!" he bellers.

I run around getting into my greens and yellow shirt, police my stuff from around the motel room, and trot out and jump into the truck. Moments later, Hanson, Allen, and Stoddard join me and we wait in the parking lot. About ten minutes later Meyers steps out of the hotel room wearing full-on greens, helmet, goggles down, shroud and collar up, web gear on, gloves on – he is ready to put out a fire. I suppress a chuckle but the others don't. They are howling with laughter and saying, "What the hell" and "Check that out." Meyers climbs into the truck and says, "Whatchu laughin' 'bout." I really didn't know what was going on with this whole detail, but I did know for certain that the fire wasn't in the damn parking lot.

An hour or so later we arrived at the fire camp outside of Hatch, New Mexico – chile capital of the world. The camp was right in the middle of some sort of fairgrounds, and looked a lot like the multitude of fire camps I would live in and work out of for the next ten seasons.

The main area of the camp was cordoned off from the public with those ropes that have different colored flags attached to them. There were blaze orange poster boards hung up here and there with arrows on them in black and red pointing to the different sections of the camp. One sign said "supply," another said "medical," another "ops," and so on. A row of port-a-potties ran north to south, and that's where I headed as soon as the truck stopped.

This particular fire, the Uvas Fire, had recently been upgraded (or downgraded, depending on your perspective), to a Type 2 fire. Fires in the U.S. are managed under the Incident Command System (ICS), a standardized approach for managing all-hazards incidents in five different functional areas: Command, Operations, Planning, Logistics, and Finance/Administration. The system is used across agencies to control and mitigate damages from unplanned and possibly catastrophic events. The system can be activated in any situation from an earthquake to a hurricane, but it's most commonly used during the wildfire season.

There are five types of incidents as applied to fires threatening citizens or natural resources or other property – they are categorized from a Type 5, which is usually a relatively small fire, to a Type 1 fire, which requires the most resources to control.

All fires have an incident commander (IC), who is the dude or dudette in charge. If the fire is determined to fall under the expertise and experience and qualifications of this person, then he'll remain in charge of the fire until he has called it "controlled." If the fire grows, and requires more resources, the incident commander may turn it over to a person or a team with more experience and qualifications.

In the hot and dusty environment of the Uvas Fire camp, however, I was not concerned about the types of fires there were. In fact, I couldn't have cared less. All I knew was that I had to explode. I max-fast-walked over to the line of porta-potties; the Augmentin appeared to be kicking in, a side effect of which is often referred to in firefighting circles under the acronym "POYA," which stands for pissing out your ass. I added dehydration to the list of my adversaries.

When I got back to the truck, I learned that Randy was talking to the operations section chief figuring out a way to get me and the two other rookies married up with Engine 341 and crew. Hanson and Allen were working as division supervisors on this fire, and thus would not be joining us. Then I was introduced to the government policy of "hurry up and wait." We must have waited there two hours before Randy came back and told us what to do next.

The two track stars and I were to prepare to be shuttled via helicopter to the fireline at a helispot where the rest of the crew were preparing to construct hand line. Oh my! I had never ridden in a helicopter, let alone ridden one into a fire.

At that point, I forgot all about being sick; the all-business side of Ben Walters emerged to prepare for the ride of a lifetime – which was going to be even more memorable than I imagined. Helicopters are contracted to the Forest Service or BLM for use during fire season. Each helicopter is outfitted with its own crew who are seasonal full-time government firefighters. This crew is called *helitack*, the foreman of which has a multitude of responsibilities. One of those responsibilities is calculating the weight of helicopter-borne loads.

There is a weight limit on your red bag. I didn't know it at the helispot, and I hadn't known it back when I was loading my bag full of canned food items and Pepsi back in Idaho Falls, either. Apparently none of the firefighters who had ridden with me to this fire had ever lifted my red bag, and I'd not lifted any of theirs, either, or I would surely have noticed that there was a discrepancy in weight. I mean, I knew my red bag was a heavy sucker, maybe 150 pounds, but I didn't see any other way around it. The helitack foreman hoisted my bag to get a weight estimate.

"WHAT THE FUCK?!" he screamed. "What the hell do you *have* in here?" He was so mad his voice cracked.

"Most of the weight's from my food, sir."

He looked from Meyers to Stoddard, spit a brown tobacco stream, then looked back at me.

I was mortified as he ripped open my bag and began taking out the food cans and chucking them into the dust 30 feet away, all the while cussing and scowling at me. I was shocked; I just stood there and watched him do it. I may have had tears of frustration welling up in my eyes as I tried to grasp how I was going to survive for the next two weeks without starving.

When he was finished, my red bag looked like a big deflated balloon sitting in the dirt with the rest of our gear. I stood there grim, but straight up and determined, like a Marine recruit on day one of boot camp. Miles away, I saw the cars moving through the town of Hatch, and the heat waves beginning to dance on the hard-packed plain through the tall cactus. A growing *whomp-whomp-whomp* sound indicated an approaching Bell 212 helicopter from the southwest direction. My anger and frustration were quickly replaced with nervousness and an adrenaline rush when the craft settled down onto the makeshift pad and the dust and pebbles and weeds kicked up all around it. We all crouched down low as per directions and followed the helitack foreman's gestures to board and fasten our seatbelts. A couple minutes passed, and an audible change in pitch of the *whomps* gave way to that funny feeling in your stomach when you change altitude in a hurry. The doors of the helicopter had been removed for utility purposes, but for me it just added to the beauty and singularity of the moment. For about ten minutes, I forgot that I was a total alien here and simply enjoyed the cool air flowing past my face as I took in the terrain of Doña Ana County from a bird's-eye view. On the ground, the temperature was approaching 100 degrees, but it felt a lot cooler up here. I was sitting in one of the back seats, and as we moved to the southwest, I could see out over the high, rocky outcroppings to the northwest, joining up next to the flat plain.

The high ridges and hillsides were sparsely covered with mesquite, cholla cactus, yucca plants, and fluff grass. It almost looked like more dirt than burnable stuff. The dirt here, I had been told, fell into one of the soil orders called *aridisols*, and it was hard as hell. I later wondered how anything could grow in this stuff.

After a few minutes of beeline flight, the helicopter made a steep banking turn back to the northeast and began dropping in altitude. A couple minutes later the pilot made another banking turn, nearly 180 degrees, and we dropped swiftly onto what's called a helispot. This was merely a flat spot in the canyon about 100 feet up the side hill from a dirt road. Dust and weeds flew everywhere as the pitch of the rotors changed back to a flatter *whomp*.

The pilot turned to us and indicated that it was safe to step off the aircraft. Meyers jumped out and ran. Stoddard and I stepped off, crouched down, and moved downhill away from the rotors as instructed. Moments later, the pitch again changed, and the helicopter was off to other duties.

I looked around for a reality check. Lined up next to a scratched, chalky, and really dusty Engine 341 were five of the hardest people I have ever seen, and one was a chick! Left to right stood Frank Morgan, Dave Farmer, Holly Nelson, Jerry Graham, and Lee Campbell. Their faces were all covered in soot and dirt like they had been working in a coal mine. Their yellow shirts were almost black, as were their green pants. None of them was smiling. We must have looked like nothing but a headache to them, exuding rookiness with our clean clothes and deer-in-the-headlights faces.

Lee, our foreman, was the first to come forward and introduce himself and the rest of the crew. He then gave us a quick hands-on lesson about starting a backfire with a fusee to save yourself in a burnover situation. We each got to light a fusee and smother it out while the rest of the crew took a break. The temperature had reached 106 degrees, but nobody complained. I knew for certain that I would soon be reaching further inside of myself for survival than I ever had before.

Those five hard-nose people I met that day ended up being something of a cadre of mentors for me for the next few years. Maybe it was like a duckling imprinting on its mother, or maybe it was just that these were people for whom you better put up or shut up, but I knew I would try my hardest for them. I always remembered Frank Morgan as the guy who repeated, "Fuck me runnin'" like a mantra whenever a situation went bad. He was also the person I remember seeing asleep in the dirt that first night at fire camp with only a jacket covering him against the frigid New Mexico night.

Holly Nelson was pretty and funny, with a pile of blonde hair, a smokin' body, and an attitude. And I would have put her up against any firefighter in the nation when it came to skill level. She had come over to our BLM district from the Sawtooth Hotshot Crew, where she worked principally as a sawyer – which is not easy work even for a big guy.

Dave Farmer was made of iron and attitude. He had a quick wit and a million-dollar smile, and now has the qualifications to fly lead planes for the airtankers that drop retardant on fires. I probably outweighed him by 40 pounds, but I never could beat him at arm wrestling. He was a sort of "golden child" of the BLM. He stood about 5-foot-8 and was just solid iron – and he knew it. The first season I knew him, I usually just wanted to punch the piss out of him, but that eventually changed. Farmer was not cool-headed on fires, but the opposite, just extremely aggressive. I once watched him take a Type 4 heavy engine up a hill that Type 6's and even 4x4 pickups were having trouble negotiating. When he reached the top of the hill, that heavy engine *actually went airborne*. Another time, he was picking up a new heavy engine over in Boise, before the engine had been governed down to go only 60 mph, so he was able to wind it up all the way. I guess they drove the entire way back to Idaho Falls going over 100 mph – he was a crazy fucker. When I first met him, he was working on getting his private pilot's license, and about six years later he was flying lead planes – years later, he would show up as an air attack pilot on fires and talk only to me. That was pretty cool.

Jerry Graham, a full-blood Shoshone Indian, lived on the Fort Hall Reservation north of Pocatello, Idaho. He was a big dude, and seriously athletic, and just a horse when it came to running and working. Jerry was *always* calm in fire situations.

Lee Campbell was one of those quintessential firefighter types. The dude was about 6-foot-3 and slim but not skinny. With his huge mustache, aviator glasses, and perpetual confidence projection, he could have been Hanson's brother, or a Navy SEAL chief. This guy, I would learn, was skilled in every aspect of firefighting, but had been doing it for only three or four seasons. Despite his height, he wore size 8 White's boots – they looked like little hooves on him. Campbell oscillated between being one cool dude and kind of a nerd – he had encyclopedic knowledge of classic rock'n'roll. He was also mechanically gifted, and whenever the district acquired a new piece of equipment or a prototype engine, they always had him test it. He was always a patient dude and kept a pretty level head. He looked older to me than his 23 years. In fact, I once asked him in all seriousness if he had fought in Vietnam. He looked at me incredulously and said, "I was four years old."

Our objective for the rest of that day, Campbell explained, was to construct a hand line from the road on which we were now standing due west over to the line the Mescalero Apache Hotshots were constructing north to south. When the two lines were tied in, we would use them to start a backfire. Theoretically, the backfire would burn into the head of the main fire, which was moving south. Our fire would essentially rob the fast-moving main fire of its fuels and effectively shut it down on this southeast flank.

Did I understand any of this right then? Nope. All I knew was that I now longed for cold tap water. I had come to the horrifying realization that the water in the bottles on my web gear had reached ambient temperature, and drinking hot water on a hot and dusty day just sucks.

Dave distributed pulaskis and shovels to everyone, while Campbell parked the engine. After a quick safety briefing, we began digging line at the dirt road anchor point, with Dave and Jerry in the lead, hacking away at the stubborn vegetation growing out of the concrete-like soil.

There is a method and vocabulary to digging fireline, or cutting line, as I would learn. The phrase bump up, as used when cutting line, means to move ahead a certain distance along the line. Tie in means to connect something to something else, as here where we planned to tie in two constructed firelines. An anchor point is a place where you begin your line construction. An anchor point is usually a feature of terrain that won't burn, like an already burned-out spot (the black), a field of rocks, a creek or a river, or sometimes even an improved dirt road or highway.

A good crew boss will scout ahead to ensure that your line follows the easiest features of the terrain and vegetation, so as not to overwork the crew. The first few people in front generally use pulaskis or other similar tools, unless you have to cut your way through vegetation that requires a sawyer and some swampers, who cut and clear trees and bigger brush. Following the pulaskis are usually the shovels. The last few diggers in the line have the responsibility to call out "take more," or "take less" to those up front. This tells these firefighters that they are not cutting enough, or they are cutting too much. The end result, a fuels-free path that's dug down to bare mineral soil, looks like a hiking trail that should be about as wide as one-and-a-half times the height of the surrounding vegetation.

In my complete and total rookieness, I had no idea about pacing myself for this task. I swung and swung with my pulaski and hit the hard earth over and over again. I was in a dreamlike state to begin with, but now I was really in a purgatorial zone. I did have thoughts for the first few minutes, and they were about the first day of high school football practice each August. I wondered how that and this compared. Otherwise, my world had shrunk to a piece of New Mexican dirt and some fluff grass being kicked up around my boots.

Not knowing or caring to observe and learn about proper form at that point, I bended and flexed only at my waist. My lower back, I knew, was taking a real beating. The muscles knotted up and burned there and in my forearms and shoulders. If I were to try that now, I'd surely be in the hospital or at least physical therapy for a while.

The midday day sun hammered down on us, and there was not even a breath of breeze as the eight of us steadily advanced across the sidehill and up the ridge. The only sounds were hand tools clanking against rocks, boots scuffing in the dust, and the occasional terse command from either the front or the back of the line. We did take regular short breaks for water, but the hot water was not at all refreshing. It was simply a physiological necessity.

At one point I looked around and noticed that I had yet to see any flames. Here I was fighting fire, but there was no fire. I also wondered why anybody would care to defend this land against fire because, from my vantage point, I sure couldn't see anything worthwhile. Sometime late in the afternoon I looked down a north-south ridge and spotted a crew of about twenty firefighters cutting line steadily toward us. My intuition was correct about this being the Mescalero Apache Hotshots, and it was good news, because that meant our lines would be tied in, and maybe we could get a longer rest period. Campbell held us up at that point, and we all set our tools down and straightened crooked backs for a moment. Even though it was now late afternoon, it didn't feel any cooler. I wondered if it ever would. Had I possibly died somehow, without knowing it? Was I actually in hell?

One thing I unconsciously learned that day was that people like to keep the rookies in the dark about what's happening. There was lots of discussion about this and that among Campbell, the hotshot crew, and the faceless voices on the radio. I remained ignorant about what was happening; it seemed there was no big picture at all. We began our backburn using the tie-in of the two handlines as an anchor point. There was no wind to blow embers across the line to where we didn't want them, and the main heat of the day was finally beginning to dissipate. Frank, Holly, and Jerry would be the burners and the rest of us would stagger out behind them and make sure no flames crossed the line. Campbell was the lookout. If something did cross the line, we were to yell "slopover" or "spot" so the burners knew to hold up and the rest of the firefighters could run up and help extinguish the getaway flames.

The burners used fusees, which are a kind of Roman-candle looking 10-minute big friction match that puts out a lot of heat. I've seen them catch even a large wet stump on fire. Fusees are easy to carry, and we all had 15 or 20 of them with us. When we got down to the engine, we would exchange the fusees for drip torches – a one-and-a-quarter-gallon metal canister with a one-spiral spout (like a child's fun-drinking straw) with a torch wick. We filled them with two parts diesel fuel to burn slowly, and one part gasoline to ignite quickly. You can steadily squirt a lot of flame with a drip torch.

Tendrils of flame and wisps of grayish-black smoke in the light grass began to stoke up as the burners passed by and touched the white-hot and hissing tip of the fusee to the ground fuels. Tendrils became 3- or 4-foot lucifers and moved swiftly down the gully. Smoke obscured the western sun and it glowed a pallid orange color through the shimmering heat waves. On the ridge above me and across the draw, the Apache firefighters were spread out and ready to kick butt should the fire do something unexpected. They too were often lost in the smoke and cinders now generated by the backfire.

Heat from the flames intensified as it gathered momentum and attacked the larger cholla cactus and yucca plants. Occasionally there would be a rush of air and a loud crackling as a piñon or juniper tree fell prey to the flames. I felt the heat bounce off my face and saw the fire dancing in the other firefighters' mirrored sunglasses. Looking over the largest northerly ridge, I finally spotted the column of smoke from the main fire as it advanced due south toward our backfire. I caught myself grinning. It was working. This was what I had signed up to do.

Eventually we reached the end of our handline and the beginning of the dirt road where the engine was parked. We came back down a lot faster than we had gone up while digging the line, that's for sure. Campbell pulled the engine out of its safe zone and back onto the dirt road headed down-canyon to the northeast. The burners extinguished their fusees with a POP! by throwing them forcefully, tip down, into the dirt.

Holly then assembled two drip torches, and after some hushed conferencing with Campbell, handed one each to Meyers and me. Yes! Hands-on time. Jerry moved off with Meyers farther down into the canyon, while Frank walked with me and showed me how to zigzag while I walked to cover more ground and increase the volume of fire I was creating. The tiny little flames came out of the drip torch spout in steady drops, but very quickly joined together and became a uniform line of fire three or four feet high, chewing up everything in its path. Would this cause me to become a pyromaniac?

After Frank decided that I had this task figured out, he walked back up the road and became one of the spotting crew. Campbell trolled the engine along slowly behind us, providing the extra backup of hardline fire hose in case we needed it. Meyers, ahead of me now by quite a ways, spit fire everywhere. Occasionally I glanced behind me and saw that I was doing likewise. Frank, Stoddard, Holly, Dave, and Jerry had spread out along the sidehill just above the road and stood at arms, scanning the line for spots or slopovers. The hotshot crew had disappeared over the high ridge back to the north. Everything was going as planned.

Then I crossed the road.

I have no explanation for why I did this. It certainly was not to cause hate and discontent, and I can't really say that I did it accidentally. I just had *no idea* what I was doing. I was walking past a small group of piñon-juniper standing on the uphill side of the road, and they looked like they needed some burning. So I crossed the road and circled the thick grass at the base of them with a ring of oily fire drops. It looked so cool that I set my torch down and snapped a quick picture with my disposable Kodak.

I began to hear yelling in the distance. Lots of yelling. I heard the turbo wind up on 341's diesel engine. *Wow, those junipers went right up*, I thought to myself.

I looked back up the dirt road to see what all the yelling was about and saw the dually tires on 341 bouncing up and down as Campbell slammed pedal to metal. The holding crew firefighters were running in my direction. Dave was screaming. "Hey, hey, stop burning, stop burning, goddammit!"

Then 341 pulled up in a cloud of dust; Jerry was there in an instant, grabbing the black hardline nozzle and knocking down the flames I had purposely put around the trees. Morgan and Dave and Holly were furiously working shovels to throw dirt on the smaller flames moving up the sidehill. Campbell was radioing for backup. Stoddard stood below the engine on the downhill side of the road, shaking his head. Meyers looked around and pooched out his lower lip. I just stood back down the road, out of the way, being about as helpful as chicken shit on a pump handle. Amid all the yelling and commotion, I again felt tears of frustration in the corners of my eyes.

My screw-up took the others almost three hours to control. It could have been a lot worse; nevertheless, 22 acres that didn't need burning were now torched, only because I was such a space cadet. The slopover I had created all by myself finally slowed down when it reached the top of the sidehill, after we had pulled one-inch hose all along the flanks to knock it down. The Silver City Hotshots had meanwhile hiked over from an adjacent division to complete the burnout that we had started. It was dark now, and I felt very small and tired, and I really wished I could just go home.

Friday, June 11, 1993, 10:30 p.m. – Campbell had parked Engine 341 on the east side of the road in a safety zone, and was conferring with the Silver City Hotshot foreman and several other firefighters just outside the dusty headlight beams of a green pickup truck parked on the dirt road. We had moved out of the hills and were now down in the flats. Hanson and Allen had shuttled the gray chase truck up to our present location, and another Idaho Falls firefighter had joined us – Eric Hall had been serving as a division supervisor somewhere on the fire. They made no effort to conceal their amused disdain at my idiocy of earlier in the day.

Across the shallow draw and up the sidehill I could see the twinkling of embers left over from where the southeast flank of the main fire had met the backfire and they had come together in hellish matrimony. I was sure this would have been awesome to witness, but I had been too busy trying to amend my mistake of crossing the road. This time of night on a fire became my favorite time in subsequent seasons – it was the time of evening when you could shoot the bull with other firefighters and compare notes on the day. The burning period is over by late evening, and unless you are running and gunning somewhere on the initial attack of a fire, the situation is usually mellowed out. Right now, though, my feet inside my cheap Redwing boots were beginning to bark out blisters, and I was feeling the remnants of some tonsillitis chills.

Campbell finally told us it was time to head back to the fire camp. He wanted Meyers and me to ride with him the 20 minutes back to camp, presumably to critique the day and have some shop talk with us. The rest of the crew piled in with Hanson in the gray Ford and Hall in his red Chevy pickup. We followed them so we could eat all the dust. Meyers wouldn't sit in the middle seat; in fact, he wasn't going to go anywhere unless I got in first. He was being a baby, and I remember thinking that I couldn't wait to throttle this guy the first chance I got. First order of business back at camp was chow – for the other crews. As hundreds of other firefighters lined up outside the food tent to secure an opulent fire camp meal of fried chicken with all the fixin's, Meyers, Stoddard, and I were ordered to "refurbish" the fire engine for tomorrow's shift. This included checking fluids on both the diesel engine and pump motor, refilling the tank with water and foam surfactant, refilling drinking water canteens, sharpening shovels and pulaskis, and straightening up the bins.

An hour or so later we were turned loose to get some food. This is when I finally learned that you don't need to bring all your food in your red bag. At the first of the line was a table with plastic cutlery, paper plates, and napkins. Next to that was a large galvanized steel livestock water trough filled with ice and cold drinks. I noticed the cans of Budweiser (which you certainly wouldn't see today) among the sodas and bottled waters. Dang, they looked so good, with the beads of ice running down the sides – I imagined getting drunk would be frowned upon, so I just grabbed a Pepsi and moved on down the line.

By about 1 a.m., we finally bedded down. When, I wondered, had we been told to get a mattress or a cot? Everyone had one. Everyone, of course, but Frank Morgan and me. He just stretched out in the dirt next to the engine with nothing but his fire jacket covering him. I figured I may as well do the same – at least I had a sleeping bag. I swallowed my last Augmentin for the day and crawled into the bag with all my clothes on.

Jerry walked past me not long after daybreak as I was putting away my sleeping bag. He spat Copenhagen through the split in his teeth, looked down at me and said, "Little bitch" and kept walking. *Huh?*

Campbell reminded us all to shake out our boots to make sure no spiders or scorpions had gotten into them. *Scorpions?*

Creatures in my boots weren't the only problem – my boots barely even went on, because of my red-hot, blistered, and swollen feet. The message here was painfully clear: rookie firefighters should not be cheap when it comes to buying boots.

Eventually I joined the food line and tucked into a good breakfast of sausage links, scrambled eggs, buttered toast, orange juice, and milk. Fire camps put out pretty good fare if you can get used to the dirt and other stuff that accumulates on your plate between the time it's dished out to you and the time you eat it.

Firefighters generally get fed pretty well, as you might imagine. They need good fuel and lots of it to keep up energy levels on those workdays that can easily be in excess of sixteen hours. Just to give you an idea, the standard for a 154-pound firefighter doing heavy work is about 4,400 calories a day, including 490 to 700 grams of carbohydrate per day – and there's not quite 50 grams in a cup of beans.

One of my favorite firefighter meal memories comes from a Type 2 fire near Silver City, New Mexico.

Meals catered in fire camps are served up buffet style. On big project fires, such as this one, the buffet is on or near a van-type semi-trailer run by the contract caterer. The catering crew worked inside the trailer, which was custom-outfitted as a mobile kitchen. Inside there it looked damn hot, too, and those people were working their asses off in 100-degree-plus temperatures – these mobile kitchen units typically are equipped with four or five commercial-size gas grills and all the other equipment necessary to feed 400 or 800 firefighters.

I first picked up my white plastic utensils, napkins, and paper plate. I climbed the four stairs to the plank that ran along the distance of the serving windows on the side of the kitchen. I was expecting some mystery meat affair like the too-common sack lunch sandwich meat, or something that was like the lunch line back at junior high. What I saw just about blew my mind.

By then I had eaten in a couple of fine restaurants around the country, so I knew what I was looking at. The meat I saw was indeed mystery meat in a way – a total mystery that they had *prime rib*, steaming and barely off the roaster, right out here in the middle of nowhere. That was window number one in the chow line. The question they asked me – "Do you want more than one piece?" – damn near made me speechless. "I'll have two, please," I answered.

I still remember how the salt and pepper and spice rub they'd put on it looked, and how the little sample bite tasted while I was in line for station number two. Perfect medium to medium-rare, and they offered both creamy and real grated horseradish along with hot au jus. I had all three. My plate already weighed close to two pounds, maybe more.

Potatoes? Well yes, meat must be accompanied by potatoes, especially in fire camp. A giant baked potato in foil landed on my plate, and the starchy smell in the steam went straight to my stomach. I dressed it with butter, lots of real sour cream, real crumbled bacon, and grated cheddar cheese.

You could then choose an ear of corn on the cob, or cheesy broccoli. I had both. Corn on the cob is pure summertime, and in a fire camp it's like a dream. Next in the chow line was a tossed garden salad – all we had to do was choose which dressing packets we wanted.

This caterer also offered a selection of desserts. The dessert table was set off to the side of the trailer and was loaded with slices of chocolate cake with chocolate frosting, very recently baked chocolate chip cookies, and even peach and apple cobbler.

I ate my fill that first night because I thought I deserved it after a day hiking and working in that godawful heat. I topped off the meal with two or three plastic cups of ice cold milk and a cup of hot coffee.

By about 7:30 the next morning we were heading back down the dirt road that turned off the main highway and led to the fire. I was looking out the bug-spattered windshield at pretty much nothing, gritting my teeth almost to the point of cracking them because of an incident while we were sitting in the cab waiting for Campbell. Country boys like me enjoy listening to country music or classic rock. Lots of city boys, like Meyers, listen to R&B or rap. I climbed into the engine first, and since I had to ride in the middle, I decided that it was my right to listen to a country station. Meyers got in, then reached over in the middle of one of my favorite country songs and turned the radio to some rap station. I turned it back. He turned it back to his station and pulled a butterfly knife from his pocket and pointed the blade at me. "If you touch that radio again, I'm fixin' to cut your throat."

I felt raw hatred; I stared at him and felt murder burning through my bones. But I hesitated, and the moment passed. I never did snitch to Campbell about it, but I still boiled inside – and I didn't forget it, either.

We worked the Uvas Fire for two hard weeks. Up every frigid morning at 5:30, putting rock-hard boots over crunchy brown socks on our swollen feet; lacing up the stiff leather laces with fumbly fingers; eating the same stuff for breakfast and lunch. Working for 17 or 18 hours straight in god-awful heat; coming back to camp after dark to prep for tomorrow's shift. No cell phone to call home. Girlfriend's probably cheating on me with that punk she works with. No shower, no fresh clothes. Nobody that wanted to talk to me or seemed to even give a crap about my presence.

But my tonsillitis was gone.

Friday, June 25, 1993, 7:00 a.m. – Engine 341 is on the de-mob (demobilization) list and we are getting ready to leave. The Uvas Fire has been declared controlled, so there isn't much left to do.

I am expecting that we will return to town, get a motel, clean up, change into fresh clothes, have a good meal and a good rest, and then drive back to Idaho. We have been gone now for over two weeks, and we were told we would be in New Mexico for two weeks. I haven't talked to Stephanie or anyone in my family for two weeks. I have been miserable for two weeks. I have been out of my element and hot and dirty and tired for two weeks. I have been with complete strangers who hardly talk to me, and I have been living *high adventure* for two weeks.

We should be back on the interstate headed north. Why are we headed southwest? Unless I am totally disoriented, which is possible, we are not driving north! What the hell is going on?

"So, uh, Lee, where we headed now?" I ask.

"I already told you, there's another big fire just south of a town called San Lorenzo that we've been dispatched to."

"How long will we be on that fire?"

"How the hell should I know?!" He must have been losing his patience with rookies. "Anyway, what do you care? We're making overtime and hazard pay."

Overtime for us was time-and-a-half, and hazard pay when we were actually on a fire was an extra 10 percent. But I still didn't understand.

"Well I know, but we were supposed to go home after two weeks," I said.

"That ain't how this business works," he countered. And that was it.

Late that afternoon we pulled into the incident command post (ICP) of the 22,000-acre–and-growing Park Fire. People in yellow and green milled about in the hot and dusty air. I'd run out of clean clothes several days before and was stuck in a soggy t-shirt, brown tighty whiteys, cardboard-stiff socks, pants, and fire shirt, and hair that felt like the carpet they put on the inside of dog houses. I ran my tongue back and forth across my upper front teeth and it felt both slick and grainy. I probably smelled bad enough to make my mother faint. This was undoubtedly the dirtiest I had ever been.

We spent the next six days just about like we'd spent the previous two weeks. This time, though, our main job was mopping up – a seemingly futile activity in which you remove the heat and smoke from virtually everything within a hundred feet or so of the fireline. This means everything from the largest juniper or pine tree down to the smallest, flattest cow pie. And we did it all day long without water.

A primer on dry-mopping: On a typical fire, by mid-morning you and your crew have received your daily briefing from the incident commander or whoever is in charge of operations on the fire. Your map leads you to your assigned spot on the division, and you pull up and park the engine and the chase truck in a safety zone. There is no way to pull hoses to your assigned fireline today, so you'll be dry-mopping, which sucks.

Even though you are on the line and should be wearing your yellow shirt, you have instead waited until the very last moment to put it on, and that moment is now. In the front right bin of the engine sits a gray and black and brown and yellow garment that smells like an old campfire. It has the look and feel of a canvas tarp, a very well-used and coarsely wrinkled canvas tarp. Already plenty warm, with the sun three-quarters of the way to its daily high, you put on the itchy garment and do a little two-armed jig to try loosening the shirt a bit.

Next, you fuel up the chainsaw. A side benefit of this chore is a minor chemical burn patch on the inside of your thigh where you spill fuel. The thigh is already uncomfortably encased within fire pants that are stiff and filthy.

Then you hike across the barren moonscape of land – rendered as such by the intensity of the fire that passed through here yesterday afternoon. There is no longer anything alive here. In the hot afternoon, this scorched place looks like the moon, but it feels like you're walking across the face of the sun. A few hot spots begin to emerge like groundhogs and kick up smoke. "Well, I guess there aren't too many so far," you sigh to yourself.

As the day wears on, however, more and more smokes pop up within the hundred-foot swath your division supervisor asked you to mop up completely. At some point he comes hiking by and decides, hmmm, maybe we ought to mop up two hundred feet in, because of the predicted high winds. *Fuck you and your high winds*, you're thinking, but you move on to the next smoking root system and swing at it with your pulaski. Dulled by hundreds of other similar swings today, the pulaski just ricochets off the main rootball and bounces off to the side. You keep at this till your lower back is screaming and the roots and stobs are all removed. That's when you realize that one of those goddamn little black stumpfucker bugs has burrowed in between the back of your neck and the collar of your stiff-ass yellow shirt. It stings and itches at the same time, and you swat at it and miss repeatedly.

The fire burned the grasses and brush so thoroughly that you are standing in ash the consistency of fine snow, up to your ankles. After a while, that gets hot too, and sometimes you accidentally step down into a root hole and get "hot foot." When dry mopping, this condition can be critical and seriously injure you. Right now, though, it just burns like a sonofabitch. Now the back of your neck has four or five itchy welts on it from the stumpfucker bites, you have a pounding lack-of-sleep headache, and still the sun beats down. You pull the cuff of your glove back to look at the dusty face of your watch and learn that this shift still has five hours left in it. Dry mopping sucks.

Thursday, July 1, 1993, 9:00 a.m. – the Park Fire has been declared controlled, and again we are on the move. I know now not to ask any questions, but just go with the flow. The flow did not move north toward Idaho, but rather, back to the asphalt yard of the BLM office.

We arrived there late in the afternoon. I felt like I had proven myself to be a good rookie over the past days by following directions and working as hard as I could. It seemed like these people weren't looking quite so hard at me now. They may have even asked me once or twice if everything was going okay.

The next few days we worked around the hot-as-the-face-of-the-sun BLM yard. We fixed up stuff on the engine, resupplied, and played hours of pushup hacky-sack. If you served yourself, you had to do 10 pushups, if you touched the bag with your hands you did 25 pushups, if you said "sorry" you did 10 pushups, and if it was your screw-up that caused the cycle to break, 10 pushups. Time was now standing still, it seemed, while I waited for the arrival of these reportedly huge Southwestern rainstorms, called *monsoons*, which should come any day now and effectively close out the region's fire season. I'll bet I spent 10 percent of my time looking up at the azure sky and hoping, willing, the rain clouds to appear. We did eat some dang good ribs at Big John's BBQ and we had excellent Mexican food at several restaurants, but we did *not* appear to be headed home anytime soon.

The Fourth of July. I had pay-phoned home the night before while I washed my fire clothes and a short load of regular clothes at the La Quinta motel's mini laundry room. I had whined and moaned to friends

47

and family, and I drank six bottles of Coors Light that Jerry had purchased for me at the convenience store (I wasn't old enough to buy it yet). The good news, I told them on the phone, was that I had dropped lots of weight and was getting tan and wiry, which I had never been before. I was hoping we wouldn't work on the 4th, or maybe if we did, it would be to drive home, yeah! Nope. We spent the day moving office cubicle dividers in preparation for remodeling the entryway of the main office.

I thought we were firefighters!?

Sunday, July 4, 1993, 10:30 p.m. – Lee Campbell, who's not nearly as excitable as Trent Allen, is rapping on the door of the motel room. "Get up and get ready," he says, "we're going to a fire. Meet downstairs in five minutes."

Five minutes later, we are rolling in 341 down the connector in Las Cruces, eventually to head north and east onto the White Sands Missile Range to assist the U.S. Army firefighters with initial attack on a running brush fire. Although I did miss partying with my friends down on the banks of the Snake River in Idaho right now, I was also pretty amped for this fire. So far, I had shown up only on fires that had already reached extended attack status (basically, burned for more than one day). We would be some of the first firefighters to attack this beast, though, so it promised to be exciting.

Radio chatter among Campbell, Eric Hall, the Fort Bliss Army firefighters, Las Cruces dispatchers, and the other responding units made me get that feeling in my stomach like moments before kickoff in a football game.

"Fort Bliss fire dispatch, from Hall."

"Hall, Fort Bliss fire dispatch."

"Engines 341, 311, 632, and I have departed Las Cruces and are rolling north on 70 at this time. En route to the White Sands Fire."

"Copy Hall, let us know when you have arrived and are in contact with Sergeant Davis."

"I copy, Hall clear."

"341, Hanson, on Tac-4."

"Go ahead Randy."

"You boys ready to rock'n'roll? I believe we've got a live one here."

"We're ready."

Forty-five minutes later we roll up on the fire, most likely somewhere near the origin, judging by the plastic grocery bags full of illegal fireworks lying on the side of the road. This thing is just ripping across the flats. Flames are so high that we'd seen them reflected in the sky ten miles before we got here. What does one do now, I wonder? Hall and Hanson convene with someone who looks to be the leader of the squad of Army firefighters. This must be Sergeant Davis.

Overhearing and eavesdropping, I get the general idea that the plan will be to cut handline on this northwest flank, because the terrain is too rocky and rough to drive the engines, while another responding Army crew from Fort Bliss burns back toward the head of the fire from a blacktop road running east to west across the range about two miles from our location. I anticipate hand tool needs and start unloading pulaskis and shovels, while also readying myself both mentally and physically.

Campbell then formally gives us directions about our small part in this plan (dig dirt), and concludes with a warning. "Keep your heads up."

Away we go, just like on the Uvas Fire, lined out pulaski to shovel, clanking and grunting in the warm New Mexico night. Embers from the fire lazily drift over our heads, while the pungent scent of newly singed sagebrush and cactus fills our nostrils. The main fire, maybe a quarter of a mile away, lights up the southern sky, while the rotating beacons of fire trucks pulse through the night haze back behind us. Headlamps on helmets focus mainly on the ground, but once in a while glare down the line.

Ten or fifteen yards ahead of us, the Army firefighters are using saws to cut through the larger sagebrush and scattered junipers. Putt-Putt-Putt, Vroommmm, Vroooooooom! as they cut through the limbs and branches.

"Motherfucker! Shit, fuck, shit, sonofabitch, godDAMMIT!"

"Fuck, get the hell OUT of here!" screams another.

Headlamps waver and fall to the ground, one of the saws goes ka-bump in the dirt and falls silent. I wonder why on earth the Army firefighters are dancing about and yelling and running through the brush. But before I even have time to go from puzzled to alarmed, a bunch of embers go down my shirt, in front and in back, and I need to fix this *now*. I don't remember *seeing* any embers, but they're burning the hell out of me. A big one is burning the back of my neck, and there are a couple down my pants – and another in my right glove.

Those aren't embers! I finally see a yellowjacket on the sleeve of my shirt, and then I begin to see them everywhere. We are being attacked by a huge swarm of yellowjackets! The Army sawyers had accidentally cut into a huge nest of them.

Someone runs up to me and says, "Get his shirt off!" It's James Stoddard.

Now I'm dancing around myself, panicking, and slapping myself all over the place trying to get them off me. I look over and see Meyers one step away from me with that butterfly knife. He grabs me by the collar and in one swipe he has the front of both my yellow shirt and my t-shirt slit wide open. Stoddard and the ever-cool Jerry Graham have hold of my shoulders and are yanking both shirts off me. Meyers is throwing dirt on me and smacking the yellowjackets off my chest.

Moments later it's over, and I have a brand new opinion of my fellow crewmembers and track athletes. They saved my butt.

Back at the engine, we made mud from the dirt and slathered it onto the dozens of stings. We did have some bee-sting medication, but I remembered my dad telling me, years ago, that he had been stung by a bunch of wasps and his aunt had remedied the pain with mud. If I was allergic, I would have probably gone into anaphylactic shock at that point and maybe even died. We were a long way from a hospital. Back on the fire, we continued digging line until we met up with an Army D-9 Caterpillar cutting a road-width fireline. The rest of the attack was relatively straightforward, as we burned off from our dirt line back to the east to remove unburned fuels between the main road and the head of the fire.

Somewhere in there, the sun had risen and the fire was determined by the IC, Sergeant Davis, to be officially contained at about 200 acres; the Army could handle it from there. We hoofed it back to 341 and drove back to Las Cruces; not to the motel for sleep, but to the BLM office, so we could continue pulling up the carpet to prep the foyer for ceramic tile.

I remembered the day back when Randy had warned me that sleep might be a luxury.

It seemed like I had been away from home for years. Even though I was starting to get along with everyone (mainly because I was beginning to accept my place as the pup of the crew), I was sick of it. Work, work, work, every damned day. Same places, same people, same motel, same restaurants. There hadn't been any fires for several days, so we hauled boxes and boxes of heavy tile, cut it with a water saw, and killed our knees putting tile in place. I didn't have a debit card or credit card, and I couldn't go anywhere anyway, so I was making a load of money and couldn't even spend it. The calendar had essentially ceased to matter to me. Two weeks had turned into at least a month. Around the middle of July, Hall and Hanson got us all together and told us we would be leaving Las Cruces and traveling to a spot somewhere on the Gila National Forest to conduct a prescribed burn.

A little fire science here. As the 1980s turned into the '90s, forest rangers, fire ecologists, and firefighters began to pay attention to the evidence that fuels for range and forest fires were loading up unnaturally. Forest fires were getting out of control much more easily, and they were burning stuff up way more severely than they had in the past. The fires were bigger, hotter, more frequent, and more expensive. Fires in timber sometimes left the area like a moonscape, even sterilizing the soil, and this caused erosion, stream degradation, landslides, and other watershed issues. Range fires burned so hot and thoroughly that the only things growing back were cheatgrass and weeds. Mosaic-type patterns of burned and unburned areas, biologists knew, were much better for plants and animals – for the whole ecosystem. These were the facts, and the USFS was seriously studying whether putting out all fires was really a good idea. But it wasn't common knowledge, and it was still debated in the 1980s whether the situation was the result of the decades-long Smokey Bear attitude of "all wildfire is bad."

Since the early part of the century, after the great fires of 1910, forest and range managers threw everything they could at wildfires in an attempt to stop them while they were still small. The 10 o'clock policy meant that fire crews would control every wildfire by 10:00 a.m. the day after it was discovered. Smokey Bear has been with us since the 1940s. At the beginning of World War II, Americans feared that the threatened (and even attempted) Japanese attacks on Pacific forests would destroy those forests and thus an important part of the national economy. The Smokey Bear campaign turned into the longest running public-service campaign in U.S. history – and Smokey is the most widely recognized character in this country. The unintended consequence of putting out all fires immediately, biologists and fire scientists now believed, was that a natural thing like fire, kept off the land by human intervention, was disturbing a natural cycle. Lightning-caused wildfires that used to burn moderately through ecosystems had created natural mosaic patterns, favoring the reproduction and growth of organisms living within the ecosystem. But if you eliminate fire, especially in a fire-dependent ecosystem, too much underbrush and other fuels are left, and the fire will burn with too much intensity. Fires that used to burn only this underbrush, leaving healthy stands of timber in place, now used the excess fuels to climb to higher fuels, working up the ladder and becoming crown fires. These tear across even the tops of trees, and sound like freight trains barreling through the forest, wiping out everything in their path and becoming about as controllable as a classroom full of seventh graders drinking Red Bulls.

The solution: prescribed fire and "let-burn" policies. The former means that humans will start fires on purpose, in controlled settings, while the latter means to not mess with fires that have already started naturally, i.e., lightning-caused fires. The science is hardly questionable, but the politics, which in this day and age, *always* seem to usurp hard science, are far more complex.

First, look at Yellowstone National Park, in 1988 (the year when I witnessed forest fires for the first time, and saw what I wanted to do). Managers of the park decided that, when the first of the fires started in late July, they would let them burn to counteract decades of fuels buildup. Managers wrung their hands as the fires grew and grew and burned and burned. A few structures were burned. Park entrances were closed.

When it was finally decided that the fires should be fought, that was a nearly impossible task – given the fuel loads across Yellowstone in areas that hadn't burned for years, along with the very limited road access to those areas. Public pressure was on to "save Yellowstone" and politicians jostled for position in front of the news cameras that brought the conflagration into living rooms across the country. Local business owners and residents railed against the Park managers and the firefighters, insisting that the Park was ruined. It was not. Politicians ordered the firefighters to put the fire out – but they couldn't. It was finally the snows of late autumn that quelled the fires. And Yellowstone came back – not at all ruined. The summer of 1988 was the driest on record for the Park's history. Almost 250 fires started in Yellowstone that summer; 31 were initially allowed to burn. A little over a million acres burned – about one-third of the Park. More than 25,000 firefighters fought fire there that summer, at a total cost of about $120 million. Yellowstone brought to the forefront what some experts had been saying for 15 years – we need to take a pro-active approach to wildland fire. Fire ecologists, biologists, foresters, range conservationists, fire control officers, ranchers, fish and game departments, members of the public, members of Congress and others discussed the interests they held in fire management. The pro-active approach of prescribed fire seemed the best option.

This involves humans deciding when and where some fires will burn. Crews go out and prep areas by cutting line, burning small hold lines (about the width of a two-lane highway), mapping natural barriers, analyzing fuel loads and fuel moisture levels, and monitoring weather factors – specifically wind speed and direction, air temperatures, and relative humidity. They even incorporate geographic information systems, differential equations, and computer models, and the fire is torched off only when all the details of the prescription for a safe burn are in order.

But you can't really mess around too much with Mother Nature. Every prescribed fire I was ever involved with did get out of control to some degree -- or it threatened to. Then there's Murphy's Law, too. Flat tires, vapor-locked water pumps, sudden wind direction changes, and even flaming wildlife running across the control line have all contributed to the most well-planned prescribed fire turning into one hell of a conflagration.

This prescribed fire on the Gila National Forest would be my first taste of it. I kept glancing over at that blue can of Skoal Mint that Campbell had left in the cab. It was early in the afternoon, and I was beyond bored with riding along and looking out at the flats around Las Palomas. I had never tried tobacco, despite the crowd I'd run with in high school. I picked up Campbell's can and attempted to pack it with my index finger like I'd seen others do. Then I opened the lid, sniffed the minty aroma, and pinched a dip the size of an arrowhead for my lower lip. Moments later, I was swept away to a land of buzzing bliss. Colors took on new flavors, R&B was good music, and the desolate New Mexico terrain became an enchanted land of milk and honey. The pint of spit gathering in my mouth I simply lurched onto the vinyl floor of the gray Ford. My 10-year love affair with tobacco had begun.

The mountains of the Gila are big, beautiful, and covered in Ponderosa pine trees. The dirt road was bumpy and we bounced along in the dust behind Campbell and Stoddard, who were cruising at two miles an hour ahead of us in 341. Jerry was driving us in the gray Ford chase, I rode shotgun, and Meyers was crashed out in the back seat. Jerry made me stay awake; he said it was government policy that the person riding shotgun has to stay awake for the driver. I don't know if I believed this or not, but I tried my best, even as my head was on the bobble. Maybe a dip of chew would help me stay awake. Oh yeah.

That night our crew camped out in a clearing under the stars and beautiful tall pines of the Gila. Nearby a small stream gurgled and bubbled over rocks, and a small breeze drifted the forest scents past my face. I was dressed in every stitch of clothing I had brought with me, *and* tucked into my sleeping bag, but I was still shivering. We were at about 6,000 feet elevation, not too far south of the Continental Divide. When I had pictured New Mexico, I had not imagined mountains and forests like this. I thought all of New Mexico was just a big desert.

At 6 a.m. we were up and drinking coffee that Dave had made for us, and I was chewing Skoal as well. It was cold enough to see my breath, and everything was covered with frost. In July. I tried to eat a chicken à la king MRE for some energy, but it was disgusting even with Tabasco sauce.

A meal-ready-to-eat is an individual self-contained package of field rations, developed for the U.S. military and also used for firefighters and other personnel when a food facility is not available. It typically includes some kind of main food, side dish, snack, and a plastic spoon, along with crackers and peanut butter and a powdered drink mix. Many firefighters have their own explanations of what MRE means, including "materials resembling edibles" and "Mr. E" (mystery).

Water and M&Ms would just have to do for me this morning. Prescribed fires do not come with caterers serving up cheesy scrambled eggs and sausage patties.

Hall explained the plan of the day, and before the sun had cleared the ridges behind us, I was driving a shovel and cutting line up a timbered sidehill, second from the back in a crew of yellow shirts. Hall and Hanson led the way, sawing and swamping ponderosas, aspens, and anything else in our way. We topped out on a flat at midday, where we tied our handline into a hiking trail running north to south. Then it was back to the engine to start a hose lay back up the line, running from 341's water pump to the tie-in spot. When this was completed, we would use fusees to burn a control line or blackline eight or ten feet wide off the trail and the handline. The hose lay was there to prevent the fire from getting out of control and either going too far down the sidehill or spilling across the trail or line and going bye-bye to the south.

Because Jerry and I were the bigger guys, it was our job to string 100-foot rolls of inch-and-a-half cotton hose from the bins on 341 up to the flats. This was hard work. I remember visualizing myself in a mirror, in my mind, on my way back down, and seeing how tough and trim I'd become. I was in the best physical shape I had ever been; I knew it, and resolved to contact Coach Mike Quick at the University of Chicago as soon as I got home, and tell him I had changed my mind and was going to play football for his team.

By nightfall we had the hoseline in place, and would now use drip torches to burn a 20-foot-wide blackline through the tall grass all the way from the confluence of our handline and the dirt road back to the clearing where we had camped the night before. About two miles. The method to do this and prevent the flame you put down from getting out of control is three-fold. First, you wait until late in the day, or early in the evening, when humidity is up and temperature is down. Second, you make sure if there is any wind that it's blowing back toward your line (which in this case was the dirt road). Third, you put the punk rookie teenager on the nozzle of the hard line, tell him to get ready to suck some smoke, and then have him knock down the flames when they get out to within 20 feet of the road.

For the rookie, this is both good and bad. It's good because it's damned exciting; you against the fire, one on one, beating back the devil. Heat and light and crackling and blue and orange and motors and pumps and yelling and sweat and nerves. Your job is very important because if you can't knock the fire down, that sucker is gonna go out of control. At the same time, it's bad because you probably inhale more smoke while doing this than the entire city of Los Angeles does in a year. Within ten minutes of Dave's dropping the first few blobs of burning diesel and gas onto the tall brown grass, I was getting more smoke than air, and beginning to experience a sensation of choking out. You simply can't cough with enough power and repetition to expel all the smoke. That's when you gag and puke – and I did. It ricocheted off the camo bandanna tied around my face and spewed down the front of my shirt. Thankfully, all I'd put in my stomach that day was one bite of chicken à la king, a package of M&Ms, and water. I wasn't about to quit at this, though. This was *way* too much fun. Morgan and Meyers shouted encouragement and helped guide the hose over rocks for me while Campbell idled 341 down the dirt road. The rest of the crew trailed along behind, watching for spots and slopovers.

Reaching the camp clearing, and thus the tie-in with the east-west dirt road, we were at the end of this blackline. For me, it felt like the end of a football game. I was absolutely soaked from sweat, overspray, and a persistent leak in the forester nozzle I'd been operating. I did a hooyah! but quickly realized that I was now staring down the barrel of a very cold and miserable night – not in my own mummy bag but in a cheap lightweight government-issue bag. Up again and drinking Dave's coffee at 6 a.m., with frosty breath, green lush canopy, camp robber jays scolding us, and several people with too much energy for this early in the morning. I am now reduced to a diet of cowboy coffee and MRE peanut butter, with a pinch of snuff for dessert. I stood there instinctively trying to reduce the surface area of my body and shivering; holding my blue tin cup of coffee as close to me as possible. I had changed out of my damp green pants the night before, but I had to wear my damp t-shirt because I had no spare anymore (after the yellowjacket incident), and I was just too prideful to borrow anyone else's.

Plan for the day: burn a blackline this morning off the handline we had cut yesterday, then monitor and hold the entire line in the afternoon while 67 Echo Golf (a Bell JetRanger helicopter) deposited thousands of incendiary ping-pong balls all over the planned area to complete the actual burn, hopefully in a manner that resulted in the mosaic pattern that was conducive to good ecology.

Incendiary ping-pong balls? The Delayed Aerial Ignition Device (DAID) system involves injecting ethylene glycol into small white balls already filled with potassium permanganate, then shooting them out of a helicopter-mounted dispenser down onto the ground. The ball starts on fire, and then starts the ground fuels on fire. First things first, though, burning the blackline up the sidehill. Allen and Holly work methodically down the line with drip torches, while everybody else spreads along the line to monitor and hold. I am down with Campbell at 341's pump helping him deliver water through the inch-and-a-half mainline stretched up the sidehill. The Briggs and Stratton pump is humming, the hose is charged, and we're beginning to see and smell smoke from the blackline fire.

Then the pump quits.

The normally cool Hanson, up the hill manning one of the red nozzles, immediately detects the drop in water pressure and starts yelling back down the line. "We're losin' it! Give us more water, we're fuckin' losin' it!" The urgency in his voice is unmistakable.

Campbell, though, is a picture of efficiency, pulling and twisting levers and knobs, troubleshooting at light speed. Morgan is there now, ready to help if he can. I look back up the hill and can see flame over the top of 40-foot trees. *Oh shit.*

There's not much I can do here. I'm not experienced enough with engines or even firefighting itself, so I just stand over to the side and wait for tempers and flames to explode – and explode they do. Campbell is getting pissed, Morgan stays relatively cool, but I can hear the forest crackling up the sidehill. Eventually, Morgan determines there is a vapor lock in the fuel line of the pump engine, and Campbell yanks it apart. A vapor lock occurs when liquid fuel turns to gas (boils) and blocks the flow into the carburetor. It happens more easily at high altitudes because of the lower boiling point. Pulling the gas line off its connection will usually get rid of the vapor lock. Campbell looks over at me standing there. "Fill up a piss pump and go help them out!" he bellers.

A piss pump is slang for a bladder bag, a 5-gallon sack you fill with water. It has backpack straps and a miniature forester nozzle that puts out about as much water as you could piss if you had been drinking beers for two hours straight and hadn't peed yet. The whole thing weighs about 45 pounds when filled. I fill one, then begin to hump it up the line.

Smoke now fills the forest, making it hard to see as I struggle up the steep trail. Sweat flies off me like rain and my lungs are seared, but I feel like I am the only hope. When I arrive at the slopover, I realize that Campbell has basically sent me to boil water (like the husband gets told when the wife is in labor) – either that or he didn't realize the height of the flames by now. A piss pump taking on those flames would be akin to a mosquito taking on a jetliner. I try to set the pump down before anyone sees that I have it, but it is too late. "What are you expecting to do with that?" Dave asks. Hanson and the rest of the crew are doing the best they can to re-route the handline above the flames when Morgan radios up on the tactical channel that they have the pump started and the lines will be charged momentarily. As soon as the one-inch branch line is charged, we take the beast head on, more powerful now that we have water pressure. Holly and Jerry each grab a red forester nozzle and sweep a water spray across the base of the flames and then proceed from tree to tree up the sidehill until all the live flame is extinguished and only heavy aspen smoke remains. Way down the hill, you could hear the Briggs and Stratton pump motor howling. The feeling of relief was palpable, but it was short-lived.

You can maintain and take care of your stuff meticulously, but strange things can and do occur. Another opponent of perfectly planned prescribed fires is miscommunication, and a third is weather. You can't just put an awakened dragon back to bed anytime you want.

When I was eight years old, I lived on the west edge of Idaho Falls, not too far from where the farm fields started. There were two irrigation ditches that ran through the area where you could often find garter snakes you could catch and keep as pets. Other kids were better at finding them than I was. I had never caught one and was itching to do so. Mike and Justin Jones and I patrolled the banks of the bigger canal one sunny summer Saturday hoping to change that.

Whoa, there he goes! A colorful little garter snake slithered through the brush, but was faster than we were and escaped into a large pile of weeds and assorted rubbish. We circled the pile and rooted through it, but could not get him out of there. That's when I had the idea – let's burn him out!

I ran home and snagged a book of matches out of the junk drawer in the kitchen. I zipped them across the sandpaper starter strip and tossed them one by one onto the rubbish pile, which gradually started to smoke and smolder. Mike and Justin and I rubbed our hands together and waited for the little sucker to exit. The flames began to consume the pile and grow bigger and bigger and hotter and hotter. Still the snake did not come out.

Soon there was a pretty good column of smoke rising, and we couldn't even see each other from more than a few feet away. I began to get scared and forgot about the snake. Mike ran home and hid. Justin ran home and told his dad. I ran over to the irrigation ditch and cupped my hands to get water to put on the fire, about a fourth of a cup at a time.

The fire left the rubbish pile and started careening down the ditch bank and across the field. I heard sirens and saw fire trucks. My first prescribed fire got loose and took out a few acres.

I had never before – and I haven't since – seen a person whipped across the bare back with a belt. Every time their dad smacked them, Mike and Justin screamed OWWWWWW! and bawled like heifers. I watched from the corner of the bedroom.

Prescribed fire experience number two. My mom and my grandma had gone to Hawaii, so my dad, grandpa, and older brother were all playing bachelor for the week. Dad decided he would burn off the old grass in the field, same as the farmers do every spring. He waited for a sunny Sunday and lit it off next to the road, as the prevailing southwest breeze would allow the fire to calmly back away from the road, down the ditch bank, and across the one-acre patch that butted up against the neighbor Carlsons' pasture.

About the time Dad had a nice strip fired off, the wind changed direction and picked up speed. Off she went. My grandpa hobbled with his cane right back to the house. He wanted nothing to do with it. My dad and brother went after the flames armed with shovels. They looked like monkeys running around through the smoke and 10-foot-high flames. I heard my dad yell, "Call someone!" Call someone?

My brother screamed, "Call the fire department!"

I did as told and the firefighters came, saving our butts. Had we not called the fire department, I'm sure that fire would have eaten up the Carlsons' pasture, including the barn full of new tractors.

I had reason to be distrustful of lighting fires on purpose. Not to mention the sweet stunt I had pulled on the Uvas Fire on my first day on my first fire as a firefighter.

Back on the Gila prescribed fire, we all caught our breath and sipped hot water from our canteens. Halftime of today's game. Some of us took the opportunity to insert some tobacco and rest our sore feet for a moment. That's when we heard the helicopter.

"I hope he isn't dropping fire yet," Allen said.

Hall attempted to contact the helitack crew or pilot by radio, but was unsuccessful the first couple of times. "67 Echo Golf, this is Hall."

Finally, "Ahh, Hall, this is 67 Echo Golf. Go ahead." Pilots always sound so cool on the radio, voices all scratchy and stuff.

The gist of the conversation was this: Have you started dropping balls yet? Yes, we have. Our blackline is not tied in yet and we have no resources, *repeat, no resources* on the north end. Okay, said the pilot, we'll stop dropping.

Where did the miscommunication occur? Who knows. Thankfully we had the experience and brainpower of the veterans on our side, or it could have been much worse. Like field generals, Hanson and Hall coordinated the resources we did have (just our Idaho Falls crew with one engine) into two groups, and we went to work getting the situation under control. The sun was high in the sky and it was hot; all was quiet but for the crackling of our blackline fire, benignly moving down the slope toward the gully. We lucked out.

Part of the crew hiked with Hall back down to the chase trucks. They would head back to the north end and monitor the fire to make sure it was within its containment line. I stayed with the crew on the south end, using the engine and the hose lay to clean up the blackline and ensure there were no more slopovers.

Was I beginning to like this stuff? I certainly was – and I was getting used to being absolutely filthy, tired, and hungry. It was strangely liberating, like being a dirty little kid who doesn't have to worry about bath time or supper time. I really wasn't even thinking much about home.

"Hanson, Hall, on Tac-4."

"Go ahead Eric."

"You better finish up on that end as soon as possible; the fire's jumped the north line and we're gonna need help."

"Wow, this is turning into a cluster," Randy said to us.

Unbeknownst to us, the helicopter had begun dropping ping-pong balls quite a while ago; small individual flames had become gangs and were now running amok. The wind had changed direction and thrown some embers over the road. We were supposed to be in position to monitor and attack this type of thing before 67 Echo Golf began dropping, but it was too late, and now we were doing damage control.

"Copy that, we'll finish up here and work our way over there," Randy replied.

"Finishing up" meant rolling lengths of hose as quickly as possible. The hose is dirty – and heavy with mud and muck and leftover water in the line. After we rolled it all, we the threw it into the back of the gray Ford, packed up our tools, and bounced our way back north, with the dust behind 341 still hanging in the air – even though Campbell and Meyers had a 10-minute head start on us.

We came around a bend in the dirt road and there in the shade was Campbell with 341. Bands of blood flowed from his nostrils through his large mustache, and on his face was the meanest look I had ever seen. At his feet sat a large lug wrench and a long cheater bar. The cheater bar had won. We all bailed out and helped haul the huge spare tire off the top of the engine while Campbell had his revenge on the lug wrench assembly. I didn't dare look at him, lest he decide to take his temper out on me.

Hall was beyond frustrated, with the north end slopover still growing and the engine out of commission. We were all angry and impatient with our impotence. Then the gray Ford refused to start.

Stoddard and I were left to figure this out while Jerry, Campbell, Meyers, and Hanson messed with 341. After rooting around the engine compartment for a minute, we found that the Ford's problem was just a loose battery cable. I grabbed a wrench out of the cabinet and fixed that.

And 45 minutes later we were back in business. We rolled down the road to tie in with Hall and the rest of the crew, who were overmatched without an engine, and getting their butts kicked. We intended to even the odds.

Jerry and Hanson stretched a hard line up the hill. Hall and Dave came back down the hill to help Campbell set up a draft line into the creek to resupply 341's water tank. Meyers and I filled piss pumps and handed them out to Holly, Allen, and Stoddard. Then we filled two for ourselves and headed up the hill. As darkness fell, we began to get the upper hand on the slopover. Hall had taken a trip back south and had determined that our other lines were holding. The main fire laid down with the rising humidity and falling temperature. I heard Hall telling Hanson that we would camp here again tonight and spend one more day monitoring before we headed out. After a decent and dry night's sleep and an easy day patrolling for slopovers, we packed up and departed the Gila. I rode back to Las Cruces in the gray Ford with the same people I had ridden with on our trip down to New Mexico. I still remember Randy saying, "You know what, boys, it's going to be October before we know it." At the time, time crawled slowly for me. But then I blinked – and somehow sixteen Octobers have since come and gone.

Saturday, July 24, 1993, 7:00 p.m. – I have just finished my sixth Bud Light as I stand in 5-foot-deep water, light rain coming down on me, with my arms folded on the edge of the kidney-shaped hotel pool. We are going home tomorrow!

The monsoon rains have arrived, and I have survived! This tour is over, baby. Hall is wasted and wandering around in circles in the parking lot yelling *Hey! Heyeaye! Hey!* Campbell is drunk and hitting on Holly, who is also drunk and stretched out with her awesome bikini-clad body on a pool chair. Hanson, who doesn't drink, is in his hotel room watching TV with Dave, who may not be drunk but has certainly slugged back a few amber ales. They discuss stealing a cool painting off the wall in the room. If Allen calls me "rook" one more time, I'm going to get out of this pool and knock him out. Jerry, Stoddard, Meyers, and Morgan are in the pool with me, chilling out and verbally dissecting moments of our detail. *We are going home*, I say again.

I am not even feeling the least hung-over as we jump on the interstate and head north the next morning. It is still hot as hell, but it doesn't even bother me anymore. I just sit back, relax, and chew some Skoal Mint. I can't even think clearly about just how happy I am. I am going to hug and kiss my girl, play with my dog, do some fishing, ride my horses, and hang out with my buddies till the night closes in.

At a roadside stand north of Socorro, I drop a few bucks on some fresh grapefruit and New Mexico souvenirs for everybody back home (including a tortilla warmer for my mom that she still uses today). The feeling of heading home after this trip is like the end of football season, the end of hunting season, or a 300-pound bench press feeling – or even that first kiss from an elusive girl.

As we achieve interstate cruising speed, I notice a bum ahead, standing on the right side of the road. I am riding shotgun in the gray Ford. Feeling good about life, I figure I'll be generous with my grapefruit and toss him a gift as we drive by. The grapefruit smashed into his sternum at 75 mph and I looked in the rearview and saw pieces of grapefruit fly out from either side and above his head as the hitchhiker was poleaxed to the ground. The guys behind me saw him get up, and they radioed to us, so I know he wasn't too badly injured. Nevertheless, Mr. Hitchhiker, if you are out there, I am very sorry.

We arrived back in Idaho Falls late in the evening on July 26. We were all grateful to be home, but sore and stiff from the drive. I spotted my black Chevy pickup parked exactly where I left it, but now sporting a sweet new matching camper shell, courtesy of my very generous father. I put my deflated red bag in the back, and inserted my semi-clean and much tanner and thinner self into the driver's seat. We were instructed to meet at BLM Station #4 in Fort Hall, Idaho, on Thursday, July 29 to finish out the season.

For the next three days, I planned to do a lot of loving, a little fishing, and a medium amount of everything else a summer warrior deserves. I had the best sleep I'd ever had that night in my own bed, with Stephanie "at her friend Molly's" again.

FIRE CREW: Stories from the Fireline

It Gets in Your Blood

Thursday, July 29, 1993, 8:30 a.m. – I arrived early at the station. Because I'd not been to the Fort Hall station before, I gave myself a bit of extra time. BLM Station #4 is on the Shoshone-Bannock Indian Reservation just north of Pocatello, Idaho. It was then considered the prime location for responding to a fire anywhere in the district. We might go to fires as far north as Dubois, near the Montana state line; south to Malad, on the Utah border; east past Soda Springs, near the edge of Wyoming, or out west past the Craters of the Moon National Monument. We could be the center of all the action.

Two crews would live at or work out of the station – Engine 341's crew and the crew of Engine 342, a Chevrolet light engine run by Jake Oman and his assistant Devin Lash. Our supervisor was Eric Hall, the "swing zone" AFCO.

The station itself was a tan single-wide mobile home on a rather depressing dirt lot overrun with tumbleweeds. Two horseshoe pits, long unused, sat on the west side of the trailer, and a dilapidated two-rail wooden fence marked off the property leased from the tribe for the BLM fire season. Parked in the ready position against this fence, their grilles aimed north out of the parking area, were Engine 341, Engine 342, and the gray Ford chase truck.

I parked on the far side of the fire vehicles, next to a sign hanging on the fence. The bullet-riddled sign read

"NO SHOOTING." I offloaded my clean fire gear and clothes and other stuff, and carried them across the lot to the front deck, sinking in the sand with every step. I was already sweating when Campbell and the rest of the crew began arriving. Most of the crew lived in nearby Blackfoot, and Jerry and Stoddard lived on the reservation itself. This was a good thing – otherwise it would have been awfully crowded in the station at night.

The interior of the trailer smacked of camps and fires and men who make their living in the outdoors. Against the back wall was a plaid couch with multiple holes, flanked by a couple of basic tan recliners. The middle of the room featured a plain brown coffee table with old hunting magazines on it, and a big gray industrial-type area rug. On the north wall sat an old color TV and the base radio station; it was alive with chatter as other stations up and down the Snake River Valley called themselves into service for the day. Campbell called us in.

"428, Station 4."

"Station 4, Fourrrrr two-aught." Kara's sexy voice.

"Engine 341 and 342 are in service for the day."

"I copy, 341 and 342 in service for the day."

"Station 4 clear."

"Fourrrrr two-aught clear."

The first order of business was PT. This is another awesome fringe benefit of employment as a seasonal firefighter – you are paid an hour each day to work out – physical training. Most people used this time to jog, and that's what we would do that day.

My time in New Mexico had hardened me physically, and it showed right off the bat as the seven of us stretched out across the parking lot and began our jog south down a reservation dirt road. I got right out front and booked it, listening to one of my favorite bands on my walkman. The only guy who could hang with me was Jerry – interesting because both of us were bigger guys. After a 3-mile loop we did a few calisthenics in the sand, then we changed into our green pants, t-shirts, and fire boots.

That year was one of the slowest fire seasons the district had ever had. In fact, if not for the New Mexico detail, I would not have gained much experience at all in 1993. August is historically a busy, busy time of year for wildland fires, and in future seasons it would be for me, but all we saw for the rest of that season was a call-up late in the month to douse a haystack that had combusted and then smoldered out through a half-acre of brush.

We kept busy during the day, though, washing the already clean rigs, inventorying equipment, sweeping and mopping the trailer, and by late August, having crew wrestling matches or playing game after game of horseshoes. We would often go to lunch together at a 1950s-type diner in the small suburb of Chubbuck, and I learned new slang and the recommended firefighter methods for picking up chicks. Evenings came to be a favorite time for me at the Fort Hall station. They began at 6:00 in the evening, when Campbell would call in to dispatch to tell them we were out of service for the evening. Almost every night the entire crew would head home to Blackfoot or Pocatello, but I always stayed. Campbell, in his supreme coolness, had purchased a Nintendo 64 for the station, and would often leave me there with a 12-pack of beer and a can of Copenhagen to play Mario Brothers for a while,

while it was still hot outside. I also liked to circle out through the adjacent fields of alfalfa and do my standard slow-walking meditation routine, which has always comforted me through the years.

Sometimes in the distant southwest there would be rolls of thunder and cloud-to-cloud lightning. On those evenings, I would sit out back on the top rail of the fence to watch and wonder whether there was a fire starting somewhere. I even caught myself on many occasions hoping for one to start, so that 341 would be dispatched to fight the fire. I was really beginning to like this life, and sometimes I wondered if I was doing the right thing by leaving to go to college in the big city.

Friday, September 3, 1993, 4:00 p.m. – Today is my last day with the BLM. Then I'll have two days to hang with my family, my friends, my animals, and my girlfriend until I make the 1,500-mile journey east to Chicago. I will leave the station early to turn my gear back in to the warehouse and its resident guard dog Avery. I'm told there will also be paperwork to fill out and a quick exit interview with Gary.

We all had a couple of beers together at lunch, which left me mildly buzzed and feeling very sentimental. It was a strange feeling, considering that these people and the fire business itself had made me so miserable back in June. I wondered whether this would be the last day I'd ever work for the BLM – or any fire crew, for that matter. I wondered how any job could be harder, more exciting, more annoying, more satisfying, or more boring, all in one work day.

The camaraderie developed by shared battle is an interesting facet of the human condition. The battle may be as intense as the fire jumping your line by racing through the crowns of 70-foot-tall ponderosa pines, or it may be as excruciating as completing an 8-hour work shift with crew members on a beautiful sunny summer day when you know everyone else is out waterskiing, hoisting frosty beers, or having a pleasure hike through tall mountains next to a cold mountain stream. The synergy and electricity born of that fire crew camaraderie can be witnessed in real-time on any incident on which a fire crew rolls up and gears up for battle.

The last items I loaded in the bed of my pickup were my yellow web gear and fire pack, hard hat, and now fully empty red bag. We all stood around the tailgate and had a laugh about that first day on the Uvas Fire, when my bag was fully stuffed with food and weighed as much as a middleweight boxer. I shook hands all around and said so-long to Jerry, James, Randy, and Lee, the new boys of summer to me. None of them were dumb enough to go to college, so they would finish out the season here at Station 4, hoping for some late summer overtime and hazard pay.

Lee Campbell is a very insightful dude, and he must have seen the wistful look in my eye, and correctly interpreted my trepidation about leaving. He said to me, "Be careful man, this business has a way of getting in your blood." He perhaps mistook my two-dollar words and good high school grades for indicators of success in a stuffy business world that has no room for dirt, trucks, trees, flames, and hot canteen drinking water. I crunched the truck over the gravel of the parking lot and didn't shift into third gear until I was long gone down the reservation road.

I Will Be Returning

THINGS WEREN'T GOING SO WELL FOR ME at the University of Chicago. Three weeks into the football season I had ruined my right knee's anterior cruciate ligament and effectively ended my football career. Stephanie had broken off our heavy high school relationship essentially because I was the wrong religion. My grades sucked, I couldn't stand life in the big city, and I had developed a hell of a drinking problem. I smoked cigarettes now as well. I realized that I had dug myself into a hole and really needed to be back out West where I belonged. Gary Eames had offered this advice to me the day I left the BLM station – "Don't let them get you down."

Simple words from a wise man. I knew that *them* was an encompassing term for the dark forces of the world that exist mainly in your mind, the forces that can make life a sad and pointless journey to hell. I considered Gary's advice as I packed up my books and clothes halfway through the winter semester at Chicago and drove back to Idaho. Had I let "them" get me down?

One day the following April, a box of Original Recipe Kentucky Fried Chicken and a letter were waiting for me on the kitchen table when I got home. The letter was from the BLM. These were the two statements at the top of the page, along with the appropriate check boxes:

☐   I <u>will be</u> returning to work with the Bureau of Land Management as a Range Technician's Aide.

☐   I <u>will not be</u> returning to work with the Bureau of Land Management.

It was with of mixture of pride, excitement, and resignation to fate that I checked the upper box and mailed the letter back. Campbell's words to me echoed in my mind, yet what else was I going to do this summer? I had thought about the fire crew all winter long and missed the boys of summer. I had read Norman Maclean's *Young Men and Fire* twice, W. Axl Rose was my new hero, and I found a new bunch of music I loved. Testosterone coursed through my body, and I sported a devil-may-care attitude about life. Stephanie was gone and my high school career dreams were essentially scrapped. But I was still a young man, and was about to run buck-wild. I had a shot of tequila and washed it down with an entire can of Bud Light. Look out summer, here I come.

Second-Year Rookie

STEPHANIE HAYES LOOKED OVER AT ME when we were both on our knees scrubbing the tile on the kitchen floor of Station 6. "You're a workaholic, aren't you?"

I'm not, really, but Stephanie right then had happened to catch me looking like one.

I suppressed a chuckle. "An alcoholic maybe. But not a *work*aholic."

I had become a heavy-duty drinker. The fire season was on, and I was ill-prepared, both physically and emotionally.

Sunday, June 5, 1994, 9:00 p.m. – My friend's brother's neighbor was Valerie the dispatcher. I hoped she couldn't see me out here in Rick's driveway, all messed up like this, shooting Cuervo, smoking Camel Lights, hoisting cans of Coors. Tomorrow was the first day of the 1994 fire season, and with that came the dreaded mile-and-a-half run. I had not practiced it once, and I was fat.

Monday, June 6, 1994, 9:00 a.m. – Seriously hung-over, I report to the dispatch office on Lincoln Road. Jerry Graham sees me and his first words are, "Your ass is just getting fatter and fatter, dude."

Randy Hanson sees me and his first words are, "Whoeee! There's a whole lot more Benny this year." Randy was a big, tall, athletic machine. He had that look of a typical firefighter, with a cowboy-style handlebar mustache and longish hair. He was a cocky sonofabitch, and as I later learned, once you got on his bad side, he was done with you.

But I did pass the run, despite the fact that I smoked a cigarette moments before the run started, I smelled like tequila, and I felt like coughing up a lung *and* my guts the entire time. Funny, others were talking before this run and reassuring each other that as long as they maintained the same speed as Ben Walters did, they would pass. Campbell asked me what had happened to me over the winter. I just told him it was a tough year and I had partied too much. No one else had changed much, except that Meyers had had enough of the fire crew for a lifetime and hadn't returned, and I had been assigned to Engine 361 for the summer.

THE EVENING BEFORE, I sat at home in the front room with baseball on TV while I looked over my gear spread out on the floor. Summer thunderstorms had not arrived yet, but a drizzly rain cell sat directly overhead and depressingly washed out the valley. Hardly the kind of motivation you need to get your firefighting gear ready. I sipped a cold beer and considered what stuff I ought to have with me this season. My more practical thoughts were often interspersed with questions I was currently asking of life – like what am I going to do now? What is Stephanie doing right now? What is Danielle (my current girlfriend) *not* doing right now? How will I get more beer tonight?

I tried to focus. The first thing I did was to ditch the cheap government sleeping bag and replace it with my maroon Cabela's mummy bag. I also put a pajama ensemble together, consisting of a Dallas Cowboys stocking cap, a thick, soft pair of navy blue sweatpants, a big fleece sweatshirt, and some chunky socks I used during hunting season. I was determined not to freeze in fire camp at night this year.

I added to my pack the rest of the stuff I had learned to call necessities. I stood and considered the pack's contents for a moment, with one hand on my hip and the other encircling a can of beer. The rain outside was now coming down in sheets. I wondered when this weather would yield to the heat waves of summer. A small chill ran up and down my spine as I thought about the adrenaline rush that comes when you know you have to respond to a fire.

At this point in my fire career, though, I had not responded to enough fires to really understand what to expect. Most of my firefighting in New Mexico the previous summer was extended attack, on fires that had started at least a day or two before we arrived. The only two initial attack situations were the White Sands Fire on July Fourth, and another smaller fire called the Radium Springs Fire. Initial attack operations are exciting mainly because of the factor called the "unknown." Because it's a fire, and because it's a situation that's essentially out of control, you never know what you're going to get when you roll up to the scene. In the past, most wildland fires occurred in relatively wild places, where the only audience was nature. But now wildland fires are occurring more often near urban areas, essentially because humans have made wild places into residential areas. The areas where development butts up against forests and wildlands are called the wildland/urban interface, and it's turned wildland fire into a much more public entity – and a much more dangerous foe. We had a lot of both in the Pocatello area.

This knowledge, along with Sean Udy's reputation for freaking out at fires, motivated me to make sure I was good and ready when the call came. I tried to make sure my pack straps wouldn't get all tangled up when I grabbed it, and tried to make sure I always knew where my hard hat and fire shirt were in the chase truck, and tried to make sure I was always hydrated and ready to rock.

A nnual fire school is traditional and required in Western land management agencies, be they state run or federal – like the BLM and Forest Service. Firefighter rookies and veterans alike come together from all over the region to attend a range of classes involving wildland fire. The first class for all firefighters is *S-190, Introduction to Wildland Fire Behavior*. It's the class I never finished in 1993 because I was shipped off on the New Mexico detail. This is the basic 101 class. The classes range upward to the 400-level courses involving advanced suppression techniques, air attack operations, and even hydraulics theories for water delivery.

That year I attended, among others, a course on the incident management system. My 150-pound red bag story from the New Mexico trip had by then become somewhat of a humorous vocational legend in local fire circles, so I was always called on by the instructors to relate it to the class as kind of an icebreaker. I guess I was always glad to relieve others of the possibility of making such a mistake, but I was also becoming aware that I could be pigeonholing myself as an idiot among my colleagues. So I tried to relate it to the class as not very funny. No one really laughed; there was a cough or two, and that was it.

The good parts of fire school include seeing people from other districts and forests, people you've met in the past. You can catch up on winter activities; you're also getting paid to be there and learn something. And you can get with your summer buddies and go out to lunch at Sizzler and screw around and wrestle and laugh and joke.

The downside of fire school is that it is excruciating to just sit there all day long. Tiiiiick-tooooock. It breeds tobacco use and caffeine abuse. And the fire school instructors are here for good hard work in the summer sun, not to nursemaid a bunch of potential blockheads. We all just endure it for two weeks.

I learned quickly that Sean Udy had a temper as explosive as a black cat firecracker, with a fuse of about the same length. This was just his summer job, his "real" job being a high school teacher and coach. Sean had been around the fire world for a long time, and had spent many a summer on a hotshot crew. Looking back now, I realize he exhibited that summer all the traits of someone who is burnt out on the status quo and badly needs the summer break that fire season provides. He seemed pissed off at the world. His personality didn't fit with his appearance, though – towhead blond hair, a plump beer paunch, and Buddy Holly glasses. His voice would get really high and whiny when he got pissed off.

Steve Lewis was the exact opposite of Sean. I don't think you could get him fired up if you put a flame to him. The day I met Steve, he was driving us down to the airport in the white Ford chase truck for some fixed-wing aircraft awareness training. The radio was set to a country station playing a really dumb song. Steve looked over at John, who was riding shotgun, and mumbled, "Country music's all right, but this is pushing it." Then he reached out to change the station and I noticed that he had the longest, boniest index finger I have ever seen, and the cocaine nail on it was about an inch long. Otherwise, Steve reminded me a lot of my buddy Jake – he was smart but really quiet. I wondered if he talked more when he was drunk.

John Ireland was an all-business and driven-to-succeed former Mormon missionary from one of the French-named towns past Soda Springs. He was about 5-foot-6 and just solid as a brick. He had a determined, respectful personality, a quick wit, and a subtle sense of humor. He was from a family of firefighters and thus was already well-versed in the culture – but this was his first year on an actual fire crew.

Because of his Mormon background, he was supposed to be at least outwardly righteous. What I think it really meant is that he just had to work harder to hide who he really was. He was never condescending to me, but I do know he would have preferred to keep me at a distance – not only did he have that religious background, but he also was in this business for the long haul and didn't need the guilt by association.

One fine summer morning, he and I were assigned to take the garbage to the Pocatello transfer station, which was on the far side of town from the station. We had to drive about ten miles down I-86, and John's driving along about 75 mph when I see the lids on both garbage cans blow off, and garbage starts flying out of the back of the truck. "Oh, we've got to stop and pick that up," he says.

"Naw, we're the government," I say, "they don't care if we litter, and we don't have time now anyhow."

"You sure?" he asks.

"Yeah, we're cool."

Next thing we know we have lights flashing up behind us – the Idaho State Police.

"What the hell are you doing!!?" the trooper screams at John. "Don't you know you're spreading garbage all over the place!!??"

The rest of the day was spent walking along the median and the borrow pit collecting all the trash to avoid a littering ticket. John was absolutely mortified, saying stuff like "This is the end of our jobs" and "I hope they don't tell Randy and Gary" and "Do you think they'll come back and give me a ticket" and "I'm going to lose my driver's license." I just laughed the whole time.

Stephanie "King Biscuit" Hayes also had roots in the fire business; her mother had fought fire for a couple of years. She was way too much of a sweetheart for the crew life, though, and way too blonde to be put in the lion's den she'd entered that summer. Sean nicknamed Stephanie "Flower" within hours of meeting her. I morphed that into King Biscuit, because at 5 p.m. on weeknights the radio station out of Pocatello aired "The King Biscuit Flour Hour." Stephanie's "King Biscuit" tag stuck for the rest of the summer.

On the afternoon after the mile-and-a-half run, John, King Biscuit, and I were standing there soaking wet – Steve had cranked the 2-inch wash hose full blast and lost control of it. Stephanie and I laughed, John growled "niiice," and Sean pressed his upper lip to his upper teeth, looked at Steve out of the corner of his eye, and shook his head.

Washing the proverbial dust off the engines was a beginning-of-the-season ritual. It was more than just a truck bath – we also washed the chase truck, and put new decals on the doors if the old ones had been scratched to hell the previous season. We checked all the fluids on all the vehicles, started the preventive maintenance and fuel logs, and did the initial run-ups of the pump and fire engine plumbing. Inevitably, there would be a leak somewhere in one of the lines or some fitting or other, or the pump wouldn't start. When (not if) this was the case, we used our acquired mechanic skills, intuition, and duct tape to get the thing fixed. We had a mechanic, Phil, but he would freak out if asked to fix something mechanical on one of the rigs. But if he saw us working on the pump, he would also freak out.

Even though it was just the first of June and everything was still green, we knew a fire could start at any time. Randy had told us that morning that they had sent a short squad of firefighters to Jumpoff Peak to extinguish a tenth-acre lightning-strike fire.

We checked out our clothes and personal gear, the same ritual as last season. I walked with Jerry Graham from the shop up to the warehouse to get our stuff. We heard the backup alarm from Engine 372, out of Station 7 in Soda Springs, as it began to chirp. Jerry Neil was backing 372 toward a parking space near the shop. He didn't see the post set into concrete directly behind him, and he hit it so hard that the front tires of the truck lifted off the ground. Jerry Graham said "niiiice" and I started to laugh. Jerry Neil looked over at me and said, "What the fuck are you lookin' at?" I decided to shut up; he looked mean.

Later that summer, as Jerry Neil was responding to a fire report, the whole district heard him on the main radio station.

"428, engine 372; we are responding to the fire report near Monsanto."

"Copy 372, let us know what you find, 428 clear."

Sometimes a mike on a radio gets keyed and accidentally stays down. This affords any and all receivers any transmissions, whether made accidentally or on purpose. The mike on 372 accidentally stayed keyed that evening as Jerry and company rolled to the fire. Among other things heard that night on all district BLM base radio stations, all from Jerry:

I'm fuckin' sick and goddamn tired of going to these false alarms down by Monsanto. Everybody fuckin' knows that it's the lights on at the mine and not a goddamn fire, but those dipshits in dispatch keep sending us there.

And later on:

I'll be damned, I do see a fire up there. Maybe those guys aren't as fuckin' stupid as I thought.

Later:

We'll just hike into this and scratch a little line around it, but I'm not bringin' my pack up there or anything else besides a pulaski. We'll wait and not call us on-scene at this fire until around 2300 hours. That way we can get hazard pay for both days. Otherwise we only get it for today, because it's only gonna take a minute to put that out.

I learned this year that Avery didn't give just the rookies the lousy worn-out gear. He apparently gave rookies *and* sophomores the crappiest gear available, because that's what I got stuck with again this season. In 1993 I had checked out pants with a waist size of 32, with medium-size fire shirts. This year it was size 36 pants, and my large-size shirt felt kind of tight.

Trench-Digging and Other Adventures

SOMETIME LATE IN JUNE when fire school was finished, the crews began to disperse to their respective guard stations. In the district in 1994 there were seven guard stations. Station 1 was about 20 miles south of the Montana border in Dubois. Station 2 was in Idaho Falls at the BLM yard itself, and Station 3 was about 45 miles west of Idaho Falls in a small enclave called Atomic City. Station 4 was at Fort Hall, and Station 5 was at a Pocatello City Fire Department building along the Portneuf River south of Pocatello proper. Station 6 was the one at the Pocatello airport, and Station 7 was at Soda Springs, Idaho, on the way to Wyoming. Station 8 would eventually be staffed in Malad, Idaho, just north of the Utah border.

The fire season unofficially started the day everybody staffed the stations, but there was still a whole lot of work to do to get the stations ready. There were two main things: turn on the water and electricity, and clean the station itself. This is where King Biscuit and I found ourselves on our hands and knees in the kitchen of Station 6 scrubbing the black scuff marks from fire boots off the linoleum. And it sucked. Shicka, Shicka, Shicka. Rest. Adjust body on floor to relieve pressure on knees. Shicka, Shicka, Shicka. Rest shoulders and cramped hands. Shicka,

Shicka, Shicka. Dunk brush in suds bucket. Repeat 800 times.

I had been thinking about what I would do after the day's shift when Stephanie asked me if I was a workaholic. Chances are I would stick around the station, I figured, despite an obvious lack of entertainment. I was under the impression, given to me at the first meeting of each season, that a firefighter was to be ready to respond to a fire within 60 seconds during duty hours, 45 minutes after hours, and just 2 hours on days off. Idaho Falls was more than a 45-minute drive from Station 6, so I had been thinking I'd better stick around the station after work.

Back on the task at hand I noticed that the water, when put on the floor, flowed pretty fast toward the south bedrooms, indicating an obvious downhill slope in that direction. I wondered if that was caused by our leveling job on the trailer when it was delivered a couple of days before.

Station 6 shared its allotted area of federal land with the Pocatello airtanker base, managed by Wade Crane. The base was expanding that summer, and that's what took most of our project time when we weren't out on fires. Mostly we just dug holes and trenches for water lines and electrical conduit, and completed whatever other menial labor Wade wanted us to do – mainly digging dirt.

If I could bet on it, I would say that moving dirt with a shovel was one of man's earliest, proudest, most enduring, and most insidious activities. Maybe it wasn't even invented by man but by the devil, and mankind is just stupid enough to perpetuate it. Wade Crane and the builders of the tanker base perpetuated it bigtime, at the expense of 361's crew, minus Sean Udy, who was too disgruntled to dig dirt.

Almost every morning after PT and showers, we were handed shovels and away we went, to dig 30-inch-deep trenches. A couple of times Crane didn't figure correctly where the trenches were supposed to be, so we had to fill them back in and start new ones. All day long a Case backhoe sat 50 feet away from us, cold and unmoving. I began to get mad about this; I began to imagine that these jerks were having us do this make-work just for something to do before the fires started. Sometimes I would go off and start cussing and chucking shovels and kicking the dirt. I kept looking at the backhoe, and I began to formulate a plan.

My main activity after a normal workday, during all my years with the BLM, was drinking beer. I loved to chill out on the redwood decks of those stations and crack frosty after frosty and consider the goings of life – one foot in the past, one in the future, and all the while straddling the present. More often than not, my crewmates were right there with me, whether they drank or not. In 1994, my main drinking buddy was Steve, although sometimes Sean would drink with us as well. King Biscuit and John, even though they didn't drink, usually joined us for the academic discourse.

One night the combination of beer and my own disgruntlement at digging dirt all day, along with the wild streak I had developed in the past year, all came together. Within about three beers, I was back to hatching my hole-digging plan, which involved the backhoe parked over there by the fence. Even though it was after hours, I was going to finish up all our conduit trenches tonight. I hadn't revealed my plan to anyone yet, just in case they would try to dissuade me.

Steve grilled chicken breasts with barbecue sauce on his Hibachi out front while I sat with John and King Biscuit and gulped down Bud Lights. The sun finally went peacefully down in the west and Sean the Vampire left the station to go do whatever he did at night. It was an absolutely beautiful summer evening, dusty and warm out by the tarmac. I lit up a Camel Light and said, "Y'all watch this, I'm gonna finish digging all the trenches tonight."

I heard John's muttered "Oh no" as I strolled toward the backhoe.

When I reached the machine, I hopped up in the cab and flipped switches until the diesel engine sputtered to life in a cloudbank of black smoke. Ever the conscientious equipment operator, I figured to let it warm up a bit before I got to work. I smoked another cigarette, chugged another beer, then fetched a few more beers from the fridge to refresh me while I worked.

I should note here that I had never run a backhoe. I really, really loved heavy equipment, though, and felt like a Tonka kid at the controls of a large piece of machinery. It's easy to imagine how this could lead to disaster.

When I climbed back up into the cab, I wasn't surprised when King Biscuit and John both disappeared into the station. Steve, drunk enough to remain witness, plopped down into a deck chair with a plate of chicken and tater tots. I examined the instrument panel and bevy of levers and selected the one that I thought would get me moving. My guess was correct and off I went.

Just to get the feel of the controls, I took a few laps up the end of the runway and around the buildings of the tanker base. This took about an hour, and at some point there I crossed over into real drunkenness and decided that what our station needed was a swimming pool. With that in mind, I steered the backhoe over to a spot west of the guard station. Perfect place for a swimming pool.

I put the brake on and swiveled the chair around backward so I could operate the mechanical shovel. I looked over and noticed that King Biscuit and John were watching out the window of the trailer. Steve was still sitting in the deck chair drinking a beer. After experimenting with the levers I found the correct ones and started maneuvering the shovel until it contacted the ground. If you've never run a backhoe, you should understand that there are two things you have to do before you can start digging. The first is to lower the front bucket all the way to the ground to provide a stabilizing counterforce in the front. The second is to set down the outriggers on either side of the cab to stabilize yourself side-to-side. I thought these two foot-type things were called stingers. And I did not put them down. Nor did I set down the front bucket.

I felt the rear tires and the cab lift off the ground a bit when the shovel in the back hit the ground. I moved some levers again and all I did was push the cab and tires higher in the air. "Okay," I thought, "I'll smoke a cigarette and drink a beer while I think about this."

I looked over and saw Steve standing/swaying between the backhoe and the station. His right hand was in his pocket, his left held a beer. He had a contemplative look on his face. He studied the shovel. "What're ya doin'? There aren't supposed to be any conduit trenches here."

"I'm diggin' us a swimming pool!"

"I need another beer," said Steve.

Back at work on the levers, I continued to lift the machine up and down, and sometimes it rocked side to side. How do I get the damn shovel to penetrate the dirt? Finally, I just jammed the lever that pushed the shovel toward the ground, and the whole machine shot up into the air. For a moment I was concerned, and in that moment I forgot which way to push the lever so I could return to the ground. I pushed the lever the same way, and over she went.

There was a crunch of broken glass and a loud squeak of bending metal when I hit the ground. This was not good. The backhoe had rolled almost all the way onto its side and some stuff had definitely been broken. Now as I stood upright, I was nearly perpendicular to the driver's side hatch and looking out at Steve, who just shook his head at me. His expression had never changed. I saw the curtain close on the station window. The backhoe engine still idled.

I crawled out and smoked another cigarette and drank a beer while I surveyed the scene. This was not good at all, I concluded, but Steve and I both made the drunken decision to just retire to the station for the night and settle down.

On our way in, Steve said, "I was going to cut down on drinking this summer, but I don't think it's going to happen."

The engine on the backhoe still idled. I was afraid to go near it.

Early the next morning, I woke up to hear someone wading through a carpet of beer cans, which led up to where I had passed out on one of the front room couches. Wade Crane looked at Steve, lying on the other couch, and asked, "Who fucked up the backhoe?"

"We don't know," we responded simultaneously.

John and King Biscuit stood tall as well. God love 'em all.

FIRE CREW: Stories from the Fireline

Fire Call

Friday, late June, 1994, 2:00 p.m. – Finally, a fire call. No more trench digging for the day, but Sean is living up to his reputation, and man, is he freakin' out. "Get in the goddamn truck! Let's go! Come on! Come on!"

Full of adrenaline anyway, John, King Biscuit, and I scramble around dropping things and tripping over them. Steve and Sean are driving away in the engine before we even get the chase truck fired up. I jump into the driver's seat and try to put on my fire shirt, do-rag, and bandanna all at the same time.

"428, Engine 361."

"Engine 361, four-two-eight." It's Kara, with an urgency in her voice.

"We have departed Station 6 and are en route to the fire."

"Copy 361, let us know when you've arrived."

"361 clear."

"Four-two-eight." It must be on purpose that they pick women with smooth, cool voices to be fire dispatchers. Or maybe they just develop those voices in the line of fire.

Sean is driving the 25,000-pound heavy like it's a Porsche. The engine on the white Ford chase truck I'm driving is wound up and whining as I try to catch him on the frontage road before he jumps onto I-86. Sean didn't even tell us where the fire was when he got off the phone, and I was too intimidated to call him now on the tactical radio channel. If I lost him, we were screwed.

Pocatello is one of a growing number of wildland/urban interface nightmares. Part of it is simply sprawl, as cities outgrow their traditional boundaries. Part of it is the lack of land use planning that's obvious in some areas, and then there's the fact that people just like their cabins and homes in beautiful areas outside of town.

In Pocatello, the interface issues cause major headaches for fire managers. The city itself is situated between two bench-type foothill areas that give rise to some tall mountains and peaks. The largest subdivision involved in interface fire incidents is the Johnny Creek area southwest of Pocatello proper. The area includes about a hundred million dollars' worth of homes and other structures.

I can't blame people for putting their homes in areas like these. It's not as if you look at a new homesite and think, "Gee, we'd better not move here, the fire department and the BLM will be mad at us." Or "if we move here, our house may be destroyed by wildfire." The Johnny Creek area is beautiful country. You've got Gibson-Jack Creek up there, Mink Creek, Cusick Creek, and all kinds of hiking trails, ATV trails, and your choice of scenic little dirt roads to take a Sunday jaunt with the family.

Dense stands of gin-smelling junipers mix with tall grass and sagebrush sidehills. In the early summer mornings you might see a big mule deer buck, his antlers covered with velvet, browsing his way through the brush on one of those sidehills. You could jog through the early morning shadows along one of the gravel right-of-way roads while the creek gurgles downstream on your left. In the fall, you might take your four-by-four a few miles up that road, not even very far from your garage, then hike through beautiful stands of orange and yellow-leaved aspens in your pursuit of an elk or deer. In the winter you could run your snow machine over the approved trails, or even snowshoe or cross-country ski through the fluffy powder snow that collects on the nearby slopes. Yet, with all this, you are only a few minutes from town and all its civilized amenities. Yes, I thought, I would live here.

But I wonder what the homeowners on Pocatello's west bench were thinking on that hot summer day in 1987 when a fire started by some kids playing with matches roared through the hills like a herd of monster devils. I wonder if they thought, "Oh crap, I wish I'd stayed on the numbered streets."

The BLM, Forest Service, and Pocatello City firefighters all responded to the fire. What they found was terrifying. Roads were narrow and overgrown with junipers and other vegetation. There were very few places to turn big fire trucks around. Water supply was minimal or non-existent. Homes were built like cabins, with cedar shake roofs and huge redwood decks with brush and grass actually growing up through them. The junipers and pines and other landscaping shrubs were planted immediately adjacent to the structures, so if the brush burned, so would the home. Houses were built upslope from one another, enabling the fire to pinball and gain traction and speed on its way uphill. Then there was the human factor. Panicked people are often stupid, and in their panic they either blocked roads trying to get out, or they naïvely remained in the yards at their homes, armed with garden hoses against the Johnny Creek goliath. Responding BLM, Forest Service, and Pocatello firefighters all operated on different tactical radio channels, and all worked out of different dispatch centers. It's a wonder no one was killed.

Disasters like this do happen, of course, but when they happen, people usually learn from it and mitigate the factors that fueled the disaster. In this case the people came back swinging. I believe that with Randy Hanson, Eric Hall, and Gary Eames involved, you could handle nearly any fire situation, and these were the leaders who – along with the fire managers and the fire marshals of Pocatello – formed the Gateway Interagency Fire Front (GIFF).

The GIFF's mission was to prevent another Johnny Creek incident. Sure, fires will start in these areas again, but this time everyone would be prepared. Fire prevention and education specialists met with homeowners and showed them how to create defensible space around their homes by removing brush piles and vegetation growing too close to structures. They distributed free packets of fire-resistant wildflower seeds and instructed homeowners about what to do and who to call if a fire started. They used Smokey Bear to educate kids about the dangers of playing around with fire. Fire ecologists planned thinning operations in the juniper stands around the area, creating fire breaks and removing ladder fuels and slash piles. Firefighters carried out the plans with their chainsaws when not fighting fires in other places. Fire managers ensured that responding units would work with an interagency system, whereby all agencies could remain in contact with one another on radios, and a single incident commander or command team would devise tactics to be employed on the fires. The plan seems to have been effective, as to this day there have been no fires in the Pocatello interface as devastating as the '87 Johnny Creek Fire. To us, the GIFF was shortened to the "Pocatello Front" or just the "Front," and through all my years with the BLM, whenever I heard that there was a fire on the Front, it gave me goosebumps, because it was going to undoubtedly be crazy – and in a heartbeat could turn deadly.

The heavy fire engines are governed – meaning they physically can't go faster than a set speed – or John, King Biscuit, and I would have been left alone to find the fire. I caught up to the engine a mile or so after we merged onto I-86, and I stayed on his tail like white on rice.

As soon as we made it around the bend in the highway, I could see the smoke from the fire. My mouth gets dry in tense situations, and right then I felt like I had a mouthful of sand. I put in a dip of chew with my hands while I steered the truck with my wrists. I glanced down and noticed I had buttoned my shirt wrong, and that I had Copenhagen snuff all over the front of it.

The radio traffic was going crazy. Pocatello City FD was on it, BLM was on it, Forest Service engines were on it. They were not going to screw around with a fire on the Front – this was dangerous fire in a dangerous place. I said a silent prayer of thanks that I wasn't the one in charge of this, and also a prayer that I would do everything right.

We pulled up and Sean stopped the engine in the middle of a two-track dirt road at the obvious origin of the fire. I didn't know where to put the chase truck, so we just sat in it and waited for instructions, which came from Sean as he vaulted out of the engine. The instructions consisted of screaming, "Come on, come on, this ain't pre-school, LET'S GO!!" He also waved his arms frantically to offer me visual cues.

I was glad when Steve came over and guided me to a safe zone – a spot where there wasn't anything that could catch fire underneath or nearby the truck. John, King Biscuit, and I pulled on our packs, gloves, and hard hats as fast as we could. In the rush, though, I dropped two of my water bottles in the dirt and the straps on my pack were twisted so many times that it hardly even fit over my shoulders. My hands shook uncontrollably as I tried to hook the chest buckle.

Dust kicked up in roiling clouds as more rigs pulled up and spit out personnel and equipment. Sean yelled, "Come on, come on!" while still wildly waving his arms. Not knowing exactly what we should come on and do, the three of us from the chase ran over to the engine. By then Sean was gone walking out through the black toward where the fire was currently consuming horse corrals.

Steve handed John and me the hard line nozzle and hose and calmly instructed us to pull it through the fence and work our way along the flank and cool out the hot spots. Stephanie's job was to help guide the hose over rocks and stobs of burnt sagebrush. This is an important job, as one of the most annoying things in the firefighting world is having your hose catch up on stuff or kink up so you can't deliver water.

Being still new to initial attack, I was unable to recognize that I was getting mentally caught up in trying to tease out the big picture of fire incidents. All I needed to worry about right now was our stretch of fireline, now grown to about a quarter of a mile. Within that scope, I was responsible for not getting myself hurt by tripping or cutting myself somehow, and I was also responsible for making sure I didn't get John or Stephanie hurt. I was also responsible for cooling off the smoking grasses and sagebrush along where we had the hose. Technically, I wasn't even responsible for the burning corral fence, as suppression of fire on man-made structures is a municipal firefighting responsibility, and federal firefighters don't do it – or they're not supposed to. That was the scope of my job right then, but it wasn't enough for me.

I wanted to be at the head of this thing, standing knee-deep in flame and taking it on like I was acting out a video game. I wanted to know who had been called, what the strategy and tactics would be, whether anyone had been burned, how big is this thing exactly – the whole who, what, when, where, and why. It was hard for me to just keep my head down and be a worker bee, but that was what was expected of me. It kept me out of trouble, it kept Sean from screaming at me, and it earned a paycheck. What irritated me most, though, was that Engine 341 from Fort Hall, my old crew, *was* at the head of the fire and kicking butt. So was Engine 351, with a future female Olympic pole-vaulting champion unwinding the hardline hose.

The fire itself, as far as I knew, had been human-caused (there had been no lightning that day), and had hit the tall grass and weeds south and east of the corrals with a pretty good head of steam. It then sliced to the right on a mission to take the foothills. As the fire began its climb, the flames grew higher and more intense, gathering strength and speed. It had to be stopped before it headed uphill in earnest, or there was going to be trouble.

This area where level ground met sidehill is where the two other BLM heavies both had two hard lines deployed and were straight-streaming. The municipal fire trucks hung back, as these Type 2 trucks didn't have the capability of moving and spraying water at the same time. The tall and raw-boned Pete Oar manned the first hose on 341 while Jerry Graham drove and Campbell scouted line. Travis Hale drove Engine 351 in a daisy-chain configuration immediately behind 341. This allowed for the use of four actual hard lines to knock the crap out of these flames, and they were doing just that. First you would see 10-foot high flames, then you would see 341, then 341 would disappear in a screen of smoke and steam for a while, then it emerged from the haze while 351 dove into it and put the final touches on the wet line production.

I could hear Pete up there shouting, "Get some, get some!!" They were having a blast. Stephanie, John, Steve, and I picked at cow pies and pieces of deep-root sagebrush with pulaskis, shovels, and the hose line. The sun beat down on my back and I remembered to suck some warm water regularly so I wouldn't succumb to heat exhaustion.

This was mopping up, and it was about as boring as boring gets, especially when your buddies are having fun in the peak of battle against the enemy fire.

We eventually worked our way around the bend and toward the foothills. Engines 341 and 351 were able to knock down the running head of the fire and had now joined us and a couple of light engines cleaning up hot spots near the line. It had finally cooled off a bit, so it was easier to get the heat entirely out of all the fuels. I looked at my reflection in the sideview mirror on the engine and saw sweat streaks through the black soot and dirt on my face. Welcome back. Another summer on the crew.

FIRE CREW: Stories from the Fireline

Fire Station

FIRE SEASONS ARE LIKE MANY OTHER SEASONS in life – they start off rickety, unsure, sometimes boring and sometimes way too exciting. A certain rhythm develops after a time, though. You get used to the activities of the day and how they relate to your attitudes and the diurnal and nocturnal patterns of your mind and body.

At Station 6, we awoke at 8:59 on a normal morning in order to be to work on time. Being to work on time meant taking a pee, pouring a cup of coffee, and drinking it in the front room by 9:01. This was one of the benefits of this job. Sean or Steve would enter the holding pattern of the stations up and down the valley calling in-service to the dispatch office in the morning.

Steve had bed-head like no other human, and he was the worst morning person I'd ever met, even worse than Sean. He would rock back and forth in the recliner by the window, cradling his cup of coffee, brooding sour and silent. King Biscuit, on the other hand, would bubble forth from her room in the middle of the trailer and greet everyone by name every morning. "Good morning Benjamin." "Hi." "Good morning John." "Hi." "Good morning Steve." Reply: a side-to-side shake of the head and more rocking back and forth in the chair. "Good morning Sean." Reply: silence.

We had an hour of PT scheduled in the morning, as mandated by the district fire operations plan. Most of the time I had other plans. How are you supposed to jog four miles when you are so hung over? I was so out of shape that summer. Most of the time I just hid near the trees a couple hundred yards from the station and smoked cigarettes. Steve and Sean didn't do PT much either, as they were often hung over, but John and King Biscuit diligently completed their PT every morning. One morning, in fact, I looked out toward I-86 and there was King Biscuit jogging down the side of the interstate. I had never seen anybody do that before. I don't know if that's even legal.

She just personified book smart and street stupid – and beyond naïve about life. Her interests included reading, knitting, and jogging – perfect background for the fire life. One afternoon we were all sitting around the station; it was hot as hell outside. Stifling hot. Airtankers were coming and going from all the fires we weren't on that day. King Biscuit decides she wants to go for a jog, and asks Sean if she can take the chase truck down to a little dirt trail she found. Fine, he says.

A few minutes later, off she goes in the truck. Sean and John and I are by then standing outside on the front deck. Around the station, out on the tanker fueling apron, and *under the wing of a taxiing airtanker* goes the chase truck with King Biscuit driving.

The pilot saw her just as she was going to clip one of the props and he locked up the brakes, heaving the huge plane forward and then back in a massive lurch. SCREEEEEEECH!!!

She never even noticed, just kept right on cruising down the taxiway, little blonde curls bobbing as she came within inches of a major accident that likely would have killed her. We just stood there stunned.

After PT each morning it was time to dig ditches or otherwise help out at the tanker base. By that time in the summer, quite a few of the big old airtankers were either on station semi-permanently, or passing through en route to other fires in the Great Basin, so we assisted with whatever we could. Then it was lunch. Then there might be a fire call, and if not, there would be more ditch digging. If there was no fire, I looked forward to the evening's revelry.

Many airports have courtesy cars for pilots to use if they are stuck at the airport overnight or for several days. At the tanker base, there was an early 1980s Chevy Caprice for the pilots to borrow for town trips. Like the Case backhoe, it always sat there unused. After a few beers one evening, I thought maybe I'd take the Caprice for a spin, make sure the battery stayed charged, check out whether the big-block 454 engine was tuned.

Sean was gone, who knows where. Steve sipped Coors Light, I chugged can after can, King Biscuit read a book, and I'm pretty sure John was silently praying as I fished the Caprice keys out of a drawer in the station's kitchen. "Come on Steve, let's take the car for a spin."

It was dark now, maybe 10 p.m., and hot and dry outside. Steve and I walked out to the Caprice. The driver's side door squealed when I pried it open. I plunked down onto the springy vinyl driver side of the bench seat and examined the dashboard. The speedometer went clean across the instrument panel in a negative parabola shape, stopping at 100 mph on the right-hand side. She fired right up when I turned the key, growling through an old-school exhaust. "Better put on your seat belt, dude," I told Steve as he climbed in. I reached for one of the cold silver cans we had piled between us.

The gas pedal looked about a foot long. I stood up on it, pushing the RPMs into the millions, then dumped the car into reverse, spewing gravel and dirt and weeds out front and across the taxiway. We rocketed backward until I stood on the brakes and skidded us to a halt. I sang the first part of the Dukes of Hazzard theme song as I shifted into drive, fished out a cigarette, and squealed out from the tanker base area and onto the asphalt.

When turned at the end of the runway, I said, "Ladies and gentlemen, prepare for takeoff," and stood up again on the gas pedal.

I will never forget the sight of the speedometer needle bouncing between 80 and 100 as we barreled down the runway, pitch black except for our high beams. Steve was slumped in the passenger seat shaking his head and looking out the window into the darkness. "Yeee-haww!" I crowed.

Try this today and you're going to jail for a while. After qualifying time on the runway, it was off to the squared sections of tall grass and weeds between the airport and the interstate. At one point, I had the car flying 70 or 80 mph through weeds taller than the hood of the car. Steve told me later how funny it looked, the serious expression on my face with a cigarette between my lips, a half finished can of beer in my right hand, and the steering wheel in my left, as I essentially took Steve's and my lives to the edge of sanity.

We finally touched back down in the parking lot of the station in the early morning hours. The tailpipe on the Caprice dragged on the ground and a collection of weeds and grass and garbage hung from the car's grille. Dust still drifted in the air over the grounds of the airport. My abdominal muscles ached and cramped and I was bent over gasping for air from laughing so hard as we made our way back into the station.

In the kitchen, I microwaved a couple frozen bean and cheese burritos and sucked down a couple more beers. Everyone else had gone to bed. After the burritos, I sat outside and smoked the day's last cigarette while I wound down. I took notice of a breeze that had arrived and watched flashes of lightning to the south and back over to the northeast. The breeze felt good blowing through my long hair, and the light show of lightning grew from faint to spectacular. I headed for the sack.

I barely noticed the traffic on the station's base radio as I stumbled down the hallway toward the bedroom. Steve and I had bunk beds, and I accidentally stepped on him as I was trying to climb into the upper bunk. "What the fuck, dude?" he mumbled at me. I looked down at the red numbers on the alarm clock – 3:30 a.m. It was strange to hear radio traffic at that hour, I thought, as I drifted off into a drunken slumber.

The Fire Pirates

Saturday, July 2, 1994, 8:00 a.m. – I am awakened by the howling jet engine and hammering prop combo of a Lockheed P2V airtanker taxiing into the base. I hop down from the bunk and make my way to the living room, where I see that everyone is awake *and* in greens and boots already. The news is that the summertime thunderstorm weather has officially moved into the West, starting numerous fires across the Great Basin and all around the West. The heavy airtanker that just landed here is on its way to Grand Junction, Colorado, to support the emerging fire situation in that part of the country. The cell that passed northeast of us last night started a few fires across the district, hence the early morning radio traffic that I had hardly paid any attention to. We have not been called to any fire yet, but chances are a few sleepers – small, smoldering, lightning-caused fires – will stoke up later today. And then it will be *game on* for fire crews.

I forgo coffee this morning in favor of Gatorade, to cut the alcohol-induced dehydration I feel. I waver between feeling hot and cold, puking and laughing, hungry and not hungry. Alcohol sucks, I conclude, then I step out back for a smoke. It's only a little after 8:00 in the morning, yet the sun bakes down onto me and causes my head to spin. I hope to God we don't get a fire call too early. I go back in, finish my Gatorade, and struggle into my greens. I grunt while pulling on my boots because my gut is all pooched out and bloated. Sean says, "Walters, go on a diet." "Yeah, yeah." I reply.

I went outside and found Steve and John already checking the pump on 361 and doing a cursory inventory of equipment. For my part, I rinsed out and refilled all the gallon canteens in the bin with the good cold water from the spigot north of the station. Then I did the same for my personal water bottles. I went in and procured some ice from the freezer and plunked a few cubes into each bottle. Maybe that would keep them cold for a while.

The rest of the day was spent in anticipation. There was radio traffic all day long among dispatch, the Soda Springs engines, the Idaho Falls engines, and the Fort Hall engines. It was only a matter of time, we knew, before we got a call. Avery was out with the pilot in the Cessna scouting for fires. Adam, up in the lookout on Big Butte, was glassing for smokes, and Gil, up on Chink's Peak, scanned the eastern portion of the valley. The fires in Caribou County were adequately staffed at present, so we expected our call to be a new initial attack situation.

A day like that in the fire world feels like being near a waking dragon. I was a punk drunk, but only after hours – and I acted like the class clown during the workday only as a cover of sorts. I misbehaved because I didn't know any other way to express my feelings. Kind of like a puppy or a 2-year-old kid – they need attention, but they usually go about trying to get it in a way that's mostly unacceptable. I did not consider fire calls funny, though, and I certainly did not seek attention during these times. I had already developed a strong sense of respect for the havoc that a fire could wreak, and while I had no fear of fire, I certainly never would mess around with it. With wildland fire, I was all business.

I could almost feel the dragon of the day waking up. It was palpable, almost audible. I could feel his respirations as the day pulsed. I could feel hot breath as it blew off the black asphalt of the tarmac. I could feel it in the dryness of my mouth and throat, and I could feel it in the butterflies in my stomach. I figured the rest of the crew could feel this, too – except Sean, because he had been through probably 8,000 days just like this one.

Wade Crane was far too busy that day to line us out with stupid hole-digging assignments. Airtankers were passing through on their way to Colorado or Nevada, or even east of us in our district, headed for the fires in the Webster Range over by Tincup Mountain. Our own airtanker, the one committed to our district for the season, came in on a turnaround from a fire every 45 minutes or so, re-fueling and loading a couple thousand gallons of red slurry. Its engines sounded like a huge but poorly tuned lawnmower, popping and sputtering and smoking.

Sean told us all to just take it easy and wait.

Angry and impatient on the outside, Sean was far from stupid on the inside. We got a call one day, and since Steve Lewis wasn't there that day, there were just four of us to respond in Engine 361. Sean took Steve's spot in the engine, along with John Ireland, and King Biscuit and I took the chase truck. One thing led to another and we ended up bouncing to a couple of other fires over the next week or so without returning to the station to get Steve. We all started getting sick of each other, so I told King Biscuit to switch places with John, so he and I would ride in the chase together and King Biscuit would ride in the engine with Sean.

She was too far out to lunch to be afraid of Sean like we were. As we rolled through Lava Hot Springs on the way to a fire, we got stuck in traffic, first with a parade and then at a railroad crossing where we watched a two-mile-long train creep by. In the right side mirror ahead of us, John and I could see King Biscuit's mouth moving non-fucking-stop as she talked and talked about who knows what to Sean. He never even looked over at her, but at each stop I could see his Buddy Holly glasses burning into the left-side mirror back at us.

We finally roll up to the fire south of Lava, and Sean lurches to a stop and leaps out of the engine. He *never* does this, so I know we're in for it, and I also know why. He runs back to the chase motioning violently for me to roll down the window. Against my better judgment, I do it. He grabs me by the collar, and in a teeth-gritted high-pitched hiss, says to John and me, "You two little cocksuckers better never do that again if you know what's good for you."

Sean knew that a sun-beaten, hang-dog crew wouldn't be any good on initial attack. He let us know that we should just hang around that day and get prepared for action. So after we were all physically prepped, we just sat inside the station or in patches of shade outside, and waited, and waited. King Biscuit sat in her room and wrote letters or knitted socks or something.

Up till that day, there had been only one or two airtankers pass through Pocatello, as the fire season hadn't really yet started in the northern section of the West. I had not yet grasped the full importance of this tanker base; I just thought it was Crane's stupid play-hobby area. As I sat there, smoked, and observed the goings-on that day, I gained a new appreciation. It was just hoppin' busy.

Airtankers are fixed-wing firefighting aircraft. They come in different shapes and sizes, and are placed in categories just the same as fire engines are, based on their payload capacity for dropping water or retardant. Airtankers carry anywhere from 800 to 3,000 gallons of retardant, ranging from the small Single Engine Air Tankers (SEATs) to the big heavies that will carry a couple thousand gallons – there are even a couple newer tankers now that will carry far more than that. The retardant these planes drop on fires consists mostly of agricultural fertilizer, with ingredients for thickening and also for inhibiting corrosion in the planes' tanks. It has a consistency, when mixed properly, similar to tomato sauce, and it works at slowing or "retarding" a fire even after the water in the mix has evaporated. The red color comes from the iron oxide component, and it helps pilots and the air attack bosses determine where each load has been dropped.

Most of the old airtankers are converted passenger or military aircraft – large, old, loud, sturdy, and strong. The P2-V Neptune, PB4Y-Privateer, C-130 Hercules, P-3 Orion, and DC-7 were all common

119

tankers in those years, but only a few are still flying today.

Each aircraft had a tail number assigned to it, and oftentimes you would recognize a particular aircraft on different fires you went to, even those in different states across the country. Airtankers were considered a national firefighting resource, and thus could be dispatched anywhere.

Being assigned to the tanker base, we got to know some of the planes and their pilots really well. These were bold but extremely professional individuals. Fire pilots – or, as they sometimes refer to themselves, fire pirates – are a special breed. Many are ex-military, many are quirky individuals, most are just as skilled as they are opinionated. The ones I knew told me stories of coming in "hot" to put in a line of retardant and described in detail what the turbulence over a fire is like. "Try playing Nintendo inside a clothes dryer – while it's running," one of them said. Another told me a story of how it was so bumpy over one fire that the turbulence broke loose the steel tie-downs of a 5-foot-tall rolling toolbox – not an uncommon item for a tanker crew to fly with – and the toolbox was flying around smashing into things in the back of the plane behind the cockpit.

It never dawned on me until I heard that how crazy flying a tanker could be. One time a pilot gave me a tour of the inside of his PB4Y. Gauges and levers and knobs everywhere. I was too awed and dumbfounded to really get any practical knowledge out of the tour. I just wondered about the sanity of these guys. If you want an oversimplified drama of their lives, watch the movie *Always* with Richard Dreyfuss, Holly Hunter, and John Goodman – it's not an accurate portrayal by any means, but many tanker pilots like it anyway.

In a true sense, we did get to know some of the pilots and crew well enough to be deeply saddened if we heard one of them had crashed and been killed – which happened somewhere in the country at least once every fire season.

That Saturday, though, I just watched from a distance as the big tankers came and went. I hoped I would be feeling better soon, but it was taking a while. I had a sick stomach from anticipation, which just compounded the aftereffects of the previous night's intoxication. I walked in circles around the station, sometimes went inside the station, and all the while thought of only the oppressive heat. It almost crackled.

Our call did not come that day, nor did it come the next day or the next – the Fourth of July. I'm pretty sure that every fire crew in this country is on shift, or at least on short standby, on the Fourth of July. Engine 361's crew was no exception. Independence Day is the day when ordinary Americans turn into pyromaniacs and flash bang munitions experts – children and adults alike. It's the day when firecrackers, bottle rockets, roman candles, and crazy jacks turn into raging brushfires and devastating house fires. People have the equipment to start the fires, but they often find it's harder to extinguish them. It's like built-in overtime for wildland fire crews.

I still harbored hope, though, of being turned loose on the Fourth. I had made plans to be with my semi-boring girlfriend and my wilder other friends down on the riverbank chugging beers and making merry. I wasn't quite indoctrinated into the fire crew lifestyle. I hadn't yet grasped that it's not just the fire crew – it's really the *fire life*. So when Sean and Steve, and even John and King Biscuit, looked at me like I was retarded when I asked them where they were going to watch the fireworks, I was more than mildly disappointed. I then realized what I should have known all along – as long as I worked on a fire crew in the summertime, I would never celebrate the Fourth of July like I used to.

And I didn't, for nine years.

On the Fourth at 6:00 p.m., about the time we'd normally hang it up for the day, the only difference being that we could drink after 6:00 (we rarely put on street clothes after work, just hung out in our greens), we instead gathered up some gear and set out for our strategic forward operating area near Kinport Peak. We waited here with Randy Hanson, the South Zone AFCO, and Engine 341 for some dummy to accidentally start a brush fire.

It was cool and breezy perched up on our overlook above Pocatello. From here we could see most of the city, and most of the city looked pretty calm. Our two engine crews found a flat spot off to the side of the two-track road and played pushup hacky-sack in the dirt until dark. I could do a truckload of pushups by the end of every fire season. We aimed to break the record of 20-something sack hits we'd set last season in the Las Cruces fire warehouse.

The meager public fireworks display started at dark. It looked weak from our vantage point. We sat in the stillness of the night listening to the sparse radio traffic. About 10:00 p.m., the radio fired up with chatter, and we simultaneously spotted a small fire, and then saw the moving, flashing lights of fire trucks heading for the southeast outskirts of Pocatello. Campbell told his crew to get ready. Our crew took the cue and made our way back to our chase truck. We listened to Pocatello City FD on the radio as they responded to the one-acre brush fire down below us. We primed ourselves and waited for the signal to move out. But just like on Saturday, my excitement and anticipation just led to an anticlimactic dead-end. Pocatello City firefighters extinguished the small fireworks-caused blaze and were able to keep it boxed in the small vacant lot where it had started. Nevertheless, we hung out on the mountain for two more hours, just in case another fire started somewhere. We headed back to the station pretty late, when the city looked to be quieted down for the evening. We pulled through the airport gates and down the access road no dirtier than when we had left, but a few dollars richer from the overtime pay.

Pump & Roll

Tuesday, July 5, 1994, 9:30 a.m. – This morning I feel better than I have for quite a few mornings, and I decide to join the crew in a game of jungle basketball down the road at the old basketball standard with its chain net. These people are surprisingly strong, especially John. He is small enough that I'd thought I could push him around easily, but I was wrong. Even King Biscuit is fast and determined. Steve and Sean, though, are just mean. My sports background is currently dormant, but still presents itself at times, and I win by a good margin. I think the crew is angry that a fat guy can still move fast when he wants to. Jerry Graham once told me that some chicks dig a dude with a spare tire, as long as he can still move with it. Our call came about 1:30 that afternoon – about the time I was tucking into a huge greasy lunch of crispy chicken fingers, white gravy and mashed potatoes, rolls with a bucket of butter, corn on the cob, and two large glasses of Pepsi at the Blue Ribbon Airport Café. Steve and John aren't stupid, they both had salads and diet Pepsis. We had a handheld radio with us, and we heard Engine 341's radio traffic with dispatch as the crew was responding to a call east of the reservation. We ate as fast as we could, so fast I got the hiccups.

As we drove up the road toward the station, we saw 361 pulling out and heading our way in a hurry. Dang it, the call must have come on the telephone again. If a call came on the radio, we would all hear the information from dispatch, but Sean would never brief us on the location of the fire or anything else if he got the call on the phone. When we met up, Sean ground the engine to a stop and kicked King Biscuit out so Steve could switch places with her. She jumped in with us, and John flipped a U-turn to get in behind the engine.

We headed up I-86 and then merged onto I-15 north. It was a beautiful blue-sky day, no clouds at all, and no smoke either. Where was the fire? The radio traffic indicated that Adam Nash, the old dude who lived in the now-defunct Big Butte Lookout, had called in the fire from clear across the valley, 30 or 40 miles away, so it must have been good-sized.

We rounded a bend around a hill that had blocked our view of the fire about the same time that Engine 341 arrived on scene. This smoke column was just beginning to morph into a monster, betraying the kind of fire that's intense enough to actually create its own weather. A cumulonimbus cloud was starting to form at altitude on the top of the plume. This sucker was huge, and moving out. It was by far the largest fire I had seen up to that point, and we were still a good 10 or 15 miles from it.

Lee Campbell's size-up of the fire, relayed to dispatch on the radio, went something like this: "428, Engine 341."

"Engine 341, 428 go ahead." The sweet voice of Valerie, who talked nicely even when the crap was hitting the fan.

"Ah, yeah, 428, Engine 341 has arrived on scene at this fire and we have a size-up when you're ready."

"341, go ahead with your size-up."

All ears in every BLM station and in every engine and chase truck were tuned to the radio. "Okay, 341 has arrived on scene, we are going to call this the Ross Fork Fire. Fire is burning in sagebrush, grass, and heavy juniper stands, on the flats and on steep south-facing slopes. Fire behavior is running. Estimated fire size is 500 acres. Resources on scene: 341 and Engine #2 from the Fort Hall Fire Department. Requested resources: Heavy airtanker, dozer, helicopter, six engines, two Type 1 hand crews, one Type 2 hand crew, one watertender."

With the allegorical stroke of a pen, Campbell had just spent at least $20,000. And far more cash would be required to get the resources to eventually tame this beast. It had started on reservation land, but was now threatening BLM and Forest Service lands, and Campbell intended to stop it.

"Okay, I copy."

Then, less formally, Campbell told dispatch about his planned initial tactics, which involved turning Jerry loose with Pete and the rest of the crew to anchor in at the road and start a pump and roll. The Fort Hall structure-fire engine would more or less stick around in a standby mode and protect the ranch house that was a couple miles west of the origin of the fire.

It felt good to be part of the cavalry, however nervous and inexperienced I was. Campbell and Jerry needed help, and we were coming to kick some butt. So were the dudes and dudettes from Idaho Falls, Atomic City, and the Caribou National Forest. Back at the tanker base, I bet Ivan had fired up the four turboprops of his PB4Y and was getting ready to roll with a load of red retardant for us. Somewhere in the

Great Basin a couple of hotshot crews were getting a phone call, as were a Type 2 crew, a helicopter, and James Beck with his D9 Cat dozer. They would soon all converge in the Ross Fork area.

In fact, all over the West on this day there were tanned, toned, type-A personalities battling, or getting ready to battle, the perennial "enemy" of forests and rangelands. On a certain mountain in Colorado, firefighters were building a helispot, as managers finally decided that a fire burning for several days on Storm King Mountain might warrant a little more attention.

I pulled on my yellow shirt, do-rag, bandanna, and chew of Copenhagen as 361 flew down the dirt road into the fire. We brought up the rear behind the engine, sucking dust. We were on track to be the second BLM resource on scene, and that meant being in the thick of things. I was way ready today, no hangover, feeling good from PT that morning, with my belly full of good greasy café food. I felt like I was running into this fire the way I ran down the field on the "suicide squad" kickoff team at the start of a football game. All testosterone and adrenaline, that was me. Bring it on!

The beauty of being a rookie or a sophomore on a fire crew is that you can exercise the liberty of being more balls than brains. Incident commanders, engine foremen, hotshot superintendents – they have far more responsibility. We young'uns could just show up, grab a hose or a nozzle or a hand tool and just start kickin' butt. This was great as long as there was some butt to kick; it sucked when you had to wind it down and grub around in the dirt for hotspots or provide menial labor at grunt work. But this fire, the Ross Fork Fire, would allow the wannabe Marine in me to emerge!

With no warm-up, briefing, or other cursory activity, we leap-frogged ahead of Engine 341 (which had run out of water by then), parked the chase in a cooled-off black area, donned our packs and personal protective equipment (PPE), and deployed the hard lines. All this in about two minutes flat – Sean did not screw around, I'll say that for him.

I grabbed the front nozzle and set it for "kill." I had the nozzle adjusted for a high-pressure straight stream – I called it "setting for stun" when we used the fog setting on the nozzle. John grabbed the back nozzle and did likewise. Steve drove, King Biscuit monitored the pump and helped with the hose, and Sean watched over us.

Pump and roll, in my opinion, is by far the best and most fun fire-killing activity. The radiant heat that's put off when tall sagebrush and prairie grasses ignite is incredible. It's far hotter than you would expect it to be, and it serves as a reminder that burning to death would be a horrifying way to perish. When you take flames and heat head-on like this, it's a rush, and really feels like you're in battle.

To keep your face from burning, you put on a Velcro-secured shroud, made of the same Nomex material as your shirt, cut to fit your face and neck. In situations like this, it's a must, even though it restricts both movement and breathing. Underneath that, you have your bank robber bandanna to keep you from choking on the smoke. Your shirt sleeves are all the way down to your leather forester gloves, which have a tab for tightening around the wrist. Your collar is popped, the way a cool guy would wear his polo shirt, and the shirt buttons are done up to the top. Your hard hat is on tight. You can cover your eyes with goggles, which is the recommended way, but mine always fogged up, so I just wore my Oakley Frogskin sunglasses – damn the sting and tears.

Steve maneuvered the engine into the smoldering black, pointed the nose north and east along the west flank, and eased up to the first flames. The thick black smoke blotted out the sun and assaulted my eyes, nose, and mouth. The rattle of the diesel engine, the white noise of the humming pump in back, and the low crackle and growl of the ripping fire all but deafened me to the rest of the world. I was smiling.

If I had stopped to think about it then, I might have been afraid, but with a job to do and my work cut out for me, I was just all business and highly focused – and quite happy. This was, for me, human earthly bliss. A workable goal, and a reason for being alive. An enemy to take down.

Steve drove only as fast as we needed to mow down the flames, chugging along on the black side of the line to avoid rocks and other hazards. Often he would stop while we took out some hotter spots. I aimed at the base of each group of them and made a slow sweeping motion. Back and forth. The breeze blew the smoke away from our faces, but the radiant heat burned right through my clothing and felt especially raw on my elbows and knees, my nose, and the tips of my ears.

Steve saw that I was getting burned and yelled at me, "Hey, put the nozzle on fog every once in a while and spray your elbows and stuff to cool them off."

Great idea – and it worked. We kept on. The heat was intense, but I barely noticed; we were kicking this thing. Now and then Steve would pull away from the flames and we could grab a breath of fresh air. The temperature was a noticeable 20 degrees cooler just a few yards away from the flames. I was drenched in sweat and water and filth, but I didn't care. King Biscuit was doing an awesome job with the hose, John was kicking butt backing me up. When I looked back, I could see only wisps of smoke where we had passed – and no flame. Engine 342, the light engine from Fort Hall, was back there cleaning up those little smokes.

We continued on for what seemed like a mile or two before we were relieved by Engine 321 from Idaho Falls. Eric Hall, who had taken over as Incident Commander from Campbell, instructed us to fill our water tank and then bump over to a dirt road that ran east to west, about two miles as the crow flies. We would tie in with Engine 341 and Engine 331 and conduct a burnout operation to prevent this fire from jumping the main east-west dirt road.

As we refilled our water tank from the 3,000-gallon watertender truck, a Shoshone Indian rancher pulled up in a beaten old Ford pickup and produced a blue cooler full of iced-down Coca-Colas. Never mind the fact that the sugar just made me thirstier, I sucked a can down in two pulls, fizz stinging my sinuses. We thanked the rancher, gratefully promising him we'd do the best we could, and took off in a rush to the north, trailing a stream of dust on the now-overused access road.

John and King Biscuit and I talked on the way over there how awesome the pump and roll had been. John and I looked like we had taken baseball player eye blacking and scrubbed our faces with it. Biscuit had a black dot on her nose and a three-inch strip of black across her forehead. Our yellow shirts were now dyed dark in ash. None of us were the least bit tired, though we'd now been going at 100 percent for about five hours.

The three heavy engines rendezvoused at a fork in the road northeast of the main fire. We put a plan together for the burnout and prepared the drip torches. Again, as with the pump and roll, our crew would be right in the middle of it – Sean, Campbell, and 331's foreman Dave Farmer had decided that 361 would be the burn engine.

Steve popped a fusee and John and I used it to ignite our drip torches. We would burn in a pattern just like I had done in New Mexico last summer, only this time I wouldn't be stupid and cross the road. We planned to light this backfire with the idea that it would head south and burn into the main fire, stopping it between these access roads. I was half expecting that someone would remind me not to cross the road with my drip torch.

Farmer said, "Hey Walters, how about not crossing the road this time."

"I'll try not to." I replied.

We were off, spitting flame like little dragons weaving through the brush. Sean had told us, "Don't screw around. Move out and move fast. We need to get some flame down."

Back and forth, back and forth we swept. John was closer to the road, I was about 50 yards inside and staggered ahead of him. I was wide-eyed at the fire we were putting down! It grew to heights of 15 or 20 feet in the taller and thicker brush, and our fire took off and ran across the prairie like a blaze-orange antelope. Looking back through the smoke and shimmering heat waves, I could see the flashing red lights of the engines staggered down the road, ready to back us up.

While John and I were refilling our drip torches, Engine 331 got a bit too close to some heavy flames and briefly caught a tire on fire. We heard Jerry Graham calmly call it out to Farmer on the tactical channel. "Um, Dave, your tire's on fire." Dave came out of the cab of that engine like a bullet from a hunting rifle, aimed the red fire extinguisher at the tire, and poofed it out.

We completed the burnout sometime after dark, parked the engines strategically down the road, and watched the backburn do its job plugging up the main fire. This wouldn't be the end of the project by any means – this was just one flank of a very large range fire. It was up to five or six thousand acres now, and that was a lot of hot spots. We'd be here a day or two.

At about 11:00 that evening, we gathered up in a flat spot on the north end of the fire and made camp. Supper was Kentucky Fried Chicken delivered right to us by the angels in logistics up in Idaho Falls. All the chicken and mashed potatoes and biscuits we could

133

eat, still warm from the curiously named "shamrocks," the gray rectangular hard-side coolers covered in slick fabric. We downed the vittles, then spread out our bags in the dirt, in the back of the chase pickups, or on top of the water tank on the engine.

I was totally warm and toasty in my mummy bag, lying in the dirt with the breeze drifting across my face. I laid myself out flat on my back, tired and happy, to watch the stars. I had a blast today. I like the fire crew. This is a good job. A good way to spend my summer.

The next day we worked around different spots on the fire. Mopping up here, pumping and rolling there, cleaning up unburned stuff with fusees and torches along the road. It was just a basic project fire day. The sky was clear and it was very hot. On Storm King Mountain in Colorado, 14 wildland firefighters were dying. None of us knew.

We returned to camp that night dirty, tired, and hungry. Over supper there was a bit of chatter that something had happened somewhere in Colorado. Someone had gotten hurt or something. I tried to piece together the rumors and snippets, but there wasn't much to go on. I dipped a Copenhagen and went to my bedroll in the dust near Engine 361.

We were up at dawn a few hours later, clustered in a circle drinking cowboy coffee with hunched-over shoulders and stiff feet and fingers. An SUV pulled up with a TV news channel decal on its door. A reporter and a cameraman chatted with Hall. They wanted to interview a ground-pounder firefighter. I was unanimously nominated, most likely because I was sort of loud and usually spoke my mind. I think everyone figured I would somehow make an ass of myself and prove them right.

The reporter was a gal in her early twenties, and I think her name was Shelly. I intended to impress her with my coolness and worldliness and gung-ho attitude. The cameraman set up his tripod, she set up her microphones and cords and stuff.

She started. "How long have you been on this fire?"

"This will be our third day."

Blah-blah, some other questions about what I knew about this particular fire, which wasn't much, I'm just a grunt. Then she asked, "How long have you been fighting fire?"

"This is my second season."

"Why do you guys like this job?"

"Well, first of all, it's a big rush to come up on these fires, get your stuff ready, and then take the fires head-on. There's a lot of adrenaline involved; it's kind of like playing in a football game."

"Do you worry about your safety?"

"No way. We'll do whatever it takes to get the job done. I mean, we look out for each other and try to prevent injuries, but it's not something that's on my mind constantly."

Oops.

Hall gathered us up after the reporter had left and gave us the details he knew. Fourteen firefighters had been killed in a burnover in Colorado. Burned alive trying to outrun an inferno. Among them were hotshots, helitack, and smokejumpers.

Hall released us from the fire back to our respective stations, as did many Incident Commanders on wildland fires across the nation that day. It was just not worth keeping firefighters on the line without their minds totally on the job. No need for more accidents just to save some vegetation. This was an awful day.

We were all stunned. We gathered up our gear and took off. There was hardly any conversation. This just as easily could have been us. We felt sick for the families and we hungered for more details.

That afternoon and evening we stuck around the station and cleaned up our gear. At 6:00 p.m. we turned on the news. There was all the information the media could give us about the fatalities. Then there was my interview, reduced to this:

Reporter: "I spoke today with Ben Walters, a firefighter on the currently eighty-percent contained Ross Fork Fire near Fort Hall, and this is what he had to say about the wildland firefighting business."

"Why do you guys like this job?"

"It's a big rush."

"Do you worry about your safety?"

"No way."

The station phone rang an hour later and it was Rick Hill, our FMO. "Come up to the office tomorrow," he said. "We need to talk."

I explained the situation and my exact words to a trio of management folks – and apologized. They gave me a lecture about keeping my mouth shut. I kept my job, but it was a little harder for me to keep my mouth shut.

The available details on the fatal fire were somewhat fuzzy for a long time, but are cleared up very thoroughly by John Maclean in his book *Fire on the Mountain – The True Story of the South Canyon Fire*, first published in 1999 and reprinted in 2009. I strongly recommend reading it.

The Airport Bar

THE CREW FELL BACK INTO the normal rhythm of the season after some time, but the tragedy in Colorado never totally left our minds. We were reintroduced to the 10 standard fire orders and 18 watch-out situations. We applied them on every fire thereafter; even Sean, who did so without letting on that he cared.

A record 34 people were killed on fires that year.

I still drank gallons of beer after work when not on fires, which was about half of the evenings that summer; it wasn't a particularly crazy fire season for us. Toward the end of the season, Steve and I met Jerry Graham at the airport bar at 7:00 p.m., after a scorching day of washing hoses near the black tarmac. Many Native Americans don't hold their liquor gracefully, and Jerry gave us a front-row seat to witness that on this sunny evening.

Steve and I arrived at the bar first. It was a laid-back and mellow atmosphere, with the sun beginning to set across the Snake River plains and reflecting in varied gold and orange hues around the restaurant area. The bar was empty save for two women in their forties and a balding middle-aged guy.

One of the reasons we came here now and then was that I was only 19, and they didn't ask me for ID. What kind of trouble was I going to cause – our station was less than a mile away up the old airport road. The bartender tilted us a couple of frosty Bud Lights and

Steve and I grabbed stools and sat down to shoot the bull. We talked about flying, hunting, fishing, or Sean. Lately we also talked a lot about the South Canyon Fire and just how fast fire situations could turn dangerous.

Jerry arrived a bit later, still wearing his greens, and copped a stool. I bought him a beer. He poured that first beer down his gullet like it was water going down a drain. Then he got a second one and did likewise. In 15 minutes flat, Jerry was preaching about his superior abilities at firefighting. He was right, he was a good firefighter, but his tone was curiously menacing. He hooked one leg on a barstool and used his other to swing back and forth, while sitting, in about a 90-degree arc, scanning the bar area for anyone who would listen to him. Steve and I, patient guys, listened to him for a few minutes until he asked me if I wanted to arm wrestle him. Jerry could easily beat me, he had before, and he had dang near broken my arm both times. I politely declined. He never did ask Steve, who wouldn't have even been a challenge.

Jerry's been here now for about a half hour. The sun's still up. Steve and I have had three beers by now and I have to pee, so I excuse myself and walk down the hall to the men's room. When I come back, I see that Jerry is now making company with the middle-aged gentleman and his two female companions. Jerry's sitting at the fourth seat at their table and challenging the guy to an arm-wrestling match. I don't think Jerry even knows him. I hear the guy repeatedly declining and one of the women telling Jerry he should just leave. Then, out of the corner of my eye, I see quick movement, the beginnings of a fracas, and a large Indian fist crashing into the temple of the man who we later learn is the owner of the Pocatello AvCenter – the guy who basically owns the airport.

Chairs, tables, drinks, napkins, shoes, fists, hair, cussing, yelling, Indian fists, a guy screaming – things seem to go everywhere very fast. Out of the rolling human ball comes the guy running out of the bar with Jerry chasing him, the two women chasing Jerry, and me chasing the whole mess so I could maybe break it up and save Jerry from an assault charge. Steve remains at the bar and finishes his beer, left hand in his pocket, right elbow on the bar, casting an uninterested gaze toward the small cyclone of humanity and tavern effects.

We all end up in the foyer of the otherwise silent "concourse," Jerry pounding the crap out of the AvCenter owner, me trying to wedge them apart, and two barflies screaming and pounding the hell out of me and Jerry with shoes and purses. Finally I pull Jerry off; he breaks loose from my grip like Walter Payton and bolts through the door, out to the parking lot, and into the government vehicle he "procured" for his trip down here. Then he is gone down the frontage road. I am left behind making apologies and trying to calm everyone, and everyone tells me to just get out of here. Guilt by association, no doubt. I pay the tab at the bar, ask if I need to pay for damages, get told again to get lost, and then leave with Steve back to the station.

I never saw Jerry Graham again, nor the inside of the Pocatello Airport Bar. His first official sentence to me had been "Little bitch" back on my first fire; I never did figure out how to take that. His second official

141

sentence to me was "Check out this arrowhead I found." Because he was Native American, I figured he had an appreciation for artifacts and maybe collected them, so I held out my hand. And he handed me a juicy wad of used Copenhagen about the same shape as an arrowhead. I was just flummoxed; we were in the middle of nowhere and I had no way to wash my hand after flinging the "arrowhead" and trying not to gag. He was an asshole, but I also know he'd have had my back in a pinch.

He was really a pretty cool customer, and he disproved for me all I'd heard and unfairly prejudged about Native Americans who lived on reservations. He was outwardly motivated and skilled at all the things impressive to me: running, pushups, fighting and wrestling, hunting, horseshoes, basketball, football, beer drinking, girls, and of course firefighting. I'll never forget his big fist smashing into the side of the head of the Pocatello AVCenter owner and the repercussions it had on my fire career. And I'll never forget his admonishing me one day for wolf-whistling at a couple of pretty girls walking down the street. "Shut the fuck up," he said. "Just look at them. If they want you, they'll look back."

A lot of things came of this incident, which at the time seemed relatively minor compared with other brawls I'd been involved in by the age of 19.

First, I decided to return to college, this time at the University of Idaho in Moscow. This would enable me to quit for the season in a couple of weeks; I was tired of firefighting for the year. Second, Jerry was fired from the BLM for improper use of a government vehicle, and coming up positive on a drug test, and not reporting to work for two weeks after this incident. Third, the decision was made to keep me stationed from then on, should I return next season, as far as possible from the south zone of the district. The bar thing must have been the final straw.

From then on I would be a North Zone Eskimo, a big person joining one of the crews we always called "the little people up north." And lastly, I learned that Sean was really not a big jerk. He got drunk with Steve and me one night and more or less explained that he knew about all the drinking I'd done all summer and the wild stuff we had pulled. He used to do the same thing, he said. He usually left after work, we learned, because he didn't want to be around that sort of thing anymore.

Our only problem, he said to us, and he was right, was that we got drunk. To me he said, *You'd better calm down your drinking, or you're gonna have major problems.*

FIRE CREW: STORIES FROM THE FIRELINE

College Bound

THE MORNING AFTER that eye-opening chat with Sean, I expected him to be a bit nicer, but he was back to his old Sean self. At one point, King Biscuit was vacuuming the floor of the guard station and Sean was trying to watch a Cincinnati Reds baseball game. She turned off the vacuum and went to plug it in at a different spot. Sean said, "Stephanie, if you turn on that vacuum again, I'm going to bludgeon you to death with it." I'm pretty sure that was the only thing Sean said to King Biscuit all summer.

I quit for the season on August 16. That gave me a week to get moved up north and settle in for my first year at the U of I. I picked up my gear from the station and cleaned up my half of the room I shared with Steve. I said goodbye to the crew and some of the people I had gotten to know at the tanker base. I was ready to be done, but I knew that in the dead of winter up north, I would greatly miss this place and this job.

I had tried to work hard and do my best, although it was made far more challenging because of my drinking and smoking and heavy weight. But partying was fun – everywhere and everything was a party to me. I was living for the good times. Tomorrow was never going to come; I was living like a rock star on the 30-year plan. Yes, I would miss this.

I climbed into my Chevy truck and fired it up, and when the air conditioning kicked in, before I was even on the interstate, a little rock chip in the windshield turned into a huge spider web across my line of sight and then some. I wondered if this had greater meaning. Before school even started up in Moscow, the smoke of the summer fires of August, from the south of us in the wilderness areas, had settled into the Palouse.

On the first day of classes, I walked along some old train tracks through an abandoned lot in the humid afternoon air, kicking the dry weeds ahead of me and thinking. All over the West right now there were young men and women sliding to a dusty stop and deploying the hard lines for pump and roll. Somewhere someone prepped drip torches with greasy leather gloves. A hotshot crew was hiking swiftly up through the shadows on a high mountain trail toward a timber fire. An airtanker was coming in hot on final approach. A delicious cold Coke was being sucked back after some handline construction. And me? I already had a math homework assignment. It was going to be a long winter.

The Girls of Summer

THERE ARE QUITE A FEW different brands of boots you can use for wildland firefighting. The required specs include Vibram soles and 8-inch leather uppers. I used Redwing something-or-others my first two seasons and they just chewed up my feet. Your feet should break in a boot, not the other way around. Wearing two pairs of socks at a time and using lots of moleskin got me through it, but jeez, you shouldn't have to do that.

A crappy pair of boots causes you to have friction hot spots in certain places on your feet, which quickly turn into blisters. Sometimes I'd work a shift on a fire, pry off my boots before bed-down, and feel like I had walked on glass all day. The next morning it was difficult to put the boots back on. I was fat as well, so I would grunt and groan and pull on the boots and be miserable. My toes and heels would burn as I took my first few steps, raw and red. No one else seemed to have that issue, and coincidentally, they all had boots that cost a lot more than mine. Get what you pay for? Yep, when it comes to boots that's certainly true. The boots I saw most often on firefighters were White's Smokejumpers, made in Washington. They're the classic, along with Nick's Boots, also made in Washington, and White's boots are the most comfortable I've ever put on my feet (*all* hiking boots included), except for the boots that the cobbler at Dubois Leather and Shoe in Dubois, Idaho, makes by hand. With top-quality boots, you're getting what you pay for, a boot that with a rebuild or two plus routine maintenance will last you for a career. Of course, I wore mine *everywhere*, and didn't rebuild or do the maintenance, so I had to have two pairs that got me through eight fire seasons. Like I was told, one fire and you've got them paid for.

Steve in Dubois and White's and Nick's can even custom-build your fire boots for you. Then you get some Obenauf's LP leather conditioner, made out of beeswax and invented by a wildland firefighter, work it into the leather, buff it out, and you're ready to go. The beeswax preservative makes the boots smell vaguely appetizing, almost as if you were wearing scones with honey butter. Once broken in, these boots will feel form-fitted to your feet and soft as house slippers. When you wear them, you stand a couple inches taller, which put *me* about six feet tall. Maybe that's why I rarely took them off. When you hike in them, you sort of feel pitched forward, which somehow adds to the feeling of getting a larger stride. Going downhill, they gouge into the terrain and offer superior stability. And I *never* got a blister with them.

This is where I found myself in 1995, traveling up to Dubois to pick up my boots, which I had ordered the day after I received the letter asking me whether I was going to return to the fire crew for the season. Again, I checked the "yes" box. My window of huge opportunities as a professional football player and doctor had, for the most part, slammed shut with the knee injury – along with several C's on my first U of I report card. I'd changed my major from Biology/Pre-Med to Wildlife Biology the second semester, hoping it

148

would be easier. It wasn't. My plan was to at least complete a degree and find a job with a fish and game department, or maybe even full-time with the BLM. It was spring break, and spring was only just now sneaking around the corner; fire season was only in the past and the future. The snow was melting so much that only blackened patches of it remained on the sides of the roads, in gutters, and in shady spots. You could ditch the winter coat for a hooded sweatshirt for the better part of a day now, and the infamous eastern Idaho afternoon wind was often unrelenting as it blew through the trees and across the prairie.

I was a tiny bit more mature and thinking about the future enough by then that I was already preparing for the first day at the BLM in June. Living with my brother in a dingy apartment all year had eliminated both fat-filled cafeteria food and our mom's loaded dinner plates, and so I was leaner this year than last. I had also worked my butt off at the Moscow Fitness Club since August, pushing weights and going through scorching cardio routines on the stair climbers and other equipment. I had come to the conclusion that I was going to shift the balance from using my brain for making a living over to using my body more to pay the bills. I'd decided that I would at least make a go of it in this fire business – be more prepared this year than last. Better body and better boots were a good start.

Monday, June 5, 1995, 8:50 a.m. – It's a bright and shiny morning. Birds are chirping, leaves are green, traffic hums, and I'm standing outside the new BLM building, which is also now home to an Interagency Fire Center. I'm wearing a black fire crew t-shirt I

149

picked up last summer, with sleeves rolled up to show off slightly pumped biceps, and standing about 6 feet tall in my pitch-black fire boots and stonewashed Levis. I even have a combed and gelled coif, and I'm wearing Aspen cologne. For work, you ask? Yes. There are several very good-looking women on this crew and others who work in the office, and I am looking for lust in my life. We're all standing around talking the usual – "How was your winter?" "Good to see ya'" – blah, blah.

Steve and John are here, as well as a couple of guys I knew from the Fort Hall light engine crew. Campbell has moved to Boise to take a job with Boise Cascade driving a forklift. Jerry Graham is no longer a wildland firefighter, Sean decided he had had enough for a lifetime, and King Biscuit has married and moved to Rexburg for college. And James Stoddard has been promoted to foreman of Engine 342. God help us.

But here at the new Fire Center in early June, all the other faces are pretty much just faces and names to me. I had seen them and knew their names, had worked and eaten and slept in the same fire camps with them, but I didn't really know them. I gravitate toward Steve while we wait for the official call to come into the new conference room for the initial meeting of the season. "So you got your Jeep, eh, Steve?" I ask him. "Pretty cool machine. Did you get your Nissan pickup sold?"

"No, I'm just gonna have to tighten my belt a little this summer. Or eat it."

"Heyyy John, how was your winter?" We exchange one of those high-five-slash-handshake things.

Not bothering to pay attention to the answer, I look around and try to act cool. This is my third season; I'm a veteran now. Maybe I'll be engine boss this year. We all kind of mill about for a few more minutes until Gary calls us in.

I enter and pick an aisle seat inside the new modular conference room with its scent of freshly installed carpet and coats of white paint. First order of business is the distribution of individual employment packets that include our assignments for the season. I receive mine and see that this summer I'll be on Engine 311, at Station 1 in Dubois. Huh, that's kind of a surprise. I did not make engine foreman, and am considered merely an advanced firefighter. The foreman for 311 will be Isaac Feltz, and his assistant foreman will be Amy Walker. The two other firefighters besides me are Alexis York and some new long-haired kid named Dave Neil.

Kim, the human resources lady, calls us up to the front of the room to fill out I-9 forms that require a witnessed signature and two forms of ID. Dave Farmer is just ahead of me, and as he roots through his wallet for ID, he drops two condoms on the table in front of Kim. What a jackass.

The paperwork and the run are finished by afternoon, and we're all out in the yard getting the crew photo. It was no problem passing the run this year, for once. I was in fine shape at the beginning of the season. I had even gone home, showered and combed my hair again at lunch. I was thinking about the chicks on the crew.

The girls that worked here were hot, all of them tanned and toned. From what I heard, none of them were stuck-up and the three hottest ones even partied.

I was still kind of shy around girls, though, and hadn't gotten to know any of them or even talked to them. Three of the best-looking ones were Amy Walker, Alexis York, and the new chick, Emily Webb. OH yeahhh, I was gonna be *living with* two of those three. The heck with the rumor that Engine 311 went to the fewest fires each season; I could give a crap.

My last two girlfriend relationships had not exactly worked out well. Stephanie broke up with me after two years when I went off to college at the University of Chicago – because I was not Mormon. That happens. Danielle, a loyal but kind of strange girl, and I broke up after a couple of years. We just never were a good fit. She was quiet, and I was too boisterous.

I was living exactly like I should have been then: like a single 20-year-old guy. I lived to the fullest, and part of that meant being with beautiful women. And then there was the strength and skill and attitude of these ladies – all were excellent firefighters. In fact, I worked with only a very few women who were *not* great firefighters. Most could hang with the average guy and even outwork him. Their stamina was often better, and they were every bit as smart. Even mediocre women begin to look really good after being out on a fire or in a remote station for a while, but that was not so in the case of the Idaho Falls girls – they'd attract attention in any situation, anywhere.

Dubois, Idaho, is maybe 20 miles south of the Idaho border with Montana, about halfway between the Sun Valley ski area and Yellowstone National Park. It's a small town surrounded by remote and rugged country. Isaac Feltz, our fearless leader, was a 21-year-old whitey from Wisconsin, who even talked that nasal

Midwest way: *nice to meetcha*. He had done two seasons with the Globe Hotshots out of Arizona, and to hear him describe it, numerous years with a volunteer fire department in some town in Wisconsin. *What the heck does he know about engine crews?* I wondered. He was kind of a high-strung guy, probably experienced enough, but disconcertingly loud and nervous at times.

Amy Walker was our assistant foreman. Very sweet, very smart girl. Looked like Darryl Hannah the movie star. She had a secret wild streak (as most women firefighters did), but acted like the crew big sister. She had an identical twin who had fought fire a couple of years ago, and her mom was a home-economics teacher at Eagle Rock Junior High School. I seriously hoped her mother wouldn't remember me as an eighth grader in her classroom, because I'd been a first-class troublemaker.

Alexis York. We sometimes called her the "90-pound menace." I doubt she *was* much heavier than 90 pounds, but she was certainly no menace. Dave "Tom Petty" Neil was Jerry Neil's younger brother. On the day I met him, I thought Dave looked exactly like Tom Petty in concert. He had long reddish-blonde hair that partially covered his face. He wore small 1960s sunglasses and an American flag bandanna tied sweatband-style around his forehead. He wore a leather jacket with lots of silver zippers, ripped old-school Levis, and polished black O-ring dingo boots. All in all he looked pretty cool, unless you didn't know him. Because I didn't know him yet, I thought, *Who is this punk?*

Frank Morgan, whom I remembered from 1993, was the foreman of Engine 312, and Felicia Lewis made up

153

his one-person crew. Morgan turned out to be mildly weird, but I got along okay with him. Felicia was just plain cool. A couple years later she received a "Firefighter of the Year" award. She was a small dynamo of a girl, but usually pretty quiet.

During fire school that year, five or six of us were called out of class one day to roll to a fire near the town of Mud Lake, north of Idaho Falls. The fire was about 2,000 acres, but it was dead-out cold, having burned in really light grassy fuels. We just patrolled around it for a couple of hours, wiped some soot and dirt on our faces for effect, then came back home.

Everybody else was jealous of our getting hazard pay for the day.

Dubois

Saturday, June 24, 1995, 2:30 p.m. – Nothing has happened yet this season. The "station" here is the typical BLM setup: a single-wide mobile home set up on a leased lot. The trailer itself seems to be at least a decade old, with serious 1980s décor: fake wood paneling, stud-sized mirrors with etching on them, old government furnishings (including very comfortable swivel rockers and couch), shag carpet in the three bedrooms, and of course the ubiquitous government bunk beds (except in the station manager/foreman's room).

Living in these trailers was always vaguely comforting, like you were living in an era of less stress. Time seemed to move more slowly as soon as you stepped through the door of that trailer.

Station 1 was in a residential area in Dubois, which is not typical of BLM stations. We had next-door neighbors, both a front and a back lawn, a fence, an aspen tree in the front yard, another in the back, and in the southwest corner there was a fire pit and a pile of cut wood. Beaver Creek ran right through town, and at the end of our street there was a swimming hole with a rope swing. The back yard bordered the high school football field, and the whole town was surrounded by sagebrush prairie. In the near distance loomed the Centennial Mountains, obscured by heat waves on sweltering summer days, brought close and crisp on cool and dewy summer mornings.

As a crew, we had a feeling of being on our own this far from the BLM yard and the main fire hub. We were our own bosses, we would do as we chose during the day, and we would live without the feeling of being watched all the time.

It is after lunch now, and our bellies are full, as Alexis and Amy had introduced us to the Cow Country Café, one of Dubois' two restaurants. I had a greasy double bacon cheeseburger with homestyle steak fries. I was hungry, taking huge bites of the burger with two or three of the big fries at time. I left the lettuce, pickle, and onion produce on the plate, and washed it all down with one of the café's locally famous thick chocolate shakes.

After we returned to the station, Feltz looked around, then told us all to just chill out in the front room for a while. I hitched a two-finger Copenhagen and settled into one of the big beanbags on the floor. Now and then I snored myself awake, then looked around only to see that the rest of 311's crew had followed suit. Morgan and Felicia were in 312 out on patrol somewhere. I thought lazily to myself, *I am making around ten dollars an hour right now while snoozing. Life is good.*

Around 3:00 p.m. we all began to stir. I got up, stretched, and stepped out onto the porch into the afternoon heat. *It's certainly hot enough to get a fire going,* I thought. But the sky looked too blue for lightning. Maybe we would go to the Legion later – one of Dubois' two bars. I was still only 20 but figured they'd serve me. *Once they see how free and stupid I am with my money, they'll never question my age.*

The first couple of weeks at the station were a string of nearly identical days. Up with a hangover at 8:59, then a 3-mile jog on the turnaround down the old highway along Beaver Creek, then crunches and stretches in the stiff grass in the front yard, then Crunch Berries for breakfast, a shower, then watch the "Price is Right" on TV until it's time to do the morning routine checks of the engine and the gray Ford chase.

There's a project list that we can get started on while we're waiting for the fires to get going, and one of the tasks is to build a jack-fence exclosure around the warm spring at Deep Creek. This one looks fun. It really doesn't matter to me what we do, I'm just so happy to be with these people. Feltz and his nervousness are fun. Dave Neil is turning out to be a heck of a cool dude. Amy, with her long blonde hair and soft voice, is always a pleasure to look at and talk to. Alexis, always cute, but getting hotter and hotter while getting cooler and cooler, is making my days and nights worthwhile. We keep finding curious and common things about one another, and she thinks it's cool that I can play guitar. I just constantly check her out in secret, trying to get a glimpse through a thin cotton shirt, watching her athletic and smooth strides, shivering if she puts a hand on my shoulder, always trying to get her alone in conversation. I considered my day a success if she suggested we do a chore together.

We all have taken to drinking at least a few beers every night around the station or at the Legion bar. We are making friends with the local people and sometimes a few will come and drink with us at the station.

FIRE CREW: STORIES FROM THE FIRELINE

The bosses down in Idaho Falls consider this a success, as repairing the relations with the locals is somewhat of a priority here after the AFCO, Matt James, broke a cowboy's jaw in a bar fight several years ago. The cowboy was one of the Meyers brothers, from a prominent ranch family in the area. You can see why they didn't warm to us in Dubois right away. I can make friends with anybody, though, especially if we get a chance to drink together and I'm buying.

Mountaintop Fire

Then the fires started.

I can't honestly say I really cared too much about fires at the time, because I was so focused on having a crush on Alexis, and so happy to just hang out at the station. That's not to say I shirked work – our first call was a lightning-caused smolderer clear down south past American Falls Reservoir. That's even farther south than Station 6, where I'd worked the previous summer.

We slowed down to exit the interstate and I could actually *feel* the transition of the weather from early summer humidity to fire-season dry. Virga – those streaks of rain falling from clouds, the rain evaporating before it reaches the ground – concealed the Wheatgrass Bench east of us, and a cool, dry afternoon wind switched back and forth with a thick heat that formed beads of sweat on the forehead. I took a shot of cold water from a bottle knowing that the rest of the water I would drink for a while would be warm.

The fire itself was a good warm-up (no pun intended) for the season. The southeastern flank did have active fire on it, and because we were the only resource in the area, we decided to travel over to that side and knock it down first. Feltz called in a size-up to dispatch from the radio in the chase truck while the rest of us deployed the hard lines to knock down the flames. The rest of the scene was just 40 or 50 acres of smoldering grass and spindly sagebrush. Then the five of us stood around in the late afternoon and kicked at dirt and told funny stories. A bolt of lightning so close we saw it and heard it at the same time motivated us to pack it up and call dispatch to get our next instructions. Fires had started all over the district, and although the light rain and increasing humidity had kept them small, it was a sure bet we would be reassigned somewhere. Feltz called dispatch with its new call sign.

"Dispatch, Engine 311."

"311, Dispatch, go ahead."

"We are calling the Horse Butte Fire contained and controlled at this time and are awaiting our next instructions."

"311, we copy, stand by for further instructions."

"311 standing by."

Our next instructions sent us even farther south into another BLM district, its call sign 429. Sweet, a detail.

Details are mixed blessings for wildland firefighters, but generally the math comes out on the positive side. The negatives are that you are leaving your home unit and you don't know for how long. Technically it could be for the rest of the season, especially if you are a college student and will leave in August. When you are working out of the area, the voices of the dispatchers aren't familiar, the FCOs and AFCOs aren't familiar, the terrain is usually unfamiliar, and you don't know when and where you will find your next meal and bed.

The benefits of details, though, are numerous. First of all, overtime and hazard pay are virtually guaranteed – the district wouldn't call for more resources unless it was for fires. You don't spend much of your money because food is paid for and there's nowhere to put stuff you might want to buy. You learn new terrain and maybe some new methods of firefighting – if you pay attention. You can network and get to know new people who might further your career, or even become lifelong friends. Last but not least, you can get phone numbers of other hardbody babe firefighters *and* local girls who dig firefighters. We arrived in Burley at about dark and reported to the dispatch office on the south end of town. Most of the other crews were off on fires that night, but we did meet Vince Gunderson, one of the AFCOs, and the members of an engine crew headed up by the big red-headed kid, Brett Anderson. There wasn't much time for pleasantries, though, as we were given directions by dispatch to check out a report of a fire on a mountaintop south of the town of Oakley. All of the district's other resources were committed to fires, so at least for now, we would be on our own to both find and fight the fire.

Stepping out into the night, it was hard to believe that fires were burning everywhere and all the BLM engine crews up and down the Snake River Valley were running and gunning. It was a beautiful and pleasant summer night. A green grass exercise yard surrounded the blacktop of this BLM yard, cool and soft in the early evening. Sprinklers on a wheel line in a neighboring alfalfa field tick-tick-ticked a mist over the beginnings of a second hay cutting. Mercury lights in the yard shone down on the collection of rangeland equipment and pickups common to a western BLM facility. I strolled over to the chase truck, sipping a red Gatorade and working a sentimental mood.

We pulled off onto a primitive dirt track around 11:00 p.m. and met the farmer who had called in the fire on top of the hill around the corner and up the canyon. He was riding a red Honda ATV, and had his grandson riding behind him. He guided us down the two-track and across an irrigation ditch bridge that caused us all to hold our breath as Feltz drove the heavy engine onto it.

After we'd parked the vehicles, the farmer gave us directions for hiking in to the fire and bid us farewell for the evening. I stretched and then started donning all my gear: yellow shirt, bandanna, pack with fire shelter, and everything else I might need to work a fire on a mountain all night. Being the biggest guy, I volunteered to pack the Stihl chainsaw, chaps, and Sigg bottles full of fuel and bar oil as well. I didn't bring an extra chain – I don't know why, to save weight maybe?

This was my first chance to impress my crewmates, mostly Alexis, with how strong I was. I intended to hump that saw right up that mountain; no stopping, no whining, no slowing down. Gradually my respiration rate increased, as did the depth of my breathing. We could smell the smoke as we climbed farther up and got closer to the fire. Then we reached the bottom of a swale and it was time to really climb.

The hill proved to be one of those killer hills. It was steep as a cow's face, but even worse, the soil was loose, so even after you ground the side of your boot into it, you would still lose an inch or two with each step. The extra weight of the saw and my gear made it harder to get a full deep breath, so I had to repeatedly reposition the saw. My lungs and thighs and calves were searing, and even my shoulder muscles were starting to bark. My mouth was sandy dry and my tongue seemed to be growing. The rest of the crew quickly passed by me, even though it's customary for the sawyer to lead the way. Feltz got more aggressive as we got closer, yet the hill seemed to get even steeper. "Cam ann!" he complained in his Wiscaansin twanginess. "Get moving, we're draggin' ass!" I might have told him off if I'd had the breath for it, but as it was, I needed all I could get just to keep up. I felt mildly humiliated that I was proving to be the slowest hiker on the crew, and I hoped Alexis didn't notice. I resolved to reduce my consumption of calories, and lose about a hundred pounds. And kick Feltz's Midwestern white butt.

And then it was over. On the mountaintop at the quarter-acre lightning strike fire. This was what dang near killed me?! One-quarter of an acre of juniper trees, and tall blades of grass, and maybe eight clumps of sagebrush. The wind kicked up now and then and a flurry of sparks would fly off with a whoosh. A larger juniper on the west side was torching and throwing embers into the breeze and down the slope into tall grass.

Feltz called the fire size-up in to the 429 dispatch while the rest of us, mostly me, sucked water and air and got our hand tools and the saw ready. The first priority would be taking down that large juniper that kept trying to torch. That would be my job. The next job would be to dig a handline around the perimeter so the fire didn't sneak down the sidehill, and lastly we would dry-mop and chunk up the larger fuels. We figured to leave sometime tomorrow with the fire dead cold.

The saw, like all others in the BLM and Forest Service, was kept in primo condition, so it fired up on the first pull after the half start with the choke. Then I realized I had forgotten to put on the required Kevlar safety chaps that I had brought with me, so I stopped the saw, set it down, put on the chaps, and fired the saw back up. I carefully walked over to the large juniper while the saw putted, holding it by the safety bar with my fingers pointing forward. The best place to dig the chain in is obviously a cold spot, so that's where I put it. Then I gunned the engine to get to work.

The tree was in pieces and parts in just a few moments, with Dave working as my swamper and bringing burnt pieces back into the middle of the black area. There was only a foot or so of the main trunk left, and it grew a ways parallel to the ground before twisting upward. I would cut it off right where it met the soil.

When I put the dawgs to the stump there were a couple of embers that flew, but not enough to worry, so I throttled it up and zipped the bar right through. It went so fast that I didn't realize the new stream of embers now flying out weren't actually embers, but sparks. *Dammit*! I had sawed through too fast and hadn't seen the rock I'd been zipping the teeth into on the far side of the stump. Gaaaame ovah for that chain. Now it wouldn't cut through a warm stick of butter.

I am batting a thousand for screwup here, I think. Out of shape and proving I really didn't know what I was doing with a saw. Feltz just said, "Well, hike back to the engine and get the other chain, I guess. Why didn't you bring a spare?"

No need to scold, really – the hike back down the hill and back up again would be punishment enough. At least I could refill my water bottles out of the big canteens, and at least I wouldn't have to pack the saw back up that hill again. The rest of the crew set to work chinking a handline around the perimeter while I took off into the night to get the spare chain. You can bet I never sawed into rock again, *or* left the extra chain at the engine.

Back on the fire a couple of hours later, the crew had finished the handline around the perimeter, so I joined them in dry-mopping all the embers. Dry mopping sucks. It's just what it sounds like; cleaning without water. Except you're not cleaning, you're cooling. You try to break the fuels into a bunch of small pieces first, using a saw or pulaski. This increases the surface area and thus increases exposure to cooling air. On pieces too big to pick up, you take your pulaski and scrape off all the charred and glowing pieces of burning wood and chunk them up. Then you mix the hotter material with dirt or sand to cool it off. We'd also put partially burning material into piles and make a kind of jackpot and just get it all burned up at once. Slow, tiring, tedious work.

I stood against a larger juniper just outside of the perimeter in the early morning hours and had a swig or two of water and a dip of Copenhagen. The stars were resplendent in the pre-dawn darkness, the major constellations easy to pick out. It was quiet on the mountain here, the only sounds being the pleasant conversation of the crew, the occasional clank of metal on rock from the head of a pulaski, and the sparse radio traffic of crews throughout the district making updates to dispatch on the status of their fires.

I caught myself smiling; I realized that for the first time since I started fighting fires, I was actually where I *wanted* to be – it wasn't so much *where* I was, but who I was with. I wasn't wishing I was back in Idaho Falls guzzling beer with the boys and looking for trouble. Isaac Feltz, Amy Walker, Alexis York, and Dave Neil had become a group of friends. These were good people, people I enjoyed being around. Had I thought about it at the time, I might have also realized that I was beginning to be *me*. I was happy to see people smile and have fun, and happy to see people successful. Happy to be a part of something good and right.

By dawn, we pretty much had this little fire dead out. You could take off a glove and safely put your hand anywhere inside the perimeter, and though you may get it dirty and sooty, and it may be warm, it wouldn't burn. Feltz called this info in to dispatch, and we packed it up and started the hike down the hill. It was not until now that I realized how hungry I was.

"Anybody else hungry?" I asked.

"Well, I had a little bit of my MRE earlier," Amy replied.

"I think I am," said Alexis.

"I could eat the butt end of a dead rhinoceros," said Dave.

"I second that," said Feltz.

"Well, what I'm thinking about is a huge chocolate shake, and some greasy fries and a giant double cheeseburger, with the juice dripping down the sides of it."

"You know what else would be good? Some fried mozzarella sticks with a load of marinara, some chicken strips with honey sauce for dipping, and of course a huge chocolate shake, so big they have to serve part of it in a glass and part of it in the metal cup they made it in." The more I talked, the hungrier I got.

"You need to stop that, my stomach is starting to growl," Feltz said.

"I can't help it dude, it's all I can think about."

"Eat some of your MRE, didn't you pack one up here?" he asked.

"You know I can't eat that crap."

The truth was, I really found MREs revolting. It was pretty much the chicken à la king puking episode back in 1993 that did it for me. I could go two days on just Copenhagen and water before I would eat anything from an MRE packet. I had done it before; I just hated being that hungry.

"Godfather's pizza, all you can eat," I said, as we reached the bottom of the hill. "Shut *up*," they all said in unison.

We got to the vehicles about noon and everybody was almost frantically putting gear away so we could drive back to town and get something to eat. I drank a warm Gatorade, put in a fresh dip, and hopped into the back of the chase for the ride back to Burley.

The bridge across the irrigation ditch failed when Feltz was crossing it in the engine. With a crack and a snap, 311's nose and grille guard and front bumper mired down in the junk and we weren't going anywhere soon. I broke open a package of MRE crackers and peanut butter – calories 8,000 and taste 0

– and surveyed the scene. This was going to require a dozer.

Hours later, with the help of the same farmer who had showed us how to get to the fire, we were unstuck and on our way. I wish I had YouTube video of me crossing that ditch in the Ford chase truck. I hit it going about 30 mph, slowed instantly to about 1 mph, spun mud 20 feet in the air, slung the tranny into the depths of hell, and gunned the engine up to heaven. *Yeee-haw!*

When we hit blacktop, I started thinking about food again.

"What's your favorite food, Alexis?" I asked. No answer.

"Dave?" Silence.

"Well, let me tell you mine," I said.

"If I could have anything in the world right now, it would be hot out-of-the-fryer mozzarella sticks and shrimp cocktail for appetizers, an Outback salad with thousand-island dressing and huge croutons, a marbled piece of medium prime rib so big it covers the whole plate, some greasy tater-tots, and a Coke in a glass with ice. For dessert, my mom's chocolate drop cookies, or hot-from-the-oven chocolate chip cookies. After that I would put in a chew and lie down on the couch for a huge nap, like two hours. Then I would get up and drink beer all night."

I turned down the radio when dispatch called on the Motorola to instruct us to continue on to another fire, this one farther north and west, as an assistance call from yet another BLM district. Judging by the location given on the map, the fire was really out in the tules – as in *no food*. I rarely verbally complain, and I didn't this time. But inside I was crying. Now my stomach growled, and when I blinked it took willpower to open my eyes back up. We drove on.

Fire Crew

Wednesday, July 12, 1995, 1:00 p.m. – Eat Dirt and Dust. And Work the Night Shift.

Sometimes an incident management team on a larger fire will set up rotating 16-hour shifts, so you work most of the night and attempt to sleep during the day. You can build a lot of line when fire behavior is slow and low, like it was last night – with high relative humidity and lower temperature, but I still hate night shift. By now we are dragging.

When we first rolled up to this fire, they had us park the chase in the black and Dave, Alexis, and I hopped onto the back of the engine (a practice I don't think is allowed anymore) for about a 10-mile ramble through the dustiest landscape I'd ever seen. Going down the main road before we went off-road was like driving over a washboard covered in 8 inches of flour.

Finding a comfortable place to sit on the engine really isn't possible either. At first the climb-on bars might feel okay to rest your rear end against, but pretty soon you feel your web gear straps gouging into your lower back. You can sit on the very top of the engine, and that feels good until one or both of your feet fall asleep, or the driver goes over a big one and you're sure you are about to be cast into outer darkness. Riding on the running boards works until your legs get so tired that your thighs begin to quiver. All the while the pump and motor are howling, so having a conversation with your fellow miserable riders is similar to having a conversation at the main street club when the music is cranked and everybody is wasted. Forget getting a drink of water. Just sit there with your goggles on, and your bank-robber bandanna up, hang on, and think of food, water, sleep, and Alexis.

The only thing I remember about our assignment that night was that it was the first pump and roll I did with the crew of 311. We had a daisy chain going with Brett Anderson's engine leading the way, and a volunteer crew using an Army deuce-and-a-half bringing up the rear. I do remember that we did pump and roll for at least 5 miles over flat terrain. No problem except for the smoke and dust. Holy crap, did we suck that down.

At 9:00 the next morning they pulled us off the night shift with instructions to grab some breakfast and some sleep.

We ate the breakfast that had arrived earlier in shamrocks from the district office's warehouse. The food was awesome, even if it was delivered in styrofoam clamshells. Cheesy scrambled eggs, four or five strips of bacon, four or five links of maple and brown-sugar sausage, greasy hashbrowns, buttered sourdough toast, even pancakes with butter in tubs and syrup in packets. Milk, orange juice, and coffee. I debated about the coffee. It had been two days since any of us had last slept, so maybe I shouldn't get a cup of coffee because we were supposed to get some sleep soon. Then Feltz said, "We've got to get a bunch of stuff ready on the engine before we bed down. Ben, you need to check all the fluids on the engine and the pump motor."

I drank three cups while we ate. The food tasted good despite the tepid temperature and the crunch and gravel from the dusty roads. We ate under a tent off the side of the main road into the fire, right next to a deep gully.

Alexis and Amy set us up with lunches and water while Dave worked on the hand tools and I refurbished the engine. All fluid levels good, tire pressure good, belts good, windshield clean, air brake system checked, pump gas refilled, and all air filters blown out. Feltz went to the night-shift debriefing that Dave Bundy, the incident commander, was holding.

Now sleep? Only a firefighter can do that in 100-degree weather in the middle of the day, surrounded by a blackened moonscape. Trucks are rolling by constantly. Generators rumble. People yell. Periodic waves of mid-July wind sandblast you. The radio crackles with updates and instructions. Sweat on your upper lip, down the front of your shirt, and a bead down the side of your face.

Sometimes I even pant like a dog. There are weed burrs and stickers stuck all over my stiff shirt and pants. The more I try to find a comfortable position near the rear wheel-well of 311, the hotter I get. By noon the only patch of shade is directly under the engine, and I'm always sketchy about hanging out there, especially if Feltz got nervous about something and decided to pull away in a rush without bothering to look under the vehicle.

I would put in a chew, then spit it out 15 minutes later. Chew a piece of gum. Drink a Gatorade. Drink a bottle of water. Try to read some from whatever novel I had brought along. Think about Alexis. Look at Alexis, still hot even though she's as filthy right now as the rest of us. Her teeth are still clean and white, and both she and Amy still have good attitudes, their long blonde locks darker from sweat and mess.

Alexis took a photo of Dave and me on top of 311 in the late afternoon of that day, prior to another night shift. We have all given up on sleep, and those food conversations are now distant memories, just like sitting down to eat food seems to be only a memory.

The heat and lack of sleep have invaded my brain. I am becoming mildly psychotic. My upper lip feels like it has precancerous wrinkles from packing so much chew into it the past couple days. Lunch wasn't really necessary for nourishment, but rather just something to do to combat boredom in the oppressive heat. Roast beef sandwiches with a partially melted American cheese slice, a bag of Lay's potato chips that I discovered had only ONE CHIP in it when I popped and opened the bag, a mini pack of Oreos, and a warm can of Mott's apple juice. And an orange that I was too tired to peel. Now I have mayonnaise and mustard from those stupid packets all over my blackened yellow shirt. The sandwich had dirt in it too.

"Damn it's hot," Amy says. For a *firefighter* to admit this, it must be really scorching.

We get de-mobed from the fire after a couple more night shifts and a day shift. It's fire stints like this one that make or break friendships. Generally, you get sick and tired of one another, but in this case, the heat and the shared misery made 311's crew closer.

You end up talking about the craziest things, telling stories about your life outside of fire, laughing at inside jokes, and getting more personal than you would with anyone else in the world – even your family. The best and worst of people tend to emerge in these situations. Sometimes the worst isn't so bad, and sometimes the best is ten times better than you thought it could be.

Alexis giggles, and when she smiles really big I just about melt. Dave and I sing along to the radio as loud as we can, cruising at 65 mph behind 311 down the interstate. It's about 10:00 in the morning and we must all be crazy by now. Dave sneezes and farts at the same time and it seems hilarious. All the windows are down and the wind is tearing through the cab. I hope we stop somewhere and grab some real food without dust and dirt in it. I hope we make it back to the station sometime soon so I can drink some beer and do a little fishing.

A song about fishing plays on the radio as we blow by the Burley exit en route to a new fire near Fort Hall. It seems like a long time since I've been fishing. We've been released by this district because now it's hoppin' up in our district. In fact, John Giles, Sam Quinn, and a little guy we called "the rooster" – firefighters from the district we were leaving – are heading north right behind us. Wow, this is runnin' and gunnin'. No rest for the wicked, or the rest of us either. Summer firefighting at its finest. I realize I love this – damn the lack of sleep.

We fuel up at Bannock Peak gas station south of Pocatello. Coffee please, and more Copenhagen. Wash the windshields on the vehicles and refuel the drip torches. Fill up personal water bottles and straighten up the Ford's cab – put away maps, throw away wrappers. Squeeze a few drops of Visine into incinerated eyeballs. Blow fire-dirt and soot out of nostrils and take a hay fever pill. Could be a long day.

I can see the column already from this new fire, the Two Mile Fire, from here, and we're still 30 miles away.

The first thing we see when we pull up is Sam Quinn stuck in his engine, high-centered and facing downhill. The fire is burning all around him in big sagebrush and tall, thick grass. The radiating heat is nearly unbearable even for us, and we are still 30 or so feet away. The crackle is so loud it's not even really a crackle, but a roar. The smoke is thick enough to make the big yellow fire engine repeatedly conduct a disappear/reappear act. This does *not* look good.

We quickly pull the chase into a washout well away from the inferno, but close enough to gear up and make a calculated maximum fast-walk over to 311 to help Quinn and company.

In firefighting and other jobs where people may get injured or risk danger, and on jobs where others may or may not witness your actions and the work is largely physical work, I think there are two types of personalities. There are project-first personalities and there are people-first personalities. Within these two groups, I think there are only a couple of other ways that people behave when a situation goes down and/or the project begins. I'm not saying that one is better than the others, and sometimes one type fits a situation better than others.

The calm type is my personal favorite. No matter what the heck is going down, this dude is always focused and on his game. No shouting and yelling and little-kid foot-stomping. No spitting and bellering and running into people, no belittling people, no grabbing stuff out of your hand as hard as he can. No brushing off suggestions and no refusing help.

Now, I'm not saying this dude *isn't* going through some duck syndrome (calm on the surface, but paddling like hell underneath), but dang, it's good-looking. It seems to always be the better way of actually *getting something done*. It's certainly easier to work with, or work for, someone with this behavioral characteristic.

Then there's the not-so-calm type. This is my personal antagonist. I have polished a genuine dislike for these guys. It comes from clear back in my childhood and, because I've been around leaders who can get the job done without losing tempers and crybabying it, I find it really hard to respect or work for this opposite personality type. Often they still get the job done, but in the process of doing it, they tend toward unnecessarily stepping on toes and leaving bruises. I have a hard time forgetting and forgiving these instances.

Then there's the composite of these two guys – which is probably how I would describe myself. By nature and breeding, I am the second personality type. I used to be a crybaby. Worrying unnecessarily, shouting too often, and losing my temper at often-innocent people. But I've had a lot of good people to look up to, and learn from, and whether they know it or not, they were behavior role models of mine whenever there was a potentially dangerous, complex, or complex *and* time-dependent situation.

Matching the two different behaviors with the people-first personality or the project-first personality, you basically have someone who sees the trees, or someone who sees the forest, to use the old cliché. Both are valuable people to have on your team. What is *not* good is when the tree guy is in charge. There's a good chance you'll end up injured at the worst, or yelled at or belittled at best. Psychologically speaking, it's a simple explanation: he's compensating for his blurred vision of the big picture and it manifests itself in rash decisions. On the other hand, if you put the forest guy in charge of a specific project, he (at best) may not get the project done at all, or (at worst) he may get himself or someone else hurt because he is daydreaming.

Of course there are all types of combinations, but the people who can see the forest really do care about the people around them. Whether or not they would admit it, or even consider it themselves, they do understand that humanity is much more important than *any* material thing. I think they realize it's the journey that makes the man, and not just the destination.

A Type 6 (light) engine crew is an interesting tool in the arsenal of Western fire managers. Often regarded as ineffective on big range fires where pump-and-roll operations are required, they still have many an advantage in the overall scheme of wildfire suppression. You don't hear about these crews much, and maybe that's because of the limited number of personnel required, and the fact that a light engine doesn't look much more impressive than a phone company rig or electrician's vehicle. But light engines are like a forward scout, sniper-type special forces team, and where they're often most effective is in stomping small fires *before* they get out of control. It just isn't economically feasible to send in smokejumpers, or hotshot crews, or 5-person Type 4 engine crews to every little lightning strike fire in the district. So you call in the two guys from Station 1 with their little Dodge one-ton 4x4. They'll get the job done.

I was sent out to extinguish a bunch of those incipient forest fires every summer around the northern part of the district. It was probably my favorite firefighting activity, second only to pump-and-roll. Besides just being on your own to do as you see fit, the firefighting itself is usually pretty straightforward, the fuel normally being just a single tree or small group of trees that got whacked by lightning that afternoon. Often there is grass and sagebrush burning too, but rarely more than you can handle as a small crew. The fire usually got called in late in the afternoon or early evening, so overtime pay was virtually guaranteed. In essence, you were going to get paid $100 to hike into God's country and put out a large campfire. Not bad.

It's five o'clock in the afternoon, an hour from quitting time, and the thunder has been booming for a while up north. The leading edge of the storm cell is passing through Pete Creek near Porcupine Pass on the Targhee National Forest. Some of the booms are just booms. Others start that way but rip through a voluminous auditory apex and then back down again, and it rattles your ribcage. Little doubt you'll be busy in some firefighting capacity this evening. At 5:30 the station phone rings and it's dispatch telling you and your crewmember to stay on standby until 7 p.m., and 15 minutes later the station phone rings again and it's dispatch again. They need you guys to take your engine up into the hills and check out a smoke report. Dispatch gives you an estimated latitude and longitude location, which you punch into your GPS.

You step out of the station and into a balmy front yard. The engine fires right up and off you go, with a stop at the one of the town's two convenience stores to grab a can of Copenhagen and a couple cans of soda. Inside you are mildly nervous, *you just never know what a fire call will bring*, but you know that no matter what happens, it will be happening in the mountains, and that's a damn good place to be.

Thirty minutes later you come to a stop on the main pass road and put the binocs on a ridge to the south. Sure enough, there it is: a wisp of grayish smoke filters up through the timber. Forty-five minutes later you near the end of the forest road where the trail up toward the fire begins. You park the engine on a good flat spot off the side of the road and gear up. It will be at least an hour's hike in to this fire, so it's imperative you bring everything you anticipate you'll need to put it out.

It's nearing 8 p.m. when you reach the fire. The hike up was difficult, but doable. The trail followed a mountain stream for most of the way, and the gurgling over the rocks helped keep you at peace. A stiff intermittent rush of wind through the pines kept your peaceful feeling in check, though, as you know that that wind could quickly cause this small lightning-ignited fire to get out of control.

First thing is to make a size-up of the situation and call it in to dispatch. This fire is about one-tenth of an acre in size, three Douglas-fir trees smoldering and occasionally burping up a couple of sparks and maybe flaming a bit. There is also a patch of smoldering grassy fuels, about the size of a two-car garage, surrounding the trees. This fire shouldn't be a problem, but if left to its own devices, it has the potential to turn into a real timber shredder. You promise to check back in with dispatch in a couple of hours.

Now comes the fun part. You take off your pack, arrange your tools, and chill out a bit. You monitor the fire for a while and munch out of a pack of beef jerky and chat with your buddy about hunting or women, the two most important things in the world, and about then you decide you'll be camping on this fire. Any camp without a campfire is lame, so what do you do? You take a burning log from the fire and move it over to an area in the black to make your own little campfire. Then you get to work putting out the fire you were called here for. This part is easy: saw down the trees, buck them up into smaller logs, scrape off the hot coals, mix some mountain soil back onto the logs, and expose as much of the burning log as you can to the cooling air. Takes about two hours of moderate work, with a break in between for a call to dispatch and a drink of water.

Then it's time to kick back and relax near your own campfire, which you'll put out in the morning. Move more than five feet away from your campfire and it just gets too crispy cold, so you stretch out on the west side of the flames and your partner stretches out on the east side. There are occasional breezes in the timber, but as the black night begins to turn grayish blue with the breaking dawn, the breezes cease and you realize that you actually fell into a light sleep for awhile, warmed by your now smoldering campfire. The lightning-strike fire you came here for is dead out, but you scratch around and pat a few random spots with your bare hand, just to make sure. Then you take a minute and extinguish your campfire.

After calling in to dispatch to update your progress, you pack up and begin your early morning downhill hike to the parked engine. Mountain birds like nuthatches and chickadees are peeping and calling, there is dew on all the grass, and the small stream still gurgles away. To properly finish off another day at the office, you stop by the little cow country café back in town, and sit down to enjoy steak and eggs and hashbrowns. Back at the station, you sack out for a few hours' sleep. This job rules.

The Point Fire

ON JULY 28 WE WERE STILL WORKING mop-up operations on the Two-Mile Fire. Thunderstorms had pinballed all through the Great Basin the past couple weeks, and there were fires everywhere. This fire was huge and we still had a day or two left of cleaning it up, rehabbing it, and monitoring what was left. Over near Boise, two firefighters from a rural fire district would not make it through the day, burned over and killed by a range fire.

I can really only imagine what I was thinking when I heard the news, first by the grapevine, and then officially from Randy Hanson, IC of our fire, during a morning "all-hands" briefing. Grasping the back railing of the engine with my gloved right hand, I merge facts with how I imagined it to really be, the four demons of a fatal fire all converging at once – scorching heat, choking smoke, suffocation, and by far the worst, terror.

Their fire had started outside of Boise, near the town of Kuna, and as is normal during the summer fire season, they had joined forces with BLM crews to battle it. They left their station a little after 5:00 that afternoon and arrived at the fire about a half hour later.

Rural Fire District people are somewhat of a different breed. In a nutshell, they fight fire because they love to do it. Period. Most of them are volunteers, so that should tell you something right there. Not only do they risk their lives to prevent wildfires from destroying the land of their county, they usually do it aggressively. Sometimes too aggressively – and while they are often just as well trained as federal firefighters, it's rare they have the money to purchase equipment as reliable as that used by the BLM and Forest Service. We're out there with hundred-fifty-thousand-dollar machines, they're out doing the same job with WWII-era deuce-and-a-half trucks and battered pickups.

I'll bet they felt the same emotions we were feeling a couple of counties away that afternoon. The call came, they booked it to the station. They laced up boots and tried to maintain a calm face among their peers. Fingers, not as dexterous now that adrenaline flowed, missed a hook on the bottom of their Redwings and when finally to the top, they found one boot was tighter than the other. It didn't matter, though, and neither did the fact that they found themselves profoundly thirsty. All that mattered was getting the rigs fired up and heading out.

The bay doors up, they ground gears and opened throttles on bulky, weary machines and crawled slowly up to speed. The engines growled and the tires hummed. They mentally went through what they would do when they arrived at the fire. They felt the heat of the day pulsate with an occasional breeze as the air couldn't decide what to do in the face of a thunderstorm advancing from the south.

Once at the fire, they instinctively and by training knew what to do. First they had to make contact with forces already on the fire and get instructions from the Incident Commander. They held nervous voices steady when on the radio, and made transmissions brief.

Their assignment was to assist the crews from Boise flanking the north line off Swan Falls Road. This assignment was similar to many I'd done in the past two seasons of fire. You deploy your hard lines, also called "live reels," and one or two firefighters will handle the nozzles and knock the flames down. In this case, though, the firefighters used nozzles attached to the front bumpers of their engines. This is kind of a cool way to cover a lot of ground and put out a lot of live flame, because you don't need to gauge your speed based on the people handling the nozzles, i.e., you don't have to worry about them tripping.

I find two problems with this method, though, and this is speaking from experience, having used bumper nozzles on a water tender to squash flame. The first is that you use a heckuva lot of water very fast. It's hard to conserve using this method. The second is that you sometimes get rolling too fast, put on the blinders, and miss small spots of flame, which subsequently start up behind you, and in no time at all they can push up a good wall of flame again. I don't know if either of these played a part in the tragedy, but I thought about it a lot.

By now the Kuna RFD guys are into the groove, the nerves have subsided for the most part, and it's all business. In tandem, the engines pull ahead of their daisy-chain partners and douse a pesky flare-up. Then a little after 8:00 in the evening, it appears to be mostly contained at about 120 acres. Mop-up time.

This is usually the point at which an incident commander can release local crews like RFDs and volunteers back to their stations. They usually have day jobs. In this case, however, the trucks stayed and were instructed to assist with mop-up work and dousing the perimeter of the fire. The IC was probably anticipating problems that could occur with seriously high winds that were predicted, along with a red flag warning. He needed all the people he had there to stay there.

The volunteer fire trucks turned around and headed back, mopping as they went. I wondered what they were thinking. Maybe, "What the heck, let's go home, the fire's contained," or were they thinking, "This is awesome, let's keep kicking butt." Could they feel the dragon breathing, could they sense that hell was brewing? Had that lethal, whipping, Idaho wind arrived yet?

One of the engines ran out of water and drove off to refill. The other stayed and continued mopping up. They reported to the other crew that their truck was overheating. Overheating an engine is just a harbinger of the engine's stall, which leaves you dead in the water, in sometimes treacherous situations. The overheating can be caused by failed water pumps, leaky or malfunctioning radiators, loose fan belts, slipping fan clutches, or – as is often the case when you're operating in dirty dusty environments – clogged air flow filters or radiator screens.

The screen appeared to be the culprit with this engine, and when the frustrated firefighters called their crewmates, they were instructed to just remove this screen. Evidently it worked for a while, because they took off and headed north up a two-track road. At some point, and for unknown reasons, they left the two-track and drove east and then north again, off-road, through heavy sagebrush. The Kuna firefighters were right then violating about half of the ten standard fire orders, not to mention the very dangerous number 11 of the 18 watch-out situations: *There is unburned fuel between you and the main fire.*

And then the fire blew up.

Two guys from the BLM, sitting in a Chevy Suburban, witnessed hell unleashed and tried to contact the volunteer crew. Although they were probably becoming frantic, they did contact Boise BLM and were already asking for an ambulance and police when the fire overtook the volunteer engine.

The engine is stalled in the middle of a sea of tall sagebrush. You are trying your damnedest to get it going again – in a place you know you shouldn't be, but hell, it's just sagebrush right? But still you're nervous and trying not to panic as you file through your mental auto-mechanic encyclopedia to see if you can figure out what is going on with this thing. You hope to God this fire doesn't blow up, but you don't feel too confident. The winds are really picking up. You can taste dust and smoke and sage and raw fuel in your mouth. Radio transmissions are scratchy, but you do hear that there is a red flag warning.

Then you see that your new worst nightmare is playing out before your eyes. The fire has blown up and you are located smack in the path of the storm. Still, you aren't terribly panicked – it's just sagebrush, right? The smoke, though, is getting thicker, you've got to do something to get this engine going, and you start thinking about getting the hell out of here. The wind whooshes and the flames, now gaining on your position, are bent at an angle with the wind. It crosses your mind to abandon ship, let this old piece of junk burn to the ground. Still, though, it's worth something; you can't just leave it. The fire has you boxed in now, and time has slowed as your body's terror reflexes engage and you unconsciously begin thoughts of survival. You feel as lonely as if you were the last man on earth, and then you find it hard to breathe, and you can't really even think straight, you can't even see ten feet or four feet or two in front of you. You can't run and you wouldn't know where to run if you could. Damn this fire.

The volunteer firefighters' very last radio transmissions, when their truck had quit:

"We're on the north line, we got fire coming hard and this thing has died."

Volunteer engine to Rural Fire District Command: "It's not going to let us out of here!"

Volunteer engine to Volunteer Engine 650: "The truck's been overtaken by fire!"

Back to Dubois

SAM QUINN'S ENGINE looked like it was about to be burned over. I saw flames shoot up and over the top of it at one point, and that was just because the wall of orange, white, black, and gray had shifted for a split second, allowing for a quick view. Feltz was frantic, and his voice betrayed him, increasing exponentially in both volume and pitch as he screamed at us to get up there and help. We moved as fast as we could up the short slope through the tall grass, pulling a hard line behind us.

I didn't know Sam at all then. He just looked like a dirty dude. Hair down to his waist, huge black punk-rock goatee. He looked like a pirate, minus the eye patch. I did know he was well thought of as an engine foreman though, and his reputation certainly didn't diminish any right now. As the flames ripped around and through and over him and his crew, I heard his voice come over the P.A. of his engine. He comically but effectively instructed his crew. "Ladies and gentlemen, as you can see, we have fire all around us. Please move to the back of the engine and charge and deploy the knockdown hose at this time. Thank you."

Two of his crew pulled the 25-foot length of inch-and-a-half hose and poly nozzle from its emergency box at the rear of the engine, underneath the pump, and stretched it out to full length. Another crewmember pulled the charge valve and the hose immediately filled hard with water. This same crewmember throttled the pump up to deliver max water pressure. The two on the hose opened full straight stream on the wall of flame that was trying to devour the engine. The roar of flame changed instantly to the hiss of a foiled cobra and then shrank to nothing. Smoke was replaced with steam, and the engine with its occupants and crew immediately cooled off. All firefighters moved with total economy and efficiency. Quinn instructed from the cab in mock proper speech. "Well done gents, now please continue to the fore end of the vehicle and employ foam and water on flame wall near right fender of engine."

This was hugely comical and awesome to me at the same time. I resolved right then to never lose my calm on a fire if I could help it. If I did panic, I intended to internalize it. I promised myself I would always at least try to *look* cool like Quinn under pressure.

Days later and back on the mop-up stage of this fire, I released my grip on the railing of the engine, and released my thoughts about the fatal incident over by Boise. Standing in the middle of a sea of cold black with a few stobs of brush and grass poking through the ash, I asked Amy, Alexis, and Dave if they knew how to start the pump with the cotton starter rope if the electric start ever failed. I had watched Steve Lewis do this yesterday and thought I should pass the knowledge on to our crew.

They all gathered round while I wrapped the rope, with its wooden handle, around the Briggs and Stratton pump motor flywheel. Amy was standing closest to me, in fact right behind me. I made the verbal instructions and then showed them, pulling on the starter cord with a wicked jerk, starting the pump and simultaneously backhanding Amy in the mouth harder than I had ever hit someone.

The beautiful and innocent face had a horrible look of shock as she took one step back, put a gloved hand up, and fell to the ground. I can't remember ever feeling so crappy about myself.

"Oh my God, Amy, I'm so sorry!" I wailed. "Are you okay? Oh crap, I'm so sorry!"

"I'm fine, I'm fine!" She was tough, but there were tears in her eyes.

It was totally an accident, but definitely live and learn. Make sure no one is standing behind you when you pull a starter rope of any kind: lawnmower, boat motor, pump motor, anything.

"Nice job, Ben." Dave tossed at me.

Alexis and Dave helped Amy up while I retrieved an instant cold pack from the first aid kit. She put the pack on her now fattened lower lip, and we decided to postpone pump motor emergency starting lessons until later.

Several days later, after lots of hard work, sweating, and baking in the late July sun, we were demobed from the Two-Mile Fire. It was time; I think we'd had enough of this one and it was time to see some new country. We had worked on this fire for six days, which seemed like a long time without beer or dirt-free food. I was eager to get back north and chill out in Dubois, especially with Alexis.

We packed up hundreds of feet of crusty, muddy hose into the bins and into the back of the chase. We packed trash bags full of old brown paper lunch sacks, juice cans, bits of plastic and Gatorade bottles in the back of the chase. We sharpened pulaskis and shovels with a bastard file in case we were called to another fire, then we put them back into the bins. Then we packed ourselves into the rigs, had Hanson sign our time sheets, and departed for the Idaho Falls yard to resupply before we continued on to Dubois. I sighed a secret sigh of relief and offered a secret prayer for no more fires for a couple of days as we pulled in behind 311 on I-15 north.

Wreck

IN IDAHO FALLS THAT AFTERNOON I helped resupply the engine with cleaned and rolled-up hose, Gatorade, fusees, MREs, and water. I also replaced a pulaski that had a long crack in the upper part of the handle. Then we milled around, bragged a little bit, and hung out with other crews from the district gathered there in the yard. It felt really humid. We compared notes from the past couple of weeks, shoptalked of the fatalities over by Boise, and asked where the parties were.

Our crew and the crews from Engine 321, 322, and 331 all went to Godfather's Pizza for an all-you-can-eat excursion. Pepperoni pizza, sausage pizza, Canadian bacon and pineapple pizza, iceberg salad with too much Thousand Island dressing, three glasses of Coke, full belly, pinch of Copenhagen, and feeling of satiation while the rest of the crew finishes.

I feel happy about the summer, but I do realize that it's August now, and Moscow beckons with her heckling reminder of boring hours in sweltering classrooms, even more boring hours doing homework in the library, and that funky, weedy smell that permeates everything in town. I guess I still have to register for this fall's classes. Right now, though, I force myself to remind myself to remember to live one day at a time. I still have three good weeks left with the crew, and I still have to get that credit card in the mail and consider buying that '91 Honda CR 500 motorbike.

Thursday, August 3, 1995, 3:00 p.m. – No wonder it was humid earlier. It was a prelude to this storm, and I hadn't even noticed the clouds earlier. It's cooled off quite a bit now, and I watch leaves and sticks and garbage blowing across the parking lot as we make our way out to the vehicles after our Godfather's pizza feast. There is no more blue sky, and I feel a drop of rain on my right ear. It's easy to see this isn't gonna be a turd-floating rainstorm, but actually one heck of a windstorm, thunderstorm, dust storm, twister spawner. We learn there is a red flag warning posted for extreme high winds today.

Something, something I've felt before, stirs inside me as the storm advertises its arrival into my world. Is it butterflies? I don't know, it feels different from nerves, but still it makes me hyperaware of my existence and my interaction with my surroundings, specifically the weather. I know this storm may bring more fires, but I'm beyond being anxious about fires this summer. It feels like something that is somehow bringing together past summer storms and hurrying home from the ball field to hide inside from the thunder and lightning, contrasted with my new macho existence, where I push my way by choice into the middle of a storm and meet it head-on.

Dave brings me back to reality. "Let's get drunk tonight," he says.

"Don't twist my arm."

"We should go to the Legion tonight," says Feltz.

The wind is picking up as we cross the bridge on Highway 20 immediately before turning right onto the I-15 North entrance ramp. Idaho State Police and Idaho Transportation Department workers arrive there simultaneously to set up the "Low Visibility – Interstate Closed" signs and markings. Not for us, though – we motate around the signs and merge into the last sparse traffic. A mile ahead of us is the beginning of the storm. The winds have increased to about 60 mph; this is actually pretty cool. Things could get "Western" here, especially if we get a fire! I can't imagine the chaos a range fire would bring right now.

I'm driving, Alexis is riding shotgun, and Dave's in the back seat. We talk about everything and anything, from the awkwardness of taking a dump when you're working on a fire, to the pros and cons of smoking pot. That 60 mph crosswind buffets the big Ford and seems to even whip through the cab. Tumbleweeds and branches and limbs somersault across the blacktop in front of us and hang up in the wire fence on the east side of the highway. Here comes a lidless red camp cooler rolling on at about 40 mph. I have not seen wind like this before. I bet the gusts are hitting 80 mph.

South of Dubois near the small farm settlement of Hamer we are interrupted violently by a bright flash in our peripheral vision. The wind is blowing the two sets of powerlines along the frontage road into each other, causing a massive arc that travels out of sight along the high voltage sets. Whoa!! There it goes again, the blast and ball of fire about the size of a small automobile.

Here come two semi trucks, about a quarter of a mile apart and traveling south. Oh my God! The first one rolls precariously side to side, more so to the east side with the direction of the wind. We can see the second one doing the same thing. Alexis asks, "Do those things ever roll over in the wind like this?"

It's quite a sight to see when an 18-wheeler is rolling along at 75 mph on nine wheels! It looks like a stunt for a movie. I feel so amazed that all I can do is giggle – I tend to do this when I can't process events, and it's gotten me in trouble before. Dave is looking out the back window – "Going, going, going ... OH, gone! Both those semis just *rolled*!"

"311, this is 311 chase on Tac-4," I call to Feltz.

"Yeah go."

"Hey dude, both those semis we passed just rolled into the median."

"Seriously?"

"Yeah, we better call dispatch and have them get the Idaho State Police up here."

"Copy, I'll do that, you guys find a good place to turn around and we'll meet you back there, see if there's anything we can do."

I don't know if you've ever tried this before, but if you haven't, then don't. Slowing down to 45 mph from 75 mph makes it seem like you're crawling. But you aren't, and I wasn't, and as I left the interstate to cross the grass and gravel median, I felt like we were momentarily flying – then we returned to Earth with a big *ker-slam* and stuff was flying everywhere in the cab and grass and dirt – and we ended up facing south on the other side of the interstate, just where we needed to be. Now double-stunned, we headed back toward the rolled trucks.

As we pulled up near them, I said another silent prayer. I fully expected to see some carnage.

Diesel fuel and other liquids were spilled all over the road and seeping everywhere. A woman and a young girl frantically motioned to us as I parked the chase safely off the road behind the first rolled truck. I really didn't know what to expect here, or what I was supposed to do.

"Are you okay?" I stupidly asked.

"Yes, I think we are, but my husband is trapped in there," she wailed, pointing at the truck.

I thought to myself, *Oh no, here come the body parts.* I looked into the cab of the semi and here was a middle-aged dude with his beer gut pooching out from under a pink t-shirt. He had curly black hair and a black mustache.

He pleads, "I need a cigarette, can you just get me a cigarette, please?"

"Dude, are you all right? Are your legs stuck? I can't get you a cigarette, there's fuel all over the place."

The dashboard of the semi cab seemed to be crushed down to where his legs were pinned under it. He kept begging his wife for a cigarette as Feltz and I tried to figure out what to do. Feltz decided that he and Amy would go see what they could do at the other semi wreck, leaving Alexis, Dave, and me to do what we could till help got here. The wind was howling, and we all got sandblasted with small bits of farm field sundry.

Dave and I crawled back into the upended cab, and we tried pulling the driver out. No luck. Tried moving the dashboard and prying it with a cheater bar; it didn't budge. The guy seemed to be okay though. I couldn't see any blood, and he was conscious and alert; and as he had somehow obtained a bent and partially squashed Marlboro Red, he was now begging for someone to light it.

We crawled back out and were discussing amongst ourselves exactly what to do with him when we looked over at the cab and the guy was just finishing extracting himself from the tangled mess. About this time an Idaho State Police trooper arrived and took over command of the incident. Both of these were a relief to us, as we just wanted to leave with the craziness of the trucks rolling, rather than the trauma of loss of life or crushed limbs or something even more over-the-top.

It was only then that I realized that the wind was beginning to die down a bit, though there still were sporadic drops of metallic-tasting rain. Time must have sped by, too; I never knew what time it was when we arrived at this wreck, but I remembered that it was not much past 3:00 when we left Idaho Falls. Now it was 6:30.

I wondered if we'd get overtime pay for this. Probably should've gotten hazard pay.

Alexis

Thursday, August 3, 1995, 8:00 p.m. – Location: Legion Bar and Grill – downtown metropolitan Dubois, Idaho. I have showered, shaved, and changed into summer shorts and a tank top. I am now sitting in a booth sucking at a glass of Bud Light poured from a plastic draft pitcher. The Legion is a typical cow town café in front and bar in the back. I call the café my home almost every day for lunch that I'm not on a fire, and the bar is my wind-down spot after work.

The café room is encircled with four-person booths with seats covered in red naugahyde, token rips and tears here and there from belts, suspenders, Levis rivets, and kids. The cups are clear plastic for small size, and red plastic for large. Fake flowers in small pots near your personal glass salt and pepper shakers. Silverware on a small napkin, with more napkins in a metal dispenser on your table. Coffeemakers and brown ceramic cups along one wood-paneled wall. At the breakfast bar, round swivel seats also covered with red naugahyde surrounded by a chrome loop. The place is staffed by the ubiquitous two old ladies – one fat, one skinny – and the super cute high-school girl, who's old enough to ogle, but too young to date, who can't wait to leave this damn small town for the lights of the big city and fallen angels.

Step through the batwing doors and walk down a greasy, broken-tile hallway and you're in a classic cowboy bar. Mirror behind the bar of high-end and low-end hooch; no dividing between top-shelf and well booze here. A big 50-year-old cash register with long white tape hanging out. Draft pullers of Bud Light, Bud, Coors, and MGD – no wussie microbrews here. Rows and rows of semi-clean glasses of just three types: beer mug, shot glass, and tumbler for mixed drinks. Weathered bar-top with cork coasters used for only the first two drinks – no one gives a damn after that. Round stools with rungs that aren't comfortable to put your feet on for very long, and a grumpy, drooping-mustachioed bartender who used to be a rodeo cowboy until the accident. Jukebox on the west wall with country and classic rock on it – and inexplicably, two R&B/rap songs.

The booth by the back door is where 311's crew makes its respite, Dave pulling up a chair at the end of the table. We celebrate a belated happy hour and a good fire detail. Talk is mostly about fire and the fire world; oftentimes this is where you really learn how to fight fire. You learn by shoptalking successes and failures with your crew. Informally you make important critiques of your practices. This crew is made up of fun and open-minded and educated folks, though, so our conversation does branch out from time to time: rock bands, college, wildlife biology, marriage, kids, sex, drugs, pro football, four-wheelers, fishing, camping, track and field, good food, and places we've been and places we want to see. Alexis introduces us to a mixed drink called Cactus Juice, and I introduce the others to a Depth Charge. We aren't getting wasted (never advisable during fire season – yeah right), but we are getting tuned up and loose and happy.

Alexis is the president of a sorority at Montana State University in Bozeman. She is telling me about her sorority activities and friends and stuff when she pauses for a second and then says to me, "It gave me goose bumps to hear you play your guitar."

The rest of the crew had left about an hour earlier, leaving Alexis and me just where I wanted to be, alone with her save for the bartender, some low light, some drinks, and some country music on the jukebox. And now I bravely (due to alcohol, I'm sure) say, "You know, I have a total crush on you."

Together, we have only enough money left to buy one can of Hamm's beer from the bartender. We take turns sipping from the can. There isn't really much conversation anymore, and we just shyly stare at one another across the bar table. She moves closer across the table, as do I. She says, "We should probably leave, they're closing us down."

We leave the bar through the "speakeasy" door and walk slowly, directionlessly, across the gravel parking lot where earlier there had been a handful of pickups parked. Where are you supposed to go now? What do you say now? What are the next steps in this age-old dance? I put my right arm around her slender shoulders and to my delight, she steps into the groove created by my arm. She feels so good to touch, so soft, but so lean.

Three blocks away the rest of the crew is bedded down, and this, between the girl and me, mustn't ever be known to them. This, of course, makes it all the more tricky and exciting. I feel charged with electricity from head to toe. The summer night is crystal clear, as is often the case in dusty Western places when a big storm blows through and washes the air clean.

Remnants of that storm today are still in evidence, as we step over inch-thick tree branches still lying in the street, green leaves attached and twigs catching on pant legs.

At the station I remove my arm from around her shoulders and begin to head left, but she says, "Let's keep walking," and points us toward the green grass football field behind the station. Encircled by a dirt running track, it also bordered a cow pasture with a little stream winding through it.

Somewhere a cow lows and I can vaguely hear cars speeding north on the interstate. The mercury lamps wash the school grounds in pale blue light, but we stroll just outside of their glow in the still darkness. Alexis has now put my hand in hers and I swear to God I can feel it in the physical organ of my heart. I know just as well that this is probably only the beginnings of the end of a summer romance – I have only two weeks left until I leave for school – but I don't care. I am 20 years old and I can think of nothing else but this petite blonde, beautiful girl I'm with.

In small towns that close at midnight, there aren't many places to go and hide, especially when you live at a fire station. We ended up sitting on the blacktop of a school playground, with our backs up against the brick and mortar of the building itself. Nothing crazy happened, just a first kiss that I'll never forget – which turned into an hour-long makeout session by two young people falling into some interval of the spectrum of love.

We eventually had to return to the station, where we found Dave asleep on the couch with the TV still on, but with the volume muted. Still on fire with lust,

Alexis and I sneaked into the room I shared with Dave and into my bed on the lower bunk, as quietly as we could. The only physical evidence in the morning was a white cotton sports bra she'd left on the floor, which I quickly hid in my pile of laundry so I could return it to her when possible.

When the crew gathered prior to PT the next morning, though, the evidence had to be written all over my face, a deep-seated feeling of flying glowing underneath. Alexis was more coy – in fact she wouldn't even look in my direction, except once when she winked at me and sent my heart flying even higher.

I still feel sentimental when I think about the girl, the night, the station, and the summer. We made love many more times – when, where, and how forever a secret. At the station and during the day, we acted as we always had, as crewmates and newly found super friends, but that's how the whole crew felt, so we just blended right in.

Stormy Weather

Sunday, August 13, 1995, 12:30 p.m. - The BLM is the main steward of rangelands in the American West. As one might assume, part of that stewardship involves erosion prevention and correction, especially along prominent streams and through riparian areas. Today we are at the Clyde Bridge across Birch Creek – a watershed becoming extremely popular in eastern Idaho as a fishing and camping destination for young and old alike. There are notable problems with erosion along its banks right here along the highway, so we're piling rip-rap along the banks and covering the rocks with a soft black fabric to hold them in place. Any project in this country is fun, especially where there's water and fish – this way we can sink a lure at lunch time. Dave is not with us today – he has a court date (someone without insurance had smashed into his truck), so it's just Feltz, Amy, Alexis, and me standing ankle-deep in Birch Creek putting rocks along the bank and talking about camping.

We stopped at about 11:30 to enjoy the lunches we had packed. I always packed awesome cold lunches for project days in the field – today I had a roast beef and cheese sandwich on a sesame-seed hoagie, three hard-boiled eggs, a bag of Cheetos, two mozzarella sticks, a Pepsi, and some chocolate Zingers (that I would peel the icing from and eat first) for dessert. At the same time we were enjoying our midday repast, somewhere along Highway 20, which runs west out of

Idaho Falls through high-desert landscape maintained by the Idaho National Laboratory (INL), some idiot was tossing a lit cigarette out a car window into tinder-dry cheatgrass, starting the first of what would be a 5-year cycle of scorched earth through Department of Energy property.

Radio chatter for this fire started in the early afternoon. The INL had an in-house fire department, but often requested assistance from the BLM or Forest Service firefighters through mutual-aid agreements.

We climbed out of the creek bed and looked south out of the drainage, through the shimmering August heat waves and over the tall sagebrush toward INL country. There it was: a convection column already reaching high into the sky and turning into a cotton-topped cumulus-resembling plume. This left very little doubt that we would soon be getting a call to respond and assist. We hastily gathered up our project equipment and tossed it haphazardly into the bed of the chase.

When the call came, we responded as normal, with me and Alexis in the chase following the engine. In my mind I battled with an emulsion of conflicting emotions. First, though we hadn't really fought many fires this summer, I was pretty much sick of fire for the year. I loved initial attack and its rush – that unknown factor, that curiosity, that fruitful proving ground of quick thinking, steely nerves, speed and stamina. I was sick of breaking up smoldering cow pies and stubbly sagebrush roots in the blazing sun, though. On the other hand, this fire, named INL Assist #1, promised to yield some serious initial attack opportunity, and I'd be able to seize the moment one more time for the season and maybe end it with a bang.

Second, I was starting to fall extremely hard for Alexis, which I knew in my heart was stupid, but I couldn't help it, and spending these last few days on a fire meant not spending time hanging out fishing or golfing or partying up in the Stoddard Creek country with the crew. As I slowed down to make the turn onto Highway 22 from Highway 28 where the hulking mountains give way to the wheat and hay fields, Alexis slid over from the right side into the middle seat, kissed me on the lips, and guided my hand onto her thigh. I removed it only when I had to shift gears, and that seemed a shame.

The fire was not eventful, and lasted only until late that evening, as a storm blew in from the southwest and quickly settled down the flames with high humidity and a torrent of rain. Lightning flashed all over the sky, though, so I realized that this fire might not be my last of the season.

Monday, August 14, 1995, 12:45 a.m. – I was correct in anticipating another fire call this night. A lot of lightning popping. Though it's raining here on the high desert, it's likely not raining every place there's lightning, so I'm not surprised that we're headed east now past the small town of Ririe after steaks and shakes at Perkin's restaurant in Idaho Falls. A full belly and the personal company of Alexis help make it okay, even though I get the hint of some moodiness brewing as we both tire out from a long day working a range fire. We're alone in the chase, and listening to country music on the radio as large, intermittent raindrops ricochet off the windshield. We are third in a line of red ant taillights marching down a section road at the foot of big-country mountains, not too far from the Tetons themselves.

Hall couldn't find the fire, and the strike team of engines and crews following him reflected his impatience. Somewhere here along the South Fork of the Snake River, someone had called in a fire. It was entirely possible that there was a fire here – heck, even probable with the hundreds of lightning bolts still zipping about. My eyelids felt heavy, and the air smelled heavy, as it does just before a heavy summer rain. I had to stick my head out the window as I drove, trying to stay awake, and when I did, I was treated to an olfactory blend of metallic rain, fresh-cut alfalfa hay, willows, and river-bottom cottonwoods.

I hoped to God no one would find the fire, as the sun had officially set on my attitude about the fire season. I wanted to glean what time I had left before school, and apply it to Alexis. Knowing my luck, though, someone would see the damn thing, we'd gear up, hike on sore feet miles into the timber, and hack up blackened vegetation until the night before I had to head north to Moscow. I rolled my head from side to side trying to loosen my neck muscles, and tried to keep the truck between the lines. I glanced down and noticed that the white-numbered shift pattern on the gearshift had worn off. Huh.

Monday, August 14, 1995, 3:30 a.m. – Now the entire strike team is parked alongside the Kelly Canyon road while Hall decides what to do. Alexis has crept over on the seat right next to me and is resting her beautiful head on my shoulder. I am happy, but

I'm also getting the super-late-night blahs complete with funky chew wrinkles on my upper lip from too much Copenhagen, with that scratchy feeling in my nose and throat. Just as I drift off to sleep, Alexis's head on my shoulder, my head on the seat belt slack, there's a rap on the window. It's Hall. "Let's just call it a night and you guys head back to Dubois. We can't seem to find this thing and it'll probably get rained on anyway. Are you okay to drive? Sleepy?" This was a lot of words for Hall. He was usually spare on conversation.

"I'll help him stay awake," says Alexis.

Now we're cruising back north on I-15 through a driving rainstorm that puddles in low spots on the road. Alexis puts her hand on *my* thigh now, and tells me something that makes my heart soar, and then gives me a big kiss on the cheek. The truck radio plays softly as a backdrop to the tires and our sleepy conversation.

THREE DAYS AND NO MORE FIRES LATER, I was finishing packing up my gear from the station, in the afternoon heat, when it hit me that I was in love with Alexis, and what was I doing going back to Moscow now? The season had started green with promise, and the season had delivered – just enough fires to get my initial attack rush fix, get in shape, make some money, and see some country; just enough down time to fish and camp and drink a bunch of beer; reciprocation of a major crush on a cute girl; beautiful summer weather and an awesome place to enjoy it. I even had received that credit card with a two-thousand-dollar limit, although I never did buy the motorbike. Instead, the first credit card purchase I made was a six-pack of Bud Light bottles at Scoggins Convenience Store on the way out of Dubois.

I still had to go back to the BLM yard to turn in my gear, but I didn't care if I had alcohol on my breath – what would they do, fire me? A couple of tears rolled down my cheeks as I drove out of Dubois for the last time this season, listening to my copy of the mix tape of summer songs Alexis had made for all of us. As I made the left onto the entrance ramp, one of her and my favorite songs played on the stereo. I managed to suck back all six bottles in the 47 miles between Dubois and Idaho Falls.

A lexis had a last surprise for me that summer. She took three days off – and I accordingly postponed my trip north – and we made a three-day "fishing" trip into the Salmon country. We ended up mainly just driving the backroads in that big country and singing songs as loud as we could, and drinking beer, and being close, and gazing at the sun's rays as they reflected across the riffles of the Salmon River; and I told her that the great spirits of summer must live in those rays – I know I would, too, if I could.

As we drove along the Salmon River in my Chevy truck it was blazing hot and the sunbeams were dancing across the water and reflecting the warmth back up at us. It was all right with me. For us, the season was effectively over. I was thinking that I hoped that moment would be one of the last memories that cross my mind right before I die.

As all things do, it ended, and I had to change faces and places back to the college student life. Alexis and I spent time together one last time the night before I left, and we both cried and hugged. As I made the 600-mile trip north to Moscow, I reflected on the season – the long, cool nights, the killer hikes, the lack of food and sleep. The season had been filled with blue-white-hot summer sun, yelling and laughter and smoke and flames. The dirt and dust and diesel exhaust and the new cow-town friends were fresh for me still, with all of these overshadowed by the feeling of love or something very much like it.

I can't wait for next season.

Southwest Fires

Monday, June 17, 1996 11:30 a.m. – Even though the convoy comprises a dozen or so vehicles, I still can't seem to maintain visual contact with any of them through this traffic. I heard on the Tac-4 radio channel that moments ago James Beck with 311 had plowed into a unit of roof shingles on the road. The shingles had fallen from a flatbed trailer and were careening down the roadway, and there was no way for Beck to avoid them. This traffic as you come into Salt Lake City is crazy. I'm not used to it; I've been living in slower places for a long while. Now I'm dodging tractor-trailers and sedans and motorbikes, all the while traveling 75 mph and trying to spot the exit that the convoy is going to take to fuel up. This ought to be a cluster.

Whoa! There they are! Slam the brakes, jerk the steering wheel, grab gears, and squeal tires as I shoot diagonally across three lanes of traffic and bobsled down the exit ramp. I steer the gray Ford chase (the same pickup as last summer) into a fueling stall, and Alexis, Dave Neil, Troy Daniels, and I deplane to fuel up, check fluid levels, wash windshields, and shop the convenience store.

For some reason, the four of us today are hyperactive. We've been giggling at everything, and it had been nonstop chatter for the last three hours as we headed south toward New Mexico from Idaho Falls. We were on our way down to relieve a group of our firefighters who had been down there since early May. All of us were starting to feel our summer oats with this nice weather, and the blue Utah sky only added fuel to our already sunny attitudes.

Oh, sweet early summer weather. A few days before the summer solstice and the sun seems like it's always in the sky. It shines down on you, and it smiles at you, and it suggests to you that you should set your spirit free, that only a fool would be anything but happy right now. The sins and sadness of the winter are washed away by this time of the year. The bad grades you earned at school don't really matter, and neither does your gradually crushing monetary debt. The tumor, in the form of a school backpack and continuous thoughts about your failures at finding love in its purest form, has been shed. It's time again to suck smoke, sweat buckets, and live like God planned for you to do.

For some reason I don't think the others in the truck with me were thinking *exactly* like that, but they certainly seemed to be free spirits now too. Take Alexis. That year, she had graduated with her Bachelor's degree in education from Montana State. Still tan, taut, and beautiful, she had also said goodbye for now to the college life and would be moving on to something new. She said she would try to land a job in the fall teaching high school history somewhere, but for now the fire crew still provided a steady summer income and the potential for some fun. She must have still harbored some feelings for me, too – we had kept in contact all winter, and although we hadn't gotten together privately yet, it was clear that the tension lay just beneath the surface. She was a master at playing hard to get, though, at least with me. This made me act goofy.

Then there was Dave. This was his second year on the crew, and being the type of guy who wears his heart on his sleeve and his zest for life also on the surface, he seemed to be exactly where he wanted to be. A little experience in this business goes a long way, and Dave knew how to parlay that experience and his naturally good disposition into a great time. He sat in the back with a mint Skoal tucked in his lower lip, the resulting bump exaggerated by the "soul patch" whiskers that ran in a red streak from the lip down to the cleft of his chin. He wore a t-shirt with a picture of Curious George smoking a pipe and the caption, "A good meal and a good pipe made George feel very tired."

Troy Daniels was the new guy, and officially the first person who could ever officially call me his supervisor. Poor kid. Troy was a poofy little towheaded dude with a military buzz haircut and a dream to fly fighter jets in the Air Force (I later heard he was successful at this – right on dude!). New to the fire world, he came off as a little like me, only louder at this point in his career.

As *de facto* supervisor of this little group while traveling south, I should have ensured that certain tasks were accomplished at the service station stop. I did not, though, and when the hood on the Ford shot open about the time I merged back into the heavy traffic after the fuel stop, at 70 mph, I thought I was seeing my final day on the job. As it was, I couldn't see much, looking through the little space between the opened hood and the engine compartment while speeding down the interstate. Just imagine what that must have looked like if you were driving the other direction on the interstate the moment it happened. I do imagine it, and no matter where I am or what I'm doing, I still can't keep from laughing. Somehow I managed to cross back into the farthest right lane and come to a safe stop on the side of the freeway. The hood took some muscle to shut now, with the crease in it, but I managed. Shaken, I pulled back into the traffic and asked Alexis, "Did you pay for the gas?"

"No."

"Dave?"

"No, I thought you were going to."

"Troy?"

"I was checking the oil."

An accidental gas-and-dash in a government vehicle with its own fuel card. Nice one.

It was tensely quiet inside the truck for awhile. Then Dave said, "That was pretty funny."

We didn't quit laughing until Cortez, Colorado, where the strike team stopped for the night.

This new fire season of 1996 held a lot of promise for me. I had finally been promoted to engine foreman. When Gary told me that, on day one of the season back in Idaho Falls, my first reaction was to say, "Are you sure?" and Gary acknowledged to me that there may have been some misgivings within the office about the decision. He merely had to say, "There's been a lot of discussion about you this winter."

Okay, what does that mean, exactly? It was obvious there were people in my corner, though, and I'm betting Gary was one of them. And Eric Hall. Either way, the bar would be set fairly high for me this summer, and there would be people watching. This was fine with me, though; I was ready for the challenge of running Engine 312 with Troy as my lone crewmember.

This detail to New Mexico was a little different from the way the forces would be organized back in Idaho. On this trip, I was the "supervisor" just while we were en route; I would be reassigned as a member on someone else's crew for the remainder of the detail. At Socorro, New Mexico, the strike team split up three ways. Alexis was assigned to the Idaho Falls engine that would be staying in Socorro. Chuck and Dave would go with Isaac Feltz over to Alamogordo and work in the Billy the Kid country of the Lincoln National Forest. I was assigned to Mike Fields' Engine 342 (from Fort Hall – Station #4) with Tom Hill, and after spending some time working on a large fire on the Bosque Del Apache National Wildlife Refuge, I would be based out of Las Cruces.

The night before we reported to the Bosque fire sucked. First of all, there would be no more Alexis for who knows how long, and I had been looking forward to hanging out with her. Second, the guys on 342 were about as straight-laced as could be, and I could not see myself having any fun with them. Third, because of some sort of snafu on the BLM's part, two full crews had to spend the night in a single room. Six guys in one Motel 6 room! I don't know why I didn't just roll out my sleeping bag on a patch of grass outside. Instead, I spent the night getting a crooked back while lying on some cheap carpet and listening to snores and farts. Not a good way to prep for the season's first fire.

Wednesday, June 19, 1996, 6:30 a.m. – The day has dawned majestically, with one of those spectacular

Southwest desert sunrises, but I can't quite appreciate it. In the east the sun breaks over the pastels of the desert country through clouds whose appearance is only fleeting before they are baked away to nothing. In my mind and body are aches that don't seem to dissipate so quickly. A long, sleepless night and no detectable humor. To someone who pretty much lives for smiles and fun, this looks like a recipe for one very boring fire detail. I swallow hard and get ready to put on the all-business Ben face; it's always lying underneath, but it's a weapon I deploy against the mundane only as a last resort.

In the parking lot of the wildlife refuge's visitor center we met the crew we were relieving as they were attempting to fix a dysfunctional pump. Wrenches and screwdrivers and pliers were scattered about on the pavement, as were various parts of the pump itself. In the distance you could hear another crew trying to recover their engine from one of the numerous bogs. They went through the unofficial checklist of rednecks trying to get a vehicle unstuck.

"Try 4-low!" Then the high-pitch whine of the engine flywheel.

"Rock it back and forth!" High-pitch whine.

"Easy easy!" Low rumble, then high-pitch whine.

A TV news crew arrived in the parking lot and began setting up their equipment. I moved off a short distance when the reporter approached Mike for an interview. Tom joined me and we listened as the reporter prodded Mike for any knowledge he had about tactics or strategy or timeframe. He couldn't provide too much; we hadn't even been to the front line yet.

Then a small bunny hopped out of a juniper bush about 30 yards across the parking lot, in the opposite direction the TV camera was pointed. The bunny was tiny, about the size of a large kitten. Tom is a predator in all ways, and he started picking up egg-sized rocks and chunking them at the bunny. He was coming close to the bunny, but it never got spooked. I also am a predator by nature and breeding, but not a person who likes to kill just for the sake of killing.

Bored watching Tom wing stones at the bunny, I walked a few steps over to the rock pile and picked up a big one, about the size of a grapefruit. There was no way it would hit the rabbit, or so I thought, but the moment it left my hand I knew I was wrong. The large rock sailed in a perfectly deadly arc and landed directly on the bunny, crushing it. Instantly sick and sad, I turned to look and saw that the camera was pointed right at the whole scene. Tom was bent over laughing. Oh no.

Thankfully, I never heard anything about it, and after we got the pump running again it was off to work on the Type II fire burning in salt cedar groves and dry grass. I put the bunny "accident" out of my mind and set to work getting back into the rhythms of another fire season. All day long hacking, cutting, spraying, and working in the 100-degree heat.

Sunday, June 23, 1996, 1:00 p.m. – We were de-mobed from the Bosque fire, we are now in the Las Cruces district. Same BLM yard as in 1993, my first season, but I am definitely more adjusted this time. The heat coming off the blacktop of the yard doesn't scare me so much. I know some of the people I'm with and I doubt they'll threaten me with a knife. I know my way around town, more or less.

Thursday, June 27, 1996, 6:00 p.m. – We have been in Las Cruces now for several days and there haven't been any fires, or really any sort of activity. Having some experience in this business now, though, I know that one of three things is going to happen in the next day or two. Either we are going to get that fire call, or the managers will start making us do busy work cleaning campgrounds or something, or we are going to get sent somewhere else for the remainder of the detail.

As time began to slow, my brain started switching tracks, not necessarily heading in a direction conducive to good business practices – I started thinkin' 'bout drinkin'. Another crew had arrived the day before from another Idaho district, and they were planning on going to the bar that night.

Mike and Tom were a bit like Bert and Ernie from Sesame Street. Tom was a former college football player. He stood about 6-foot-6 and was solid as steel. He was a predatory type, and hunting and fishing were pretty much all he thought about. Mike, standing about 5-foot-7 and also solid as steel, seemed to live only for firefighting. His "real" job was teaching fifth grade, but he lived at a Pocatello Fire Station and volunteered on fire calls. That is true fire love.

The difference between these guys and me was simply my lack of attention to detail. I was easily bored with mundane stuff, and these guys could do it all day. It annoyed me. For example, no fires are burning, no real projects happening, I figure I'll just settle down and read a magazine. Mike would appear and say, "We should probably go wash the engine."

Always I would join him because he was my foreman, but I couldn't help my frustration at his perfection and its busy-work consequences. That engine would be spotless, yet here we were soaping it down again.

As soon as I knew I'd been promoted to engine foreman, though, something changed inside me. I felt I should be in charge of something, anything. I'd never been a boss before, and I was ready to give it a try. It was secretly irritating to be taking orders from someone who was essentially the same rank as me. This secret angst I just stored inside with the rest of my perceived irritations. To a heavy drinker like I was, this practice is poisonous.

I had been doing well on this trip, hadn't drunk once, but seeing Mike and Tom so happily scrubbing and polishing an already clean vehicle put me over the edge. It was well over 100 degrees out there. I'd have been spent if we got a fire call. "When we get done with this, we should re-roll all the hose." Tom proclaimed.

Gimme a break.

"Sounds good," I heard myself say.

Right then a little voice in my head determined that I would be going out with the guys from the other Idaho crew tonight, and I was gonna drink some beer.

Friday, June 28, 1996, 7:00 p.m. – We're stepping through the doors of a local joint called Coyote's somewhere in the center of Las Cruces. It looks to be pretty happenin', with a five-piece band jamming on country-rock favorites and knocking them out really

221

well. Las Cruces is home to New Mexico State University, and we saw plenty of co-eds with long, tan legs and pretty halter tops. There's the guys from the other Idaho crew – I know two of them, Dave and Alex. Mike, Tom, and I join them at a tall round table near the mini-stage. A freckled blonde babe of a cocktail server takes our order – a Bud Light bottle for me, diet Pepsis for Mike and Tom.

A bottle or two into the evening I begin to feel the slack in the tension wire. After all, *it is* summertime, and I'm a free-wheeling 21-year-old on a free-wheeling fire detail. I alternate between talking about fires and scanning the room for girls.

I spotted them on the east side of the bar. Three blondies with no guys hanging on them yet. I wasted no time hopping out of my seat, swaggering over, and introducing myself. Joanie and her two friends were college students at New Mexico State University.

"Are you guys firefighters?" Joanie asked.

Absolutely!

Back at the table and now joined by Joanie and her two friends Laura and Kim, we get the party started. I remember telling Mike and Tom "just one more brewski and we'll jet" several times, but eventually they lost patience and left. It was now down to three guys and three girls.

Beer after beer made the lights and sounds blend together in a kaleidoscope, with Joanie and her pink shirt and white shorts at the center of it. At one point just prior to closing time, she was sitting on my lap, my left arm around her waist. Damn, she had nice legs. The only dilemma for the six of us then was where the after-party was going to be, or more specifically, how we would get there. I couldn't tell what was happening with the other couples, but I knew Joanie and I were close to kissing, and I just couldn't have the night end right there.

The next thing I remember is cooking hot dogs and hamburger patties on a stainless steel grill on the back patio of a huge and beautiful house. Rock music was blaring on a stereo. There are only snippets of memory after that; jumping fully clothed into the kidney-shaped pool, falling into a table umbrella, riding a four-wheeler through tall weeds in an adjacent field.

Then I was waking up next to Joanie in an upstairs bedroom. A soft breeze clicking the curtain rods, and birds chirping, brought me to a state of semi-consciousness. It's the foggy game called "name that ceiling."

I looked over at the girl lying next to me. "Joanie," I whispered, rubbing the corners of my eyes and hoping that was indeed her name.

"Hmmm." The girl replied sleepily.

"What time is it?" I asked.

My heart started to race and I was instantly, if only temporarily, sober and wide awake. If I didn't make it back to the hotel before Mike, Tom, and Hall left that morning, it would not be good. Likely there would be some blowback, possibly with employment consequences and discipline dessert. I leapt out of the bed and skidded down the stairs. Everywhere I looked I saw empty and half-empty beer bottles, wine bottles, liquor bottles, paper plates with bits of mustard on them and bread crumbs. The tile floor of the kitchen was sticky when I crossed it. The clock on the microwave read 7:32 a.m. I was wearing only underwear and only now beginning to realize what had happened. Why do I always have to turn a good relaxing time into a wild-ass party? If some is good, is more *always* better? Moderation, it seemed, was my nemesis.

On the floor were horizontal bodies. I kicked one of the bodies that looked a firefighter, and it mumbled, "Dude, whass goin' on?"

"We gotta get out of here and back to the motel, that's what's going on. We're late."

Joanie padded into the front room looking so fine, rubbing the sleep from her eyes and yawning. "Whass goin' on?"

"I'm sorry babe, we've got to get going." I replied.

"Okay," she said, wrapping her arms around my waist and burying her head into my chest. "Call me. I hope you're in town tonight."

Her hair smelled like a strangely alluring cross between Aussie shampoo and cigarette smoke.

I prodded the other two firefighters to get going, and soon we were trying to figure our way out of the neighborhood and back to the motel. It was going to be a scorcher today.

I met Hall, Mike, and Tom leaving the hotel carrying their red bags. Mike carried mine as well. I hung my head, apologized, and climbed into the engine into total silence. No mistaking the fact that I had made another bad decision. I really was sorry, but why was I? Do I always have to apologize for having a good time? Did that make me half-sorry?

Saturday, June 29, 1996, 9:30 a.m. – Not as sorry as you are now, sucker! Who put us up to this? Picking stones off a trail that leads up to some historical site? A tuberculosis sanitarium?

My temples feel like they've been rapped by a small hammer. My stomach lurches. I am hot, itchy, and sick. The brown-bottle flu. The one-day flu. A major hangover. Thirty minutes of sleep and thirty beers. Every time I reach down to pick up a rock, the blood rushes and pounds from side to side in my head, like a big fat guy pounding down a water slide. Ohhhh me!

"Have a few too many last night?" Mike snickers.

"Got that right," I reply.

His comment pissed me off, but I don't think he was trying to. I realized there was nothing to eat. I needed something to eat. I had drunk too much water and Gatorade that morning as prophylactics. Now I splattered those on the side of the trail.

Frank Sinatra said, "I feel sorry for people who don't drink. When they wake up in the morning, that's as good as they're going to feel all day."

By that evening, I was starting to feel human again. We had supper as a crew at Red Lobster, and it put me right. I was still acting humbled, though, so I kind of kept quiet and accepted the jabs from Mike, Tom, and Hall. Must be nice to be a teetotaler, though not nearly as fun.

The next morning we were turned loose by the district, with orders to head north to assist with firefighting efforts in Arizona. I tried unsuccessfully to contact Joanie, and that *was* disappointing. Apparently Joanie had become someone for me to commit to memory, and nothing else. It was dusty and dry, and the prairies and hills and forests seemed like nothing more than fuel right now. It was so hot out that everything seemed to have a whitish hue. Frankly, I was surprised we never got any fires.

In Socorro, we picked up the rest of the Idaho Falls crew. We would travel to Arizona as a strike team now, and that's when the real fun started. As it happened, the riding arrangements made me kind of the odd man out. It was either ride in the middle seat of 342 or take up Hall's offer to ride shotgun with him. I accepted his offer, but with reservations. Hall is spare with conversation, and I hate sitting there in uncomfortable silence mile after mile.

Eric Hall should write an autobiography. Though he's not much for conversation, I'm long on memory and can remember almost everything Hall ever said to me. His life would make a great book.

Eric was from back East somewhere, and like Teddy Roosevelt or Gifford Pinchot in the early 1900s, Eric must have come out West for more than just the fresh air and wide open spaces. He was as skilled a woodsman as there ever was, maybe a lot like the great ranger himself – Ed Pulaski. To me, his greatest skill was his ability to think and act clearly and calmly in chaos. If you asked him, he'd likely say he was most proud of the fact that he built his house from the ground up. The house was not a split-level on a residential street; it was a beautiful log cabin in a beautiful place, near Pine Creek south and west of Jackson Hole, over the pass. He sawed down the trees and hauled the logs himself. I remember this because he told me he went through a bunch of chains on his saw because he would never use bar oil on his saw because it would discolor the logs. His dedication and attention to detail are legendary in many fire circles. I also appreciated the way he could piece out the big picture of things.

Only once did I ever see him out of control, and that was the infamous evening before we left New Mexico in 1993, when he was dee-runk. Only twice did I hear him raise his voice – both times at me.

Here we were now, driving at the head of the convoy and cruising through painted desert country. This is the landscape you often see depicted on Western paintings and on the covers of Western novels. Inside the cab it was totally silent, save for the standard road noise experienced in pickup trucks. I rode shotgun and projected a blank stare across the rocky canyons and through the low scrub oak as it whizzed past. Gritting my teeth and biting my tongue were not working. I was going to piss in my pants if we didn't stop soon; and I mean SOON!

"Eric?"

"GODDAMMIT, YOU'RE LIKE A LITTLE GIRL!" He screamed, startling me enough that I darn near did piss my pants.

Three-quarters of a mile later he led the entire convoy down the highway exit ramp so I could get out and relieve myself for the six or seventh time in the last couple hours. Then it was back on the interstate and up to cruising speed. Fifteen minutes passed.

"Eric?"

I was really regretting my decision to drink so much coffee and water at lunch.

We made one more stop at the top of a mountain pass near Jacob Lake on the Kaibab Plateau. We were nearing our destination; I could tell by the blanket of haze and smoke surrounding us and drifting through the forest. We were waiting at a pullout for the rest of the convoy to catch up, so I figured I could zip over into the trees and take a pee. The moment I opened the door Hall bellowed, "GET BACK IN THE TRUCK!"

Again, I nearly peed my pants. I believe these are the only two things Eric said to me in five hours of driving.

Sunday, June 30, 1996, 7:30 p.m. – We are standing in the chow line at a Type I fire camp on the Kaibab Forest near the north rim of the Grand Canyon. I feel happy again because I'm reunited with my friends, specifically Dave and Alexis. Alexis is standing in line in front of me wearing a gray sweatshirt with Montana State University written in yellow on it. She has on blue warm-up pants and a baseball cap. Even at her frumpiest she is hot. She gets hungry and deprived stares from men on handcrews who've been out all summer long on fires and haven't seen anything quite this pretty.

At supper that night, we all managed to find a couple of picnic tables in the chow tent in proximity to one another. It was fun catching up on each other's tales of the last week or so. Then everything fell eerily quiet. Three or four hundred firefighters under a tent eating supper and talking and then it's instantly silent – except for a nearby commotion that's beginning to get louder. Metal chairs banging into each other; tables and chairs and cups falling over. A person coughing and making a loud wheezing noise. A fight maybe? Somebody having a heart attack?

I look over and see that there's a man grasping his throat, lurching in a jagged semi-circle back and forth and stumbling around. He is choking. Absolutely *no one* does a *single* thing, including me. Everybody just stares at him for several moments, till a woman rushes over and starts the Heimlich maneuver on him. Otherwise it's still completely silent, except for somebody way in the back, who yells, "Don't do that, he's still breathing!"

After what seems like an eternity, he spits up the bolus, onto a table, and the scene inside the chow tent returns to semi-normal. Sitting across the table from me is Steve Lewis, who never even looked up from his food. "Dumbass," he mumbles, shaking his head.

Steve Lewis was cool and level-headed, but he surely did not look the part of a firefighter. He was about my height, but he was scrawny. And he looked like Charles Manson, especially when he wore a goatee.

Sean Udy, when he was our foreman, just seemed to hate us for being young and stupid – and his temper was explosive. One day we were pulling up to a fire southeast of Pocatello, and Sean needed to get the engine turned around on this tight road, so he had Steve get out and spot him. King Biscuit and I were sitting in the chase with the windows down waiting for him to turn around, and then we would do the same. Steve appears behind the engine, and he's eating a raspberry pop-tart with one hand and guiding Sean with his other hand. Meanwhile, the fire is just *ripping* up the other side of this gulch, so Sean is freaking out, and he's such a shitty driver he's just grinding the gears and nearly doing wheelies. And he's screaming. Finally he jams on the brake, jumps out of the engine, runs back to Steve, and yells in his face, "Put down the goddamn pop-tart and pay attention!"

Steve, with his mouth full of pop-tart and no expression at all on his face, yells back at top volume, "It ain't my fault you don't know how to drive!" Sean just goes ballistic and screams unintelligibly all the way back to the engine cab. I still crack up to remember it.

About two weeks later we were out in the yard in front of the station cleaning out the engine after several trips out on fires. The bins on the engine tend to collect garbage and shit after being out for a few days. You just get too lazy to clean up and throw stuff away. Steve is pulling out old lunch bags and juice boxes and junk and a pink blanket falls out; he simultaneously spills a half-bottle of Pepsi down the front of his shirt and that's just the final straw. He goes crazy, throwing shit out onto the ground and screaming, "This is a *fire* engine, not a kindergarten bus!" I start laughing and the more I laugh, the madder he gets. I can't think of that one still without laughing, either.

Fighting fire in Arizona was nothing like I thought it would be. First of all, I had the mistaken impression, like I'd had with New Mexico, that I would be fighting lots of range fires in sagebrush and Taco Bell cactus and mesquite. Nope. This was textbook tall-timber forest firefighting. This part of Arizona boasts the largest contiguous stand of Ponderosa pine on the continent. The mountains and rolling park-like areas were all ringed or carpeted with

Ponderosa at its most exquisite, although the trees seemed tinder dry.

This particular fire near Jacob Lake was actually one in a complex of fires that had reached the Type I project fire stage because of the enormity of acres and resources involved, as well as the growing political concerns over the touristy location. It had started several days ago, and I was curious to know how it had become a crown fire so easily. I wondered about this because of the noticeable lack of ladder fuels – those graduated levels of grasses, brush, dry saplings and deadfall that allow a fire to climb to greater heights. The landscape appeared conspicuously clean. The vegetation seemed to be laid out in that perfect mosaic pattern that I had learned, in my wildlife classes at the U of I, was excellent for sustaining ecosystem health. This was how forests were supposed to look.

The large fluctuation in temperature was not what I had expected either, and I had a hard time adjusting to it. In the daytime we would easily get into the high 90s, working our asses off (especially with Mike and Tom). At night, though, it was frigid. Even my mummy bag wasn't cutting it. One night it was so cold I was forced to throw small pebbles at Steve and John to make them wake up, so I wouldn't have to suffer alone. Steve finally sat up, and in the moonlight I saw his bed head silhouetted against the trees at the edge of the clearing. The hair stood out on the back of his head like a rooster tail on a 5-year-old after naptime. He started scratching the rooster tail with his right hand and trying to figure out what was going on. I sailed a small dirt clod at him.

"Zood, wass the hell?

Ping, another small pebble off his back.

"Knock it off!"

I smiled, lay back, and took in the billion-star Kaibab planetarium. Shivering.

One night, while battling cold-induced insomnia, I looked over where Alexis was lying, and after my eyes adjusted, could see in the moon shadows that her eyes were open.

"Hey!" I whispered.

"What?" She hissed back.

"Let's take a walk."

I'm guessing it was about 2:00 in the morning when we padded through the tall dry grass of the meadow, across a little wash; we headed into the pines. Life was good.

After a couple of weeks of this, it was time to head home. We had been de-mobed from this fire. In listening to regional reports, I had come to find out that the monsoons were beginning to arrive, which signaled the end of the Southwest fire season and the beginning of the fun in Utah and southeast Idaho.

I bought a red zip-up sweatshirt, with all the fires of this complex and their locations on it, from a vendor near the visitors' center. I gave it to my dad when I got home. I rode a lot of the way home with Mike and Tom in Engine 342. Once I learned their ways, I started getting along well with them. Mostly that meant working my ass off and keeping up – they were basically firefighting machines.

The Legion Bar Fire

Thursday, July 11, 1996, 6:25 p.m. – Well, in *my* mind I'm a celebrity now. A reporter from the *Post-Register* (the local newspaper) called me at work the day after we arrived back in town. He did an interview with me about our New Mexico/Arizona detail, and it came out in today's paper. I thought I made a good interview and kind of felt redemption for the 1994 interview that I had screwed up.

To celebrate that as well as to celebrate just being alive and being on the crew at Station 1, the four of us who stayed in Dubois after work walked the few blocks down to the Legion for the happy hour. It was my first happy hour of the season at the Legion, and it was probably going to be more of a power hour.

In 1995, unlike '94, I made a conscious effort as often as possible not to get blitzed while on call. This was not just because it was highly discouraged by BLM managers, but also because fighting fire is inherently hard, physical work. Doing physical work, requiring cardiovascular effort, while drunk, just plain sucks. In 1996, that advice to myself was usually disregarded. The six other guys I lived with were just too goddamn wild to ever think about doing something less than 100 percent – and that included drinking. Anything I suggested, they would partake in, and vice versa. In fact, I ended up being pretty much the wildest one.

That first happy hour at the Legion, we were attempting to each drink twelve beers during that 60-minute time period. Well, about eight beers into it we hear the city fire bell start ringing. This thing is *loud,* you can hear it all through town. I looked at Rob Emery, the assistant foreman for 311, and asked, "Is that the fire alarm?"

"I think so," he replied.

"Does that have anything to do with us?" I asked.

No one replied. Everyone just kind of looked at me with wide eyes. The bell had been ringing for about five minutes when I walked out to the café and saw the Mayberry-like volunteer fire truck speed past the windows on the café side of the building, sirens wailing. I thought they responded only to house fires and stuff, and most of me began to hope that it was somebody's house burning down and not a brush fire.

Still holding a red plastic cup full of Bud Light, I did an about-face, swallowed a foamy gulp, and strolled back through the batwings into the bar. I was trying to act cool, but I was gradually forming an ice-ball in my stomach, and quickly losing my buzz. As the highest ranking firefighter on the crew that evening, I was responsible for making the decisions on initial attack if any brush fires started. That meant that not only would I be responsible for the actions of the crew of 311, who were mostly inexperienced, but I would also be the incident commander of the fire. I may have thought before now that I was ready for this, but all of a sudden I felt very unready. This was not how I had envisioned my first incident command fire. In my thoughts and daydreams, the first fire was always during the regular shift, I always had a full crew, I was not nervous, and I was sober. This could turn out to be a nightmare. Now I was reduced to making a quick request of God. "Oh, please don't let this be a brush fire." Maybe if we ignored the siren and just stayed in here drinking beer it would all stop, I thought to myself. I knew though, I just knew there was a brush fire. "I better go have a look outside." I said to the bar in general.

I took one step out the side speak-easy door, and there, towering above even the tall cottonwoods across the street, was the messenger telling me it was time to come to the proving grounds. The tall, thick, black smoke column made for a literally sobering moment.

"Shit, we gotta get back to the station!" I yelled back into the bar.

I did have the presence of mind to inform the bartender that we'd be paying our tab later. Didn't want to make bad neighbors.

Trying hard not to break into a full sprint, the four of us took off for the station. Through the fog of the beer, and the thin line between nerves and hysteria, I tried to somehow quickly rehearse what I was supposed to do. My big picture was now quite blurry. I was a long way beyond that first fire years ago in New Mexico, but this new role as incident commander and foreman, arriving when it did, promised to expose me as a green rookie.

We could hear the station phone ringing by the time we got to the left turn. If cell phones had been more common in those days, dispatch would have contacted us by that method. As it stood, though, there was just the landline and the radio. In retrospect, I probably should have brought a handheld radio to the bar, or called dispatch to let them know where we were going to be. In future fire seasons they would often call the bar looking for me or other firefighters – *the bar's phone number was actually listed as a secondary contact number for us in the dispatch office!* I snatched up the phone and it was Jim, one of the dispatchers. "Where were you guys, there's a fire outside of town."

"Yeah, sorry, we just got back," I knew I was slurring. "We'll sake 311 and respond," I said thickly. "I half here Rob, Dan, and Chris, we'll respond."

Even after the constant rehearsing I had done for the past seasons, and the quick rehearsal on the way back to the station, I still felt like I was now running in circles trying to don my fire gear. After what seemed like an hour, but was probably more like five minutes, we piled into the vehicles and departed the station.

"Dispatch, Engine 311," I called.

"311, Dispatch."

"We have departed Station 1 and are en route to the fire east of town."

"Copy, let us know when you've arrived."

The proximity of the fire to the station made it a quick trip, maybe five minutes – and I'm sure I was driving the engine like it was a Corvette. So far, so good, except that in self-critique I felt I was acting way too excited – just like what used to bug me about other ICs and foremen. If there was a scale between the lady in New Mexico in 1993 who hyperventilated, and the ever-cool Hall, I knew I was riding on the side of hyperventilation. Even though I was aware of it, I couldn't stop my hands from shaking or my voice from quivering.

We arrived at the fire and pulled the vehicles into the safety of the black. The only thing left on this end of the fire was some curlicue smoke from burnt sagebrush stobs and singed brush. On the northeast flank, though, a 10-foot wall of flame galloped across the prairie. The volunteer firefighters were going after it like angry hornets, and kicking some butt.

I took a swig of warm water from a bottle and used my tongue to wet my lips and clear the upper part of my throat. Then I called dispatch to tell them we had arrived and to give them an initial size-up.

Size-ups are something experienced incident commanders should be able to deliver calmly, clearly, concisely, and professionally. This is no longer kid stuff. It's for real. I know this because it's one of those things where I could never start laughing, no matter what (that's how I gauge whether something is important or not). There was a checklist you were supposed to follow, but even after tearing through all the paperwork in the engine and in the chase, I couldn't find a copy of one. I was just going to have to wing it.

"Dispatch! Walters!" I yelled into the radio.

"Walters, Dispatch," Jim calmly responded.

At this point, you're supposed to proceed through the checklist and allow dispatch some time to copy down the facts. The info is straightforward: location of fire, size of fire, fuels, fire behavior, topography, localized weather conditions, resources on scene, resources you anticipate you'll need, and outline of suppression strategy and tactics. Not me. Not this time. I just keyed the radio mike and yelled, "We're here and it's huge and it's burning in *sagegrash* and *bushbrush*! It's ripping!"

"Um, Walters, could you please repeat that transmission."

"The Dubois volunteers are here!" I yelled back into the mike.

Thankfully, I had with me some cool dudes. Dan, Rob, and Chris stayed calm, and that helped me get hold of myself. By the time I did, the volunteer firefighters had knocked down the head and effectively stopped the fire. This made my job simple when I had to transition back from IC to engine foreman for a moment. "Take the engine and work up the west flank and around to the north and back again," I instructed. "Let's make sure the line is good and cold. Then we can mop up."

I stayed at the chase truck and calmed down for a few minutes before calling dispatch with an update. All told, the fire burned about 20 acres, and for that I was thankful. It could have been much worse.

I analyzed and reanalyzed and went through the events of the fire over and over in my mind for the next couple of days, hoping I could make a better showing next time. I knew, though, the next fire would likely present an altogether different scenario, and I would have to learn to love that part of the job. It never occurred to me to slow down on the drinking – in fact, after I called the fire officially controlled that night, we took our sooty selves back to the Legion and got re-drunk.

The Front Fires

I would likely maintain that the remainder of the summer of '96 I spent in Dubois was the finest and happiest of my life. Hands down it was the famous "Summer of '69" for me. It was my time for fun in the sun.

I believe that if it hadn't been fire season, and a good busy one at that, I would have spent every cent of the money I was earning on alcohol, tobacco, firearms, and all the fun those things imply. Our Station 1 was like a mini version of the Animal House fraternity house and all that implies. As the resident John Belushi or Good Time Charlie, I made sure to spend at least three-quarters of every paycheck buying rounds for the bar and keeping the jukebox stoked. I even quit drinking beer out of glasses; I just drank it straight out of the pitcher. Everybody in town knew me, and I had about seven girlfriends, including a rekindled romance with Alexis. I made odd choices of people to look up to as role models. I had no savings account. I was living only for the moment, only hoping the moment could last.

As the high summer of July waned, and the dog days of August loomed, the fire season began to peak in number and intensity of fires. The weather patterns began to get predictable in the valley: cobalt-sky mornings with no early-summer dewy feeling or late summer/early fall chill, followed by the noontime pre-heat, early afternoon oppressive heat, and late afternoon stacks of airborne cotton balls in the southern sky. We were at the apex of the season. The cotton ball cumulonimbus clouds often turned dark and you would hear the *kaboom – baboom-boom* of thunder in the distance, often accompanied by a light show as well.

It was only a matter of time before the Pocatello front went up. Now, though, I had the responsibility of an engine and a crew, and possibly the responsibility of being in charge of one of those crazy and dangerous wildland/urban interface fires. Randy Hanson, the south zone AFCO and firefighter essentially in charge of the front, was a natural teacher, and he had often suggested that it was time to put the ball in the court of the younger foremen and ICs. Even though I was from a station in the far north, the potential for commanding a fire on the front remained, for if all engines and ICs were committed elsewhere, they would move us all down south.

Each boom from those distant electrical storms caused me to have butterflies in my stomach. In an attempt to beat back that apprehension, I often discussed at length the many "what-ifs" with other more experienced foremen. I tried to imagine the many possible scenarios, along with the proper response. I knew, though, that with my completion of formal Type IV incident commander training, and its subsequent notation on my red card, I was setting foot in an area that required more thinking. There may have to be derivation and manipulation of different strategies and tactics. Facts would now have to be interpreted and sometimes rules and methods bent, broken, or otherwise changed. Not much was going to be cut-and-dried from here on out. A plus B would not always equal C.

Monday, August 5, 1996, 3:00 p.m. – Troy and I have just arrived back at the station after a long patrol in Engine 312 through the Medicine Lodge country. We found no fires, but we did get paid to witness the beauty of sage grouse and antelope country as it rolled, cut, and climbed into foothills and finally rested on tall, windy, and lonely granite peaks. Heart Mountain was my favorite lonely peak in that country, and even now, in the heat of August, it was high enough that snow still wisped off its crest in the ever-present wind.

We had returned because 311 and the crew had been called to a fire near Fort Hall, leaving only Troy and me to cover the entire north zone. Since that happy-hour fire there had been quite a few fires where I was just responsible for Troy and myself, and two fires that I had worked as a Type IV incident commander. Both those IC fires had been just single-tree lightning strikes where we hiked in and worked them overnight. No big deal, about like putting out a large campfire. Therefore, I really hadn't had any more experience on a ripping fire and was still apprehensive when we got the call to head south and stage at Station 5 in Pocatello. Now there was nobody left in the north zone. The seams had evidently split in the south zone and they were going to need some help. Would this be when I would confront my fears and actually IC a fire on the Pocatello front?

"Well we better head out, Troy," I said, "you ready for this?" I was asking the question more to myself than Troy.

"I hope you know what you're doing," he replied.

All the way down to Pocatello that afternoon we had front-row seats to a lightshow out the windshield and audio entertainment from the Motorola radio as the various crews updated dispatch on the main channel and conversed with each other on the tactical channels. Throughout the 2-hour drive I again rehearsed my jobs and applied them to imaginary fires. I knew that if we got called to a fire on one of those steep sidehills bordering the city that I would be seriously wishing I was in better shape. So far this summer I either hadn't had time, or hadn't had the ambition to do much running. Also this summer, we had been able to drive the engine to almost all the fires we had been to, so I hadn't had much hiking time. Any power hikes over the next few days would have to be done slowly or I would was going to end up having a heart attack or puking on the hill. Knowing this did not help my confidence.

Dark clouds, a steady wind, and bolt after bolt of lightning greeted us in Pocatello. A large black thunderhead was perched over the peaks south of town. This must have been what was starting all the fires. So far down here, the fires had been caught while still small, but there had been a bunch of them. I learned later that this area alone had had something like 60-plus fires in the past two days. It was only a matter of time before one of them got out of control and took off. Moisture was sparse or nonexistent; the few drops of rain quickly dried on the windshield. When the window was rolled down, you got that rapid temperature fluctuation as the ambient air couldn't decide whether it was going to be humid and hot or cool and breezy.

Dispatch instructed us to stage at Station 5 in the Portneuf area of town. This was the station that the BLM shared with the Pocatello city fire department. We pulled into the parking lot and backed the engine into a stall reserved for BLM vehicles. Then we went inside to chat with anybody who might have been left at the station. I looked over at Troy and noticed he was licking a tootsie pop like he was a little kid. On *any other day* I would have chuckled or overlooked this, but today I was too keyed up.

"Troy, get that stupid sucker out of your mouth."

"Why? I just started on it and it tastes good."

"Dude, I'm telling you, spit it out. We have to go talk to the Pocatello guys and I don't want to look like a couple of dorks."

Obediently he deposited the sucker in the trash can just outside the doors of the station. I instantly realized what a jerk I had been.

"Sorry dude, it's just that I'm game-face on this. We'll probably be going to a fire soon and I want to be ready." I realized the apology really had nothing to do with the sucker, but it was the best I could do at that point. "I'll buy you another one when we go fuel up."

"Whatever."

The station was deserted. The trappings of a typical BLM station afternoon were present – magazines, soda cans, TV still on – but the crew wasn't home. Everybody was on a fire. For the next two days we staged. That meant for the next two days we ate MREs, chewed pounds of Copenhagen, slept in sleeping bags on couches, watched the one channel on the TV and read out-of-date mechanic magazines and auto sellers. We got more and more nervous. The radio crackled non-stop, as did the thunder. Still no rain, and still more fires. And still Troy and I sat around. I called dispatch several times on the telephone, and was told simply to stay put and stand by for initial attack.

On day three in the early afternoon we were released. There was a smoke report south of Dubois they wanted us to check out. Finally we could get out of Station 5 and do something. They hadn't sounded too enthusiastic about this fire report, though, and we were roughly two hours away, so Troy and I didn't move fast. We even stopped at the convenience store on the way out of Pocatello so I could buy some tobacco and a lollipop for Troy.

As we rattled along I-15 northbound, I thought about what it meant that we didn't get called to any fires on the front. On one hand, I was secretly relieved. Wildland/urban interface fires are scarier than the dentist, so I was glad I hadn't screwed anything up. On the other hand, I knew that the inevitable had only been postponed. It was going to happen eventually. Gradually my thoughts became more focused on what I was going to do that evening. We did something fun every night in Dubois when there wasn't a fire. We either went to the bar and sang karaoke, or hung out with the local girls and partied, or built bonfires in the backyard and played guitars, or went fishing or went swimming or went shooting. Hell, one night I rode an ostrich or emu or some other huge bird that a guy kept in a pasture in the middle of town. It bucked me off and then bit me on the ass before I could leap back over the fence.

I hoped the guys from 311 would be in Dubois, too, but if not, I could start a party and keep it humming by myself, even if that just meant hanging out and drinking beer with Troy and the gaggle of blonde cowgirls who considered us the true boys of summer.

I was still immersed in these daydreams when we came over a rise just north of the small enclave of Hamer. Instantly, I was brought back to a hard reality. We had been originally called away from Pocatello to go check out a fire report. I looked left and then right, and then I looked left and right again, and as far as I could see across the horizon was a perfectly straight line of 15-foot-high flames. Why hadn't I noticed the smoke? *Oh shit.*

"Troy, there's the fire!" I yelled. He had been dozing in the passenger seat.

"Whoa, dude!" He exclaimed, now wide awake.

Have you ever been faced with a problem and you know the answer, but you can't figure out where to start? That was me right then, and I made the mistake of verbalizing that initial confusion.

"I wonder what we should do," I said aloud.

Troy had gold caps on two of his teeth, one on each side of his upper set. Whenever he was laughing, or when he was agitated, the teeth appeared. Now he was agitated and concerned and the gold flashed. For some reason it pissed me off; I wanted to blame my lack of confidence on him. I wanted to blame everything in the world on him right then.

"We have to call dispatch!" he exclaimed.

"Don't you think I know that? I was talking about how we're supposed to get over there to it, for starters!" I roared.

I was aware that I was betraying my inexperience, but I felt powerless to control myself. Here was another totally different scenario than the dozens I had been going over in my mind. It was frustrating. We were stopped on the side of the interstate, with the red and white overhead flashers on, but no real plan formulated. Momentarily paralyzed.

Then I attempted to call dispatch and discovered the radios were down. Not just the radio in the truck, but the whole system in the district. I knew this because I tried contacting dispatch with just the handheld radio, as well. It was as if someone was keying the mike and not letting go. All you could hear was a frustrating buzz. For all intents and purposes, Troy and I were all alone and would have to do something about this fire on our own.

I swallowed hard and tried to make a conscious effort not to slip into a panic. Cars were stopped all over the highway watching the fire shred the Camas Wildlife Refuge, and here we sat, merely watching it with them. The people would look at the fire, then look at us, then look back to the fire, then look at us, and then give us the palms-up "Why aren't you doing anything?" gesture. What they failed to realize was that there wasn't a whole lot we could do right then anyhow. Going after a fire this big with 250 gallons of water would be a lot like taking on a charging grizzly with a fly swatter.

I figured to drive to the next exit, about three miles up the highway, and then backtrack down the frontage road until we could turn onto the refuge road. To the people stopped on the highway, it was going to look like we were running away, but I figured this would be our best bet for safe access. Plus, if the Idaho State

Police didn't hear about this soon and clear this traffic, these people would be running away themselves. Those flames were bearing down on the highway.

Troy, now highly agitated, with gold flashing galore, and all of his two months of experience, said, "Just cross the median and we'll cut the fence and head right out to it."

I replied by tersely telling him to just shut up. I realized immediately that wasn't the most tactful way an engine foreman should maintain order, so I added, "First, we don't need to be cutting through any fence. Second, we're liable to get high-centered in that far ditch, and third, we can't just pretend there's a damn anchor point right here in the middle!"

I was mildly proud of myself for actually thinking a little. We still couldn't get through to dispatch, though, and after a final attempt, I grabbed the mike by the cord, cursed, and slapped the mike hard across the dashboard. Then we took off for the exit.

"We're gonna need a damn airtanker here before too long," I growled, knowing full well that all this district's airtankers were already committed to the sling-load of other fires burning in the valley.

When we turned off the frontage road and drove west into the refuge, I began to realize I was most likely in over my head, as far as acquired skills go. I also knew, though, that at 21 years old, having lived the life I'd lived so far, I had acquired big enough balls that I would have taken on hell with a bucket of ice water. Of course, that attitude is all fine and good when you're just responsible for yourself, but now I was responsible for Troy, a nationally known migratory bird stopover, and potentially all the idiots parked alongside I-15. This was going to require not just balls, but gray matter as well.

Then a weird, calm feeling came over me. I realized the summer was waning, and this could be my last fire and real excitement for almost a year. I also thought, you know what, I can handle this engine; I've been to tons of fires over the past summers and I've paid strict attention to what the incident commanders' strategies have been. Perhaps most important of all, I came to a realization that there was nobody to bail me out here. I would be calling the shots, and I would be making sure they were carried out.

The first order of business was to establish an anchor point. This meant we were going to have to cross the barbed-wire fence, and there was no gate in sight.

"I knew we were going to have to cut the fence." Troy complained.

"We ain't gonna cut it," I replied. "Hold on!"

The sound produced when you run a Type 6 fire engine at high speed through a barbed-wire fence is certainly unique. When we hit it, even over the roar of the unwound diesel engine and the droning buzz of the radio, we could hear the tension rising exponentially in the wires. It sounded like a giant tuning his giant guitar and then accidentally breaking a string. Wayeeeeeeee – ka-ping – ka-ping – KA-POW!!!! The lines sprang apart and we flew through. Now I was hoping none of the wire had got caught up in the wheels or the driveline.

Now we raced across the mostly tall grass plain as the flame front, buffeted by steady wind, careened across the prairie like a fiery riptide. I knew I was breaking one of the cardinal rules of firefighting – putting fuel between you and the main fire – but I couldn't see any other way to reach a safe anchor point. I prayed to God the engine wouldn't break down.

When we did reach that anchor point, Troy jumped out and grabbed the hardline while I started the pump. Our plan was to pump and roll until we got back to the east-west dirt road. That is, if our water supply lasted. I was now unable to see more than a few feet ahead of us, so it was a matter of keeping one tire in the black and moving as fast as we could. Still no contact with dispatch.

As we worked up the line, I kept seeing the fire flare up behind us. This is one of the reasons fire engines "daisy-chain" while doing a pump and roll. We had no choice, though, so we just gave it our best shot. And we damn near made it.

By now, the fire was bumping up against the dirt road that we had driven in on, and there was a truck parked on that road. From 50 yards away, I hollered at him to get the hell out of there. Simultaneously, the low-water safety switch on the pump activated, and the pump automatically shut down. We were done.

Fifty yards! If we could have made it that far, we could have essentially stopped the fire. Now the guy on the road screamed and frantically waved his arms. "What are you doing? Spray until you get to the road!" He yelled.

"We're out of water." I yelled back.

"I said spray it out until you get here!" He indignantly pointed down to an imaginary spot on the ground.

I felt my face instantly flush with fury because I knew we had tried our hardest.

"Mister," I angrily shouted, "You better get in your truck and get outta here, or I'm gonna kick your ass out of here!"

I left the engine and started to walk toward him, and that put him in gear. He jumped in his truck and sped away.

The fire was speeding away, too. I believe its next plan was to bump the interstate hard, probably jump it, and then take off in all directions. Head down, I went to the back of the engine to grab a Gatorade and think about what to do next.

"You want a Gatorade, Troy? We may as well hang for a minute and think what to do next," I said.

"Yeah, please, grab me one."

Gatorade bottles back then were sometimes still glass. Unbeknownst to me, one had broken all over the top of the engine. When I put my hand up there to pull myself up, I accidentally found a shard and it sliced my hand right open. Blood everywhere. Nevertheless, I grabbed two unbroken bottles of Gatorade, tossed one to Troy, then guzzled an orange one myself. I was too amped up to be worried about blood.

As I went around to the passenger side of the engine, I suddenly caught a flash of yellow. "Whoa, here comes the cavalry!" Troy exclaimed.

"Hell yeah!"

Here came Engine 311, leading a comet trail of dust up the road, as well as another heavy engine and a Forest Service light engine. Back in the game!

The Idaho State Police had contacted our dispatch via landline and given them a brief rundown of the developing situation. Included in that rundown was the fact that a light engine was up there by itself and needing some serious help. Engines 311, 331, and Forest Service Engine 1511 had just returned to the yard from another fire when dispatch alerted them. Jerry Neil, one of my best friends, was the foreman on 311 this summer. When he heard the report and relayed it to my other friends on the crew, that was all it took.

By late that evening, we had won. The fire was contained and controlled, thanks to the arrival of the cavalry. That is doubtless one of the coolest things that an embattled fighter can ever witness: the coming of his closest friends to jump in and help kick some ass on a common enemy. Having been on a fire crew cavalry before, I now knew what it was like on both sides. When that call comes, you always get nervous, but when you find out it's someone you know, those nerves vanish away, replaced by determination and focus to help your friend. I've felt it on football teams and fire crews, and when it's personal, it's utterly intoxicating.

We never did get a call in to dispatch until we had the fire squashed. It was unnerving to have no communications, and I hoped it never happened again.

Friday, August 16, 1996, 2 p.m. – As hard as I've tried this summer, I've been unable to slow or stop time. This is my last day on the crew for the season and as usual, I'm bummed out. It seems like it's going to be especially hard this year. Why am I leaving something so fun and concrete for a future that's cloudy at best? Well, because I'm expected to, I suppose. I expect it of myself. I know myself enough to understand that I likely couldn't be satisfied with this for my career. It's too crazy a lifestyle for me to maintain. I want a family and a real life. But man, so much *fun* this summer! I could stay and work until probably December before I'm laid off, with all the fall projects, but it's probably best that I go.

I felt really down that final day on the crew in '96. Smoke filled the valley from the fires burning everywhere. I really never even got to say goodbye to anybody, as they all had to respond to more fires. It was quiet and lonely inside Station 1 as I packed up all my summer gear.

I had saved up a total of 60 dollars this summer. It did not bode well for me, economically, for the school year. In fact, it bordered on near-disaster. Before school even started, I was using credit cards to buy groceries and sinking into a bottomless pit of debt.

I had an overwhelming sense of discouragement as I thought of Alexis. It was fairly clear that this would be the last of that two-summer romance. The next time I saw her, she treated me like someone she used to work with, nothing more. It made me sigh and want to take a nap, dreaming of better times as I drifted off. In fact, those times were so wonderful they could have been just a dream; I'm glad they're saved here, proving they actually happened.

Over the winter I really pined away for the fire crew, and could not wait for spring. As the days got longer and warmer, I began to feel it all through my body and soul. I knew that summer would come eventually, just not soon enough. I knew just as well, though, that a repeat of last summer would likely never happen to me again. I was glad I had tried to wring every bit of fun out of it while I could.

After the 1996 season, the innocence of the crew, as in my life itself, seemed to rapidly drain away. Maturity seems like it should grow in a person as the innocence ends, but that wasn't the case with me. I tried way too hard for the next three seasons I had with the BLM to recapture those times. It was a titanic task that ultimately I couldn't complete.

Being on the fire crew was somewhat similar to being a farmer. I learned this over the first couple of years, when I sensed the boom and bust nature of the business. Firefighters do like fire. Not only does it get us away from the station and the mundane routines of washing fire trucks and doing inventories, it's also fun. It's an adrenaline rush, it's good hard work in the sun, and we make significantly more money while a fire is burning. As soon as that fire is officially controlled, we no longer get hazard pay. Economically speaking, it would make sense for firefighters to never put out a fire. We do have a social conscience, though, and enjoy applying our skills to new challenges, so we inevitably try our hardest to put out the fire.

I also learned that each season, after the threat of fire was essentially over, the firefighters who stayed to work through the fall would be employed on BLM re-seeding crews. I believe this is a necessary step to returning something of a balance to the ecosystem, but I also maintained a malicious little thought that all they were doing out on the prairie was sowing the ground for next summer's harvest; the crop being fire.

For some reason, it never occurred to me that there would be a year when there weren't many fires. I really hadn't ever paid any attention to fire cycles, my mind being too focused on drinking, having fun, and blowing cash that I didn't have. If I assumed anything, it would have probably been that each season I would return from the University of Idaho in May, hang out with my high school friends for a couple of weeks, then greet my fire friends at the first of June. We would go to fire school, get the stations ready, maybe go on a Southwestern detail, then return and fight about 20 fires: ten small ones, seven medium-sized ones, and three big ones. I would drink too much, have too much fun, save no money, pack up my gear in August, be sad, then go back to the University of Idaho.

I should have predicted some change, though. I have anxiety problems, and for me the best way to combat this is to avoid change at all costs. Here's the problem: I have a nasty little crush on change. I see it out there in all its sexiness, looking at me too long, sharing too long a laugh with me, and coming physically too close to me. I know it isn't good for me, but I know it's inevitable that we'll eventually have a love affair. It won't be just a little love affair either; it will cause a drastic change in my life, and set me on a course into uncharted waters. Most of the time it catches me by surprise, but there are also times when I actively seek it out. Pre-empt its attack so I can have more control over my life.

All winter and spring my life had run a rollercoaster of changes, and it didn't stop when my BLM job started in June. I learned that I was not going to be in

Dubois this summer, and even worse, I was going to be stationed in Idaho Falls!

The changes up at school had put me into a digressing behavioral pattern, and being stationed in town probably wasn't going to help. The salient fact was that I was a mess. I was simply a man trying to mine a fun motherlode that was all but tapped out.

It must be sad to witness a guy doing that, always chasing the buzz and the good time. My family was pretty sad about it, for sure, but there just wasn't much they could do; I can be a stubborn ass. This fast life of mine was straining them and I knew it.

The fire crew guys didn't know me through the rest of the year – they just knew me as a crazy and fun summertime party animal. It was expected that I would be drinking beer and having a good time whenever there wasn't a fire. And I was.

Strange Season

Early June, 1997. Fire School, Eastern Idaho Technical College. Don't cross Randy Hanson if you want to keep progressing in your fire career around here. I learned that the hard way today.

I won't pretend I was some sort of Captain America firefighter early in 1997, but I'm not a jerk either. My circumstances in life and at the BLM right then were such that this job was actually kind of bringing me down. It had all started with a morally defeating year up at college, and my dog who'd been my best friend since I was a little kid had died. It continued on with the news that I would be stationed in Idaho Falls for the season. I was newly in love with a girl, though, so that was definitely a positive. For better or worse, she was where I directed most of my attention. But everything else kind of kept a chip on my shoulder.

On one of the scheduled breaks from the fire school class Hanson was teaching, I scurried down the hall to a payphone so I could make sweet talk with my new girlfriend. At the end of the allotted 10-minute break, I didn't hang up the phone because I didn't want to cut her off mid-story, so I arrived back to class five minutes late. Another guy did, too – a huge and mean-looking Samoan firefighter.

Hanson decided to make me do pushups in front of the class as punishment for being late. He made it clear I would be the only one doing pushups, not the mean-looking Samoan guy.

"Well," I said, "I'll do them if he has to do them too." I gestured with my chin toward the Samoan, who sat quietly staring forward.

"Nope," said Hanson. "Just you, Benny."

All was now silent in the room – at least a hundred firefighters sat unmoving as the showdown developed. I looked around at everybody and felt my face flush. This is bullshit. I'm tired of being humiliated by this guy.

"You know what Randy?" I said, "I've done enough pushups for you in my career, and I'm not doing any more."

"OOOOOOOOOOOOOOOoooooohhh," the class responded.

Everybody was intimidated by Randy Hanson, and he encouraged that. He had left the BLM that year for his new job as a Forest Service AFMO. I'm not sure this split had been amicable.

He looked at me. "You just fucked up bigtime."

Outwardly I smirked, but inside I was sick; I knew I'd just hit the apex of my fire career. But my pride wasn't going to let me apologize or backpedal when I thought I was right. I can put up with only so much shit.

I kind of assumed the situation would blow over, and within an hour, I no longer even considered it a big deal. When I pulled back into the BLM yard that afternoon, though, Gary Eames was there to meet me; he looked at me over the top rims of his aviator shades.

"Why didn't you do pushups for Randy today?" My God, news travels fast.

"Because he singled me out unfairly. There was another guy who was late, too, and Randy didn't tell him to do pushups."

"You probably just should have done the pushups," he said, almost apologetically.

I just shrugged.

Then Dave Farmer came strutting up and wanted to give me a high-five. "I heard you basically told Hanson to fuck off. It's about time someone did."

From the corner of my eye, I swear I saw Gary smile a little. Evidently Hanson's arrogance had worn thin around here. And Hanson never spoke to me again.

Monday, June 2, 1997, 9:00 a.m. – In the time it takes me to walk from my truck to the fire center door, I get absolutely soaked. Of course, so did everyone else, and most of them have long hair. Guys *and* girls. When they step through the steel fire door they all have to shake their heads from side to side like dogs just out of a lake. Emily Webb, my crewmember this summer, struts down the short carpeted hallway with her eyes crossed, trying to focus on the auburn bangs hanging into her face. She is wearing a black t-shirt with a screenprinted name tag on it. It reads "Hello, my name is Satan."

"This weather sucks," she says.

All of us waiting in the dispatch anteroom concur by nodding or grumbling.

By June, in this part of the world, nature has usually shaken off the gray skies and showers of late spring. Usually even the gusty southeast Idaho winds are temporarily calmed. We expect muggy days full of brilliant colors. Yard grass should be thick and full, and it should be sharing landscape margins with the pinks, reds, deep purples and blazing yellows of flower gardens. Fresh bark bedding should be surrounding newly planted aspen and maple trees. The streets, malls, ballparks, and greenbelts should be full of children with all kinds of summer plans and dreams. Families should be planning picnics.

Down at the BLM yard, we should have been busily preparing for another run-and-gun summer. Instead, we just stood and peered out the dripping windows at the growing puddles. We had our initial meeting, we had fire school, and we drove out and opened the stations. We stood around the yard. Then the Snake River flooded.

As part of the incident command system, fire crews are prepared and organized to respond to other natural disasters besides wildfire. When the flow of the river, caused by higher than normal precipitation and runoff, exceeded the capability of the channel to hold it, it became an official incident. Firefighters became floodfighters.

For the first three weeks of June, our days were taken up with filling and distributing sandbags to create artificial levees. All day, every day, we showed up at different farms and homesteads, and worked at controlling the floodwaters. Usually, we had limited success, but it's beyond the scope of the human mind to just let Mother Nature run her course.

We have to try something.

Once again, I became locally famous because of a photo on the front page of the newspaper. My net score on media spin returned to zero as the unflattering photo depicted me munching out of a bag of ranch-flavored Doritos and holding an oversized bottle of pop. That was in the foreground. In the background were 20 or 30 other people busting their butts on a sandbag line. For the record, that was the only break I had that afternoon, and I'd been working at least as hard as everyone else that day. Damn the luck!

Wednesday, July 16, 1997, 2:30 p.m. – "An idle mind is the devil's workshop, and idle hands are the devil's tools."

It's one of those old statements that are actually true. The one job for my crew today was to pull the pump and pump motor off a light engine that was going to be scrapped. It took a couple of hours of fast-paced work to do it. Then we met the boys from Dubois for one of those Godfather's lunch feasts. I had been hung over for two weeks straight, so the greasy food helped me feel better, but when we came back and there was nothing to do, I felt bored and tired. I saw two options here: go find a shady, hidden spot somewhere and nap for a while, or find things to screw around with in the mechanic shop. Chad Brady, from the Dubois crew, is on my crew today, and not so much directly because of him, but because he is one of the representatives of the wild Dubois days, we chose the latter option.

Mechanics use overhead cranes to move heavy parts of automobiles around in the shop. We had to use one earlier to remove the pump and motor from the engine. Now the crane sat unused, with the hook hanging down and the top of it attached to a winch, which in turn was hooked to the 30-foot ceiling. It ran on a trolley system so it could move anywhere inside

261

of the large shop. It moved side to side and up and down –quite fast, actually.

"We should make a swing with it," I announced.

After some welding and pipe-bending, and drilling and screwing, we had a pretty neat shop-crane swing assembled and attached to the crane hook. Emily egged us on.

"You go up in it first, Chad," she said.

Up he went, as high as the ceiling. Emily swung him around and moved him speedily to and fro.

"Let me try it," I said to Emily.

She handed over the controls, which consisted of a bright yellow box about the size of a large TV remote control. There were up/down buttons, and forward/back buttons, and the hoisting speed controls, which I switched to the picture of the rabbit. I had Chad flying around like Peter Pan, and we were all giggling like kindergarten kids when I saw the smile instantly disappear from Chad's face. At the same moment, I felt a presence behind me. The presence was Gary Eames. I felt the cold chill of impending job loss.

"This does not look good," Gary calmly said.

"Oh jeez, sorry Gary," I groveled. "We were just practicing how to use the crane."

"Don't bullshit me."

Gary is not stupid. Fortunately for me, though, I'm sure that Gary had had his wild days and knew what happened when Type A personalities got bored.

"Get him down from there," Gary growled, and then stared at Chad as I let him down.

I will never, ever forget the look on Chad's face as I let him down from the ceiling. A moment ago childish smiles were plastered on our faces. Now, as the crane's chain chunk-chunked him out of the air, he had a look of total fear and seriousness. That in itself was worth it, just seeing that instant change, seeing him sitting in the swing, being lowered down to the shop floor while Gary watched. I am laughing right now.

Gary knew that I wouldn't do it again. So he left it at that and walked out of the shop shaking his head. I wonder if he too was trying not to laugh.

There were a handful of people in my fire years that I really looked up to, and Gary Eames was one of them. He was the guy I imprinted on, like a gosling, because of the way he approached the business. He was one of those *wise* people who seem to be able to comfortably observe life from an experienced position and make their calls from above without adding arrogance. I realized Gary was wise within hours of meeting him; I sensed he could see through my bullshit bluster and class clown antics. There was nothing I wouldn't have done for him. He was also mysteriously nearby many of the fires we went to. He always beat us there, like he had some kind of Jedi power. He looked the part of a Fire God, too – short and stocky with a big bushy mustache, fading brown hair always perfectly parted down the center. It was rare you ever saw him without mirrored aviator sunglasses or without a cigarette held inconspicuously between index finger and thumb, hidden in the palm of his hand. If he wanted you to know he was addressing you and only you, he would cock his head toward you at an angle where you could see his eyes over the rim of his shades. That look meant you had better listen.

It was during the summer of 1997 that I began to wonder whether I should keep working for the BLM. I knew one thing for sure, being stationed at the yard in Idaho Falls totally sucked. I am not good at finding busy work, so I spent my days pacing back and forth from the shop to dispatch and back again. I wore out the soles of my first pair of White's boots. One day I was so bored I crawled under a fire engine, spread some tools around to make it look like I was working on it, and then duct-taped my hand to the driveline and took a nap until my hand fell asleep. Another weekly routine was to call the old woman at the front desk and have her page Hugh Jazz for a phone call, or Richard Head. She never did figure it out.

Thursday, July 24, 1997, 5:00 p.m. – "Ben Walters, please report to dispatch. Ben Walters, report to dispatch."

Usually that means there's a fire, but this summer the only fire calls in the entire district have been three or four false alarms from people burning their fields. I am not too excited. So I stroll toward dispatch from the shop, kicking an egg-sized rock that was somehow deposited out here.

Moments later, I emerge from the dispatch office with heart racing.

"Emily, let's go! There's a fire east of Blackfoot. This one's for real."

I am nervous because I was not at all mentally prepared for this. It's like a football player who played tons of games the season before, but no games this season. You get out of practice. I might be called upon to be an IC for this one, and here I was again on the verge of panic.

Emily and I vault into Engine 323 and fire up the Ford diesel engine. Geez, that's funny, it has a hell of a rattle, and we're belching black smoke. Screw it, we're not missing this fire.

I pull out onto the main road and lurch into traffic, hoping the engine will just warm up and run smoothly enough to get us there. At the first stoplight, I quickly run dry of hope as the engine clanks to a halt and steam comes out from under the hood. We are dead in the water. Lime-green antifreeze pools underneath us.

I'm sick of this summer. Pushing a stalled fire engine through a busy intersection is professionally humiliating. The only thing I can say about the seized-up motor is that it allowed me to quit a little earlier in the season and go get surgery to repair an old football knee injury.

A strange season and strange weather. I thought long and deep as I drove back to Moscow that year. Here was an awesome fire season, then a crappy school year, then a crappy fire season. I was *really* broke this fall, and I had a steady girlfriend, too. This is not a good combination. I crutched around campus and got pretty good grades for a while. Then I got bored and depressed about missing summer. Aw hell, a lame fire season was bound to happen sooner or later. It couldn't have been a new precedent. It won't be like that again. I guess I'll give it one more try. I'll do another season. I check the "yes" box on the "are you returning" letter from the BLM, and then sit back to see what that implies for my life.

The Sunshine State

Tuesday, June 9, 1998, 9:00 a.m. – "Well, I guess this is where you finally get killed," my brother said to me.

He meant: This is when the job kills you. He had taken time from his job to come down and see me off to Florida – something he had never done any other time I had left the state on a firefighting detail. I wondered if this was a bad omen. But bad omen or not, we were going.

In 1998 the state of Florida caught on fire. Wildland fire suppression resources from around the nation mobilized and headed to the southeast part of the nation to lend a hand. It sounded like it was going crazy down there. For us, that meant we would be releasing two engine crews to take part. Everybody wanted to go. A detail to Florida! What an experience that would be. Names and engines for the trip were drawn from a hat. Engine 311 and Engine 381 were selected.

First piece of good news for me this year: back in Dubois with 311. Second piece of good news: drawn for the Florida detail. This had the potential to be one of the coolest things I'd ever experienced *in my life*. I didn't care if it killed me.

"I hope this doesn't kill me, but if it does, you can have my guns," I told my brother.

He and I had a handshake and a hug, something we very rarely did as brothers. This gave me a serious morale boost. I told him and my parents goodbye, as he was there also as a proxy for them, then I tossed my stuffed red bag into the bed of the brand-new maroon Chevy 4-door four-by-four chase truck that 311 would use this season. It was time to go.

I drove the chase for awhile, with Emily Webb and a new girl named Andrea Prost as passengers. Jerry Neil drove 311, with Lee Snow, a Forest Service transfer, riding shotgun. For seven 12-hour workdays we rumbled across America, joining a large migration of other firefighters to Florida.

Monday, June 15, 1998, 5:00 p.m. – We have arrived and have been given a preview of our enemy. It is going to be hot like I've never known hot. It's also going to be humid like I've never known humid. The air feels near solid, like a sauna. On the way down here, I had tried to acclimatize myself as we passed through the deep South by turning off the air conditioning and wearing a long-sleeve shirt. Now that we are here, though, I am mildly nervous about it – I am soaking wet, and I mean *soaking* wet.

For this trip, and for the summer of 1998, I was demoted, if you will, to assistant foreman. It was just technical, because I was Jerry Neil's assistant foreman, and most of the time he worked as an incident commander, which would leave me in charge of the engine and crew. Along with the title demotion I had received a raise. It was pretty much my dream come true – I was making more money and had less responsibility.

Jerry was one of the few human beings I have ever spent any time around who actually understood my quirky ways. As we arrived at the incident command post outside Bunnell, Florida, I was doubly glad he was foreman. I had no idea where we were, what was going on, or what we were supposed to do. I would have figured it out eventually, of course, but not with the ease that Jerry seemed to have.

Fighting fire in Florida was the ultimate in wildland/urban interface firefighting. It actually made the Pocatello Front seem like child's play. Have you ever been nervous about something to the point that you thought about it all the time? You think about it when you eat. You think about it when someone you love is talking to you and you look like you're paying attention. You look in the mirror while you're brushing your teeth and you don't even see yourself because you're thinking about it. It attacks you especially when you lie down in bed at night and it's quiet, and you find yourself with your eyes wide open thinking about it. You know that eventually you'll face it, and you hope you can respond like the world expects of you. You hope you can emerge victorious, or at least handle defeat with grace.

Eventually, one of three things happens. Either you face this fear, emerge victorious and continue on in life with new confidence, or you face the fear, lose, and respond to that – maybe with grace. The third option is that you become so immersed in it that the whole idea of it doesn't seem so intimidating anymore.

During my first season playing varsity football I was one of the deep men on the kick receiving team. All I thought about in the days leading up to our first game, which was a home game, was that first kickoff. I tried to visualize successfully catching the ball and making at least a decent return. Whenever I weakened, though, nerves would creep in and all I daydreamed about was bobbling or fumbling the ball and thus making a hell of a mistake. Then the moment arrived, the kickoff came, the ball fell into my hands, it fell out of my hands, the other team arrived, the other team recovered the ball, and that was that. I did not accept this failure with grace.

An example of the de-sensitizing option was the wildland/urban interface in Florida. In amongst the tall pines and sawgrass were neighborhoods full of pricey homes. About one out of three of these homes was now nothing more than a smoking ruin. The families would be outside picking through the ashes to find anything that might be saved. There were tears, there was terror, and there was anger. On one radio station we heard a woman ask, "Why aren't they sending in the Marines?"

With all due respect to the Marine Corps, we wondered, "Lady, what are the Marines gonna do, shoot the fire?"

The finest the nation has are down here trying our hardest. From the most experienced crack smokejumpers to Type 1 hotshot crews to powerful engine crews – it's the best we've got, and if we can't do it, no one can.

Most of the time we were successful saving houses, but at one point, we were actually assigned to do a triage of sorts. We drove around in neighborhoods and tied different colored surveyor's tape on the mailboxes of houses, based on possible survivability should the fire approach. Survivability was loosely based on things like type of shingles and siding, volume of junk in the yard, defensible space between structures and natural fuels, and escape routes for firefighters. People quickly figured out that an orange flag meant they were screwed, a yellow flag meant we might be able to do something, and a green flag meant we would probably be able to save the house. Dealing with the fire was one thing, dealing with the human emotion was an entirely different proposition. I became somewhat cynical after seeing so many structures lost, but I also found solace in the fact that I wasn't the foreman right now, or the incident commander. Those jobs I was glad to leave to the most experienced among us.

I found it rather annoying that other engine crews ran code – lights and sirens on – through the neighborhoods on the way to fires. Hell, the whole area was a fire, what was the point of screaming and yelling to add to the chaos?

To give you an idea of the scope of the conflagration, consider this: at one point we had to use the parking lot of a shopping center as a safety zone after a fire overran crews. After being pinned down there for five hours, I became bored and read a *Sports Illustrated* magazine and sipped Gatorade while thick black smoke choked the entire sky and various booms and rushes of hot wind punctuated the air. It was a very futuristic, apocalyptic, Mad Max type of situation, but it certainly seemed to be sanding the rough edges off my fears about interface firefighting.

At night, after a 16-hour shift, we stayed at the opulent Palm Coast Resort Hotel, abandoned now that all guests and staff had been evacuated. For a fire crew, it would have been a crazy fun rendezvous, but working all day in the heat exhausted everyone. The best we could muster for energy at night was to gather around the huge pool area and chat amongst ourselves or with other crews staying there. The pool became black with fire soot from the air and from washing off the bodies of firefighters. What a time, though, this huge beachside resort vacant except for the hundred or so firefighters.

Monday, June 29, 1998, 9:00 a.m. – Sitting around in heat like this is morally defeating. Even early in the morning, the stifling nature of it knocks all the work ethic out of me. A persistent heat rash in the crooks of both my elbows has forced me to cut the sleeves off my fire shirt. It's now a yellow fire vest. The sky *looks* cloudy, but it's not really – there's no precipitation on the way. That's just a haze created by the statewide firestorm. The chase truck has to be running all the time, with the air conditioner on high. That may seem like government waste, but this was a safety measure against heat exhaustion. We could work outside for a little while, mopping up the weird burned local flora, but if your sweat doesn't evaporate, you're going to go down. So we took turns literally chilling out in the chase.

We got up each morning at 5:00 in the coolness of our hotel rooms. Then we would pack up our personal gear and meet out at the trucks by 5:30. When we stepped outside of the hotel the contrast in temperature and humidity was like walking into a door. Even after two weeks, it was still hard to get used to the immediate sogginess of our clothing. We would drive a few blocks to the incident command post, eat a standard breakfast of bacon and eggs and grits, and then do the usual fire camp stuff – fueling up, watering up, getting our daily assignment.

Half the time we were sent out in the boonies and glades and wetlands to work creeping forest and sawgrass fires. These areas were full of awesome reptile species. We often had to draft water out of ponds and marshes to fill up the tank on the engine. Every time we did, we would see various sizes of alligators ascend to the surface of the water to check out the commotion. At one pond, a water moccasin crept up to where we had our draft line in the water, and when we tried to retrieve our filter and bucket, the bastard came after us!

On other days we were sent to do structure protection at interface locations around Ormond Beach or Flagler Beach. This is when things got bizarre. First of all, the vegetation that was burning was totally green. Nothing looked dry to me, and besides that, in the Great Basin where I was used to fighting fire, fuel would *never* burn in this kind of humidity. Second, the heat and intensity of these fires was absolutely incredible. With all its power and technology and water-delivering capabilities, 311 was no match for these flames. In contrast, though, we could never seem to get a backfire going. It was frustrating to present such a passive defense to this enemy.

So many structures were burning to the ground and gas stations exploding and lumberyards going up in smoke that it became almost strangely comical. People quit panicking about it. They just walked around like zombies. There seemed to be no rhyme or reason to what we were doing, no overall plan – our crew was skipped around everywhere to different locations all day long. One morning we found ourselves protecting an exclusive gated community clubhouse. By noon, we were working with a bulldozer to put a line around a house with a huge outdoor pool. In the early afternoon we were foaming down a burning pile of tires at a junkyard; what a losing endeavor that was.

One of highlights of the Florida trip was the backwoods barbecue near Ormond Beach. Florida is *full* of rednecks, and that's not something I'd thought much about prior to our 1998 assignment – I mostly thought about the Miami Dolphins, hot Puerto Rican and Dominican babes, Miami Vice, and old retirees in golf carts. I'm not fully redneck, but I definitely lean that direction, so these were my people. On one shift, we found ourselves right in the middle of redneck heaven helping save someone's house and barn.

They had been out there pissing in the wind trying to stop this hot but slow-moving lava-field type fire as it crept in on them. They were getting their asses kicked. Then the cavalry arrived – our strike team of engines and a dozer. We were successful in steering the fire away from the buildings and saving them. The food goodies that arrived afterward were nothing short of amazing.

We were all standing around in the dirt driveway mingling with this family and some of their neighbors when five or six jacked-up pickup trucks came roaring in off the country road and into the driveway. The people in them looked something like the characters in the movie *The Road*. A dude who looked exactly like Leon Russell stood in the back of one of the pickups and put both hands on the chrome rollbar and in a booming voice addressed all of us firefighters standing there. At first we thought he was pissed.

"Y'all have come down here from wherever ya came from, driven over our fields and through our yards and over our ditches. Some places ya couldn't even help us keep our places from burnin' down, but I'm here to tell ya, y'all will jest never know how much we appreciate ya. Now we're here ta feed ya and clothe ya and tell y'all thanks."

And with that, the cast of *Mad Max Beyond Thunderdome* all bailed out of the pickups and set us up a feast I'll never forget.

They had brought card tables and picnic tables and grills, and coolers full of food and drinks. It was true-to-life, down-home, and beyond delicious. The Leon Russell dude himself was kind of like an emcee for the whole event; he went around and made sure everyone was getting enough to eat and drink. He slapped people on the back, shook hands, and kept everyone smiling.

The feast was centered around a huge pile of baby-back ribs slathered with the very best barbecue sauce I've *ever* had. I loaded a whole plate with slabs of those ribs, grabbed a Coke and a two-inch stack of checkered napkins, and sat down with my back against a huge shade tree. With still some room to spare, I went back up to a table that was loaded with ceramic crockpots full of baked beans and spooned up a bunch of those. This table also had potato salad, macaroni salad, biscuits and dinner rolls, you name it – all homemade. A couple of my buddies ate huge double cheeseburgers that a guy had grilled for them.

If you still had room, they had brought for us all kinds of desserts as well. I was too stuffed by then, but remembering the chocolate brownies in pans on a card table still makes me salivate. They even had boxes of T-shirts and Florida souvenirs they wanted us to take home. I still have the BootHill Bike Rally tank top I picked out.

We thanked them profusely and waddled back to our hotel with full bellies. It amazed me how grateful these people were, even though we were successful in saving their property only about half the time. I still feel bad that I never got any of their names to send thank-you notes for taking such good care of us.

Any way you looked at it, this detail was another one of those BLM situations where hard work and misery were generously spiced with good times and good humor. I just don't think we could've survived any other way. The hardest times were the hottest times – 9:00 in the morning until 6:00 at night. That's when smiles firmed up into tough young faces setting out to do a job; not unlike I picture a soldier's face in battle. Even the jokesters like me settled down into the routine. Eventually our own forests and rangelands out West would catch on fire, and we needed to be back there protecting them.

But not before one last wild party at Daytona Beach.

Saturday, July 11, 1998, 7:00 p.m. – God bless the BLM. They are not going to make us drive back to Idaho. Our plane leaves tomorrow at 11:40 a.m., and our engines and chase trucks will be trucked home on a low-boy flatbed. Duty calls back in the Great Basin.

We'd met up with the party-savvy crews from the other Idaho districts earlier in the week, and they said the place to party in Daytona was at a club called

Razzles. It is there that we will be winding down this fine final Florida evening. We have been working our asses off for the past three weeks, and it's time for some fun. I would like to get to know some of these Florida women. They're the finest I've ever seen, and rumor has it they dig firefighters.

It was easy to see why the guys sent us to Razzles at Daytona Beach. It's a very happenin' beachside club teeming with the most beautiful women on the planet. The ace in the hole for Jerry, Lee, and me is our vocation; it's certainly not because of our money. We purposely wore new t-shirts with fire logos on them to get noticed. The women did notice, and most of our drinks were free. We danced and partied and made out with the pretty beach babes till the place closed. We pretended we were going to be here tomorrow, though sadly we wouldn't be. Lee, absolutely wasted, drunkenly attempted to go home with a girl, but Jerry and I had to prevent it. The end result was Lee back at the hotel with two black eyes and me with a twisted ankle. The fond memory of that night will stay with me forever, and I'm sure it's one of the reasons I decided I want to live in Florida some day.

The next morning we found our seats on the jetliner that would take us on the first leg of our journey home. The captain announced to the passengers that there were ten firefighters from Idaho on board, and we got a standing ovation. We tried to act cool, but inside I'm sure everyone else's smile was as big as mine.

The Florida detail, besides being one of the high points of my life, was also really the only noteworthy experience of the summer. Besides the night at Razzles, I didn't drink at all in Florida, because I would have simply perished in the heat the next day. When we finally moved into Station 1 in mid-July, I more than made up for that sober period. I was back at the Legion bar, happy hour after happy hour, night after night. Without realizing it, I didn't even spend much time camping in the nearby mountains or fishing in the sparkling creeks and rivers in the area. I was just staying near the station and drinking too much.

Friday, August 14, 1998, 2:30 p.m. – The ritual last day of the season for me has arrived. I load my stuff into my pickup for the drive with confusing and opposing thoughts about the future. I'm going to graduate with my bachelor's degree in Wildlife Resource Management from the University of Idaho next spring. After that I am unsure of my future. I will supposedly have the training and capabilities to be a wildlife biologist, but I'm having second thoughts about how much I would actually like doing that for a living. But what else will I do? I can't fight fire forever, can I? I can't make this a career. Besides that, I've got a steady girlfriend who lives outside of Moscow and I'm wondering if I'm maybe even going to get married in the spring. This is a fork in the road that I'm not looking forward to. I think about my time on the fire crew. I was totally miserable when I first started, but I'd gradually figured out what's up over the past six seasons. I think I'm finally somewhat proficient at it; maybe even rather skillful. Now that I've gained that experience and been given that training, I feel like I'd like to apply it to more situations where I can call the shots. As I told everyone goodbye, I got the feeling that I might never see them again.

The Wagonbox Fire

Friday, April 2, 1999, 3:30 p.m. – "You're getting old, dude," Jerry says.

"I feel old," I reply.

"Well, are you coming back this year or not? If you want, you can run 312 in Dubois this summer. It's a brand new Ford F-450."

Moments ago, I had been sitting on my couch in a rented single-wide trailer, staring at the snow/rain mixture falling outside and trying to keep from crying. At a time when I should be rejoicing about the impending conclusion of a frustrating journey here in Moscow, I was instead more depressed and unsure than I ever had been in my life. This call from Jerry might have been what saved me.

The afternoon of Jerry's phone call happened to be a rare one; one of the few times that spring that I was able to sit back and meditate. A whole lot was going on in my life that ate up most of my free moments. I was attempting to manage my overwhelming stack of bills, and any chance I had to think quietly would inevitably end with me just sad and scared. I tried to stay busy, working three jobs and going to school full time. One of my jobs was volunteering at least 20 hours a week as a fireman and EMT with the Moscow Fire Department.

But here I was at the end of my college days, and I felt like I had nothing positive to show for it. The possible marriage to my girlfriend at the time? She'd started seeing someone else on the side, and it was breaking my heart. Now, no matter how many generic cigarettes I smoked, or how many times I swept my hands down my face or raked my fingers through my hair, I couldn't erase the doubt. Doubt about my past, my future, the here and now. What was I going to do?

"Hell yes, I coming back," I heard myself telling Jerry. "I'd love to run that new 312."

"Okay, I'll let Eric know. See you in June."

"And another thing, Jerry, I'm staying for the whole season this year."

There, I'd said it. My future was set, at least for the next couple of months. My heart was noticeably lighter. I had some direction. Once again, the fire crew snatched me from the doldrums of the northern Idaho spring and a directionless life.

I put on my now tight-fitting jogging clothes and stepped out into the breezy April afternoon. A day reminiscent of an April day in 1993 when I first attempted practicing the mile-and-a-half run back home in Idaho Falls. I smelled diesel exhaust when I passed by a farm on my jog and it immediately brought me back to fire season.

Early June, 1999. Fire School – Sometimes you come across a fire school instructor who takes himself way too seriously. Jim Butler was one of those. This guy was just as dry as a dirt sandwich when he taught, and everything was the most important thing to him. As an added torture bonus, they usually made him teach the boring classes.

The class that day was some sort of hydraulics class. I'm sorry, but I just knew I would never practically apply that knowledge, so I was tuned out before class even started. But, being the helpful lad I am, I told everybody in my group of senior firefighters that I'd grab their little desktop name tents for them and fill them out with a marker while they got coffee that morning.

From Jim's perspective, he saw people's name tents in our row, but the students themselves couldn't see what I'd named them because the names faced away from them, and evidently none of them ever bothered to check. All morning long, Jim was forced to look at, left to right in the front row, Courtney Craven-Morehead, I.P. Standing, I.P. Sitting, M. Dick Burns, and the *coup de grâce*: I.M. PIGFUCKER "oink-oink" – which I'd lettered on Bryan Clark's name tent. My name tent simply read "Ben W."

I'm not sure what got into me. I like to fuck around in general, but I'm usually not a practical joker like this.

Every time Jim passed by us as he lectured, he would stare down at the name tents. I wasn't sure if he had noticed them yet, or figured it out, but then he stopped in front of us. He took off his glasses, wiped them on his shirt, and put them back on. He looked one more time at the name tents.

"You know what? You BLM people come here and start wasting everyone's goddamn time the minute you walk through the door. I'm up here trying my hardest to get this material through to you blockheads, and all you want to do is screw around."

The guys I'm with are just looking at him with complete blanks. They have *no* idea what he is talking about.

"What if," he continued, "you get into a situation with a hose lay and need to figure out if you can get water up to someone who really needs it. Then you'll be damned sorry you came here and wasted my time and yours."

Brian "I.M. PIGFUCKER" Clark says, "Dude, what's your problem, we haven't said a single thing since class started."

And truthfully, all of us had sat there totally paying attention. Well, everyone but me anyway. I seriously don't know if I've ever had to try that hard to keep from exploding into snot-and-tears laughter. I was actually dripping sweat.

"This is what I am talking about, Mr. Pigfucker." Jim turned Brian's name tent toward him where he could see it.

"I didn't write that!" Bryan pleads.

"Yeah, whatever," Jim replied, obviously pissed.

"Yeah," I repeated out loud, "you guys are wasting my time and everyone else's."

They all started looking at their name tents, then at mine, and I got some of the dirtiest looks I'd ever seen.

Tuesday, June 15, 1999, 3:00 p.m. – This new F-450 fire engine is a beast. We're crawling up a steep washed-out trail and I think it's doing every bit as well as a jeep could. I doubt my pickup could make it up here. Of course, this is a government vehicle, and they seem to go better in tighter and tougher places than a personal vehicle, if you know what I mean. I have just two gripes about it – the rims are too big and the tires too small, so I've unfortunately gotten to where I can change a flat as fast as a NASCAR pit crew. Also, the stabilizer bar in front keeps shearing off on one side or another when we bump into anything.

We're working our way into a small lightning-strike fire called in by a pilot. I'm with Troy Daniels (from the '96 crew) and Kelly Hayes (King Biscuit's younger sister). We're on a two-week detail working out of a BLM district in Cedar City, Utah. Since we arrived here, our little crew has become somewhat of a standout for our ability to find and extinguish a bunch of little fires before they've gotten big.

GPS, though commonly used at that point by pilots, mariners, and scientists, was not considered mainstream yet. I happened to own an early model GPS receiver unit that my dad had given me for hunting. I brought it down here on this detail and they had me working with air observer platforms to find these little fires in the incipient stages. A small airplane, like a Cessna 172, would fly out on patrol, and when they found a smoke, they could call in the latitudinal and longitudinal coordinates to dispatch, who would relay them to me. I then could punch those numbers into my GPS and easily find the fires. It made me look like I knew what I was doing, and it felt good.

So it was with a feeling of increasing proficiency bordering on cockiness that I returned to Idaho Falls in late June after the detail. Yeah, life outside the fire crew sucked, but the fire crew is not really a job, it's a life. I felt like I was becoming a more career-minded firefighter. I had worked my way through being slow and stupid, to sophomoric zeal and gung-ho, then started slow again as an engine foreman, Type IV incident commander, and crew leader. Now I was becoming comfortable in these roles, comfortable enough to call in size-ups and devise suppression strategies in my head, all while on the move. One time I even found myself talking to dispatch on a cell phone, talking on the radio to air attack, reading a map, tuning the FM station to classic rock, and punching in GPS coordinates, all the while munching on a Big Mac and driving a heavy engine down the interstate in heavy traffic on the way to a fire.

Still, though, I hadn't really been tested in the commander role on a heavy duty wildland/urban interface fire, and that still remained in the back of my mind. I felt if I could be successful at that a few times, then I would be worthy enough to apply to some of the Assistant Fire Control Officer jobs or Engine Module Leader jobs coming open around the region. That could essentially result in a career as a firefighter, not just a summer job.

Friday, July 9, 1999, 10:30 p.m. - Location: Goose Creek Area, Sawtooth National Forest, approximately 18 miles south of Oakley, Idaho. The remainder of this season, I'd wager, is going to be busy, bordering on frantic. We got home from our Cedar City detail only a couple of weeks ago, and I hardly had time to drink a beer before we were running and gunning to fires all over our district. Now Kelly and I are down here assisting this other district on another detail. Then we'll probably ping-pong back north to our district when fires break out there again – it happens every time a series of electrical storms passes through. I love this. Money, money, and action!

Now it's late in the evening, nighttime actually. While many people are getting ready for bed, we are out here with a strike team of engines to see what we can do about this new fire. It's a rapidly spreading monster, eating all the junipers, mountain mahogany, sagebrush, and grass in this drainage. Access to it is evidently going to be an issue, something that shouldn't be attempted in the dark. It's been named the Wagonbox Fire.

And all we can do now is watch it. It's too dangerous to attempt to do anything, so we stand around and talk and watch the flames from a comfortable distance. I put in dip after dip of Copenhagen and try to stay awake. One of the engine foremen is the Type IV incident commander at the moment, and he has driven up into the gulch to try to make a size-up. This fire isn't going to be a Type IV when it's all said and done, I can guarantee you that. Before too long he arrives back at the staging area and instructs us to head back out to the flats to start a camp for the night. More forces are en route, many due to arrive tomorrow morning. We'll decide what to do then. All we can hope for now is that the higher humidity and cooler temperatures of the late evening will slow it down some.

The next morning, after about one hour of sleep in the dust next to the engine, we met with the current incident commander and discussed a tentative plan. We were to accompany a Forest Service engine up a long and deep canyon toward Middle Mountain. After a while, a hotshot crew coming in from California would be up the canyon as well. The hotshots would conduct a burnout back down the road that led up the canyon, and the job for our engine and the other engine would be to prevent the hotshots' backfire from jumping the road and thus running up the other side of the canyon into another drainage. I guess that's what I heard, anyway. To be fair, it was just 15 minutes before that I had peeled myself from an exhausted deep sleep and fished a cocklebur out of my sock. My hair had that dog-house carpet feeling.

Kelly and I gratefully accepted the sack lunches from the Burley logistics ladies. Then it was time to lock in the four-wheel-drive hubs on the engine and begin making our way up the canyon. The Forest Service engine followed closely behind as we bumped and ground our way up the two-track road. The sun was just beginning to peek over the eastern horizon, and judging from the picturesque morning Empyrean, it was going to be a July scorcher. Just another day at the world's coolest office.

Reaching a bend in the road and a pullout of sorts, in an otherwise tight canyon, we stopped to get out, stretch and kill some time. It was cool and shady where we stopped and I thought it best that we enjoy this bosky area before the work of the day began. Besides, the hotshot crew was going to be a while making it up the rather rugged canyon road in their crew vehicles – the hotshot crummies. I slugged down a Gatorade, put in a fresh dip of Copenhagen, and took a stroll by myself a few hundred yards up the road.

To say I never thought about the past few reckless years I'd had would be lying, and solitary times like this afforded me space to analyze them. There was no hurry, so I just put my hands in my pockets and walked and thought. I looked up at the high steep hills on either side of me. The grass on them was tall and still had dew on it. The stands of piñon-juniper were thick and mature. They made perfect hiding places for deer. Gin-smelling juniper berries and pine needles littered the ground everywhere. A small creek gurgled over rocks through a little coulee on my right. In just a few hours, if all went well, the right side of this canyon would be a blackened moonscape.

I was like this canyon when I was eighteen: new, green, quiet, full of potential, tall and strong. Like this canyon, with a fire to come, my life had faced and was now facing all sorts of drastic changes. Some things here would die and never return. I saw the metaphor between the canyon and my own innocence.

We planned to burn this canyon to save it – and keep the fire from becoming huge and running wild. In just a year, the grass would be greener and newer here on the right-hand side of the canyon. Life would emerge from the ashes like the phoenix itself.

The deer would think it's better eating on the right-hand side, but then we can go hide on the left side when the sun is high in the sky. The new grasses and sage and piñon-juniper stands will think, wow, we can get so much sunlight and water now! People who might not even grasp the strategy of a backfire could see, in the results, the benefits of a pro-active approach. It was risky, but that's the *only* way to make it anywhere in this world. You have to take risks and you *cannot* be afraid of failure.

Where the hell is that hotshot crew? I've walked too far, thought too much, and I haven't had enough sleep or enough food.

By noon we were all wondering just what had happened to that crew. We radioed the incident commander, who in turn contacted the hotshot crew, who in turn reported that they were working up the canyon as planned, but it had been slower going than they had anticipated. Even though I was not yet the world's greatest fire strategist, I was getting mildly irritated at the delay. I knew that as the air heated up, especially in a tight canyon like this, flames will start to do funny, unanticipated stuff. A backburn in fuel this heavy is going to be tricky to hold, especially when there are only two light engines assigned to the task. They would have sent a heavy up here, but the terrain is too rough for a vehicle that big. I had volunteered to come up here, because I knew that this new F-450 was a veritable mule in four-wheel-drive country like this.

There was no shade anymore. And by 2:00 p.m. I couldn't stand waiting anymore, so Kelly and I decided to crawl the engine up the canyon a ways and scout the topography up ahead, see if it opened up at all. The Forest Service guys would wait here at this spot; an area wider than we had seen all morning, but still tight enough that it barely fit both the engines, and would require at least a six-point turn to get headed back down the canyon. I shifted the transfer case on the Ford into four-wheel drive low range, and moved slowly off the pullout and onto the dusty road – which was quickly petering out to a two-track jeep trail.

Almost an hour later, and still no word from the hotshot crew, we made it around the large bend in the canyon and came to a place where we could see a ways in front of us and a ways behind us. What I observed in either direction was not something that made me very happy. I felt a tinge of nerves, the kind I hadn't felt since back in the '96 season, when I had first been made engine foreman. I became angry at myself for thinking too much about things that had only metaphorical reference to this job. I hadn't been in the "here and now" enough to be aware of my surroundings, other than to compare them to my life itself.

Ahead of us the canyon came to an abrupt, box-like halt. In fact, they call these box canyons, and at the head of them there is always a topographical feature called a chimney. It acts like a chimney on your house, and it's the type of place where pilots crash their airplanes when they realize they can't turn around, and firefighters burn to death when they realize they can't turn around. To the southwest of my position and the right of the thousand-foot chimney, I could see thick black smoke and the tips of the flames from the main fire beginning to crest the skyline. When I went around to the other side of the engine and looked northwest, I could see a darkening smoke cloud down-canyon behind us. There was fire there as well, and it was growing in intensity. The jaws of a deadly trap were closing in on Kelly and me and the Forest Service guys parked down below. Hell's gates were closing.

The road here was so sketchy that the engine sat at a precarious angle. With as calm a voice as possible, I told Kelly to just stay in the cab because if she opened her door on that side, it was going to be hard to close it. I went around to the back of the engine and put a hand on the rack near the hose reel and closed my eyes for a second. My stomach suddenly felt queasy, and I was pissed at my overconfidence in 312 and myself, and really pissed that I hadn't remained vigilant about my surroundings. I had become complacent and had unwittingly violated many of the standard fire orders, and now I had a real situation on my hands. *What would Hall do?* I thought.

See-sawing between murderous anger at the stupidity and vanity of the hotshot crew below us (they sometimes don't give a shit about engine crews), and the fear of being burned over and at the very least destroying the brand-new fire engine, I tried to get hold of myself and return to some modicum of pragmatism. I'd been suddenly thrown into a fight for life here. It was game-on, time for all-business Ben Walters again. I realized I was smiling inside. Then I gritted my teeth and realized I was smiling on the outside. Am I crazy to love this? I am in a life-or-death situation here and it *feels so good*. Why is there such a fine line between terror and thrill with me? I want to be normal, but I just can't seem to be satisfied with it.

I was unconsciously referring to my football days again when I made my fight plan. In football, the harder you try to hit a guy, the less it hurts you. Whenever I pussyfooted on the field, I inevitably got my ass kicked and it hurt, but when I went balls to the wall and tried smashing into people like an 18-wheeler into a dynamite plant, it was only loud, and it never hurt. Now was time to be that smashing machine and take the fight to the enemy. If I operated with fear or hesitation, I would very likely end up taking this little 19-year-old girl, myself, and three other guys into a tragically fatal ring of fire.

Here were my problems: I had fire above me at the head of the box canyon, which would crest the skyline and work its way down to us in the bottom; the hotshot crew below us had begun firing off without ever making contact with us (this was their bad, bad mistake); I had two engines in tight spots without good places to turn around (essentially, no good escape routes or safety zones). This problem was one I should have detected and solved before ever settling in for the day. The main fire and the backfire were likely to meet up just about where we were parked right now.

I steadied my voice and attempted to make contact with the incident commander on the main channel with my handheld radio; of course, no luck. I waited a couple of minutes, then said into the mike, "No contact with Wagonbox Incident Commander. Break. Mendocino Hotshots, this is Engine 312."

I tried this twice with no luck, then checked to make sure I was actually transmitting by calling the Forest Service engine on the same channel. They responded, and judging by the inflection in their voices, they had become aware of the developing sinister situation.

"Engine 1611, this is Engine 312."

"312 go ahead."

"Can you guys hear me calling the IC and the hotshots?"

"Yeah we read you five-by."

Which basically means loud and clear.

"Okay. Hey, you guys need to get turned around and start working your way back down the canyon. This is a box canyon, the main fire's crested the ridge and evidently the hotshots have started burning below us. We'll have to get down there and help them hold it. I wish they would have called and told us they were starting."

"Yeah, we copy. We're getting turned around right now."

"Copy, we'll turn around and meet you down there," I replied.

I hopped back in the engine and told Kelly what was going on. This was her first year on the crew and I didn't want her to get freaked out, so I just kind of gently explained that we were in a tight spot here, so hold on.

With the transfer case in four-wheel-drive low, I cranked the wheel left and went as far as I could on the sidehill before spinning out. Then I cranked the wheel right as far as it would go, shifted into reverse, and slowly backed down. I made it about ten degrees around the unit circle. Do the math, and you'll come up with about 18 times I had to do this before I had my one-eighty completed. I breathed a little sigh of relief. Then I began to pick up the chatter on the radio between the hotshots and the incident commander.

"Wagonbox IC, this is Mendocino Hotshots."

"Mendocino Hotshots, Wagonbox. Go ahead."

"Hey, we really need those engines up here. We've lost it across the canyon, so we've got fire running up both slopes."

Goddammit! We are up here! We've been waiting on you guys! I furiously thought to myself. They were screwing up, yet we were being blamed for it!

The hotshots' radio transmission contained the last words I wanted to hear: They'd lost the fire and it was headed up both slopes. I had worried that this might happen. Now our one and only escape route was cut off. We bumped on down the road until we met the Forest Service guys at the spot where we had split up earlier, the small turnout area. They had seen a wall of flames plowing through the junipers, headed up here, so they had turned around and come back. Now I could see the flames just around the bend, about 300 feet away.

One of things you are taught and drilled about, even though it should be common sense, is that one of the safest places to be if you are about to be burned over is in the black, where fire has already been. It's not likely to go there again. In remembering this, I had planned to use this little turnout as an area to light off and burn, then we could stay put and wait till the fire left, with the engines into our burned area as a safe zone. It would be hot and smoky, probably pop the tires on the engines and maybe blister some paint, but we would survive. Now that option had been taken away from me. The hotshots' backfire had gained too much steam and was barreling up the draw at us, leaving no time to create our burned-out safe zone. We barely had enough time to turn around and get in behind the Forest Service engine before the flames ripped through that area.

On instinct, we hammered it up the two-track jeep trail behind the Forest Service engine, going much faster than we should have been for this terrain. Kelly and I, now seatbelted in, got tossed around the cab like a carnival ride. Shit from under the seat, behind the seat, and off the dashboard flew around like asteroids. There went my GPS. Now an empty Copenhagen can, my extra pair of sunglasses, a map. I had salty grit in my mouth from the dirt and dust kicked up in the cab.

We continued up to an area halfway between the main fire up-canyon and the hotshots' fire behind us down-canyon. Here is where we would make our stand. The problem was that there was no damn space. We were choked off by a steep washout that dropped down to a trickling stream on our right side, and a steep, juniper-covered sidehill on our left. The Forest Service guys hesitated in front of us. No time for that now. I saw a slight opening in the junipers. "Hold on," I yelled, "'cause here we go!"

I pinned the motor and made it through at least three gears before I cranked the wheel and smashed through the scrub brush up the slope. U-joints screeched and axles moaned and leaf springs ka-pinged; the front tires grabbed at the loose dry soil and the back end fish-tailed to the right. We made it about 30 or 40 feet before coming to a dead halt. I was out of the engine like a calf-roper off his horse, making sure the Forest Service guys had gotten to a safe spot. The Forest Service foreman and I were popping fusees like grapes off a vine and laying down fire all around our defensible space. We had our crew members stay inside the engines; it was most likely the safest place right then.

After we had our fire burning, we each grabbed hardline hoses and adjusted the intensity of the flames impinging on our vehicles to where they wouldn't do too much damage. The heat, when our fire hit the junipers 10 feet away, was likely the most intense I will ever feel in my life. The sun had been blotted out by now, leaving only a hellish orange/ochre hue. The decal on the side of 312 bubbled with the heat and the plastic headlight borders on the front were melting, but other than that the engine seemed okay. I used the trick Steve Lewis had taught me in 1994 by spraying myself off when the heat began to sear through my fire clothes. I remember that through it all, a strange calmness pervaded my psyche. It was almost just like, okay, there is a job to do, and I'm doing it. We're being proactive and so far, it seems to be working.

When we were fairly certain we had saved the engines, I jumped back into the still-idling 312, with its glorious air conditioning, and just waited. There was nothing more we could do now. The heat was so intense you couldn't touch the windows without burning your hands. The environment inside the cab was strangely calm; I was glad for this because I didn't want to sour Kelly's experience about the fire crew. If we didn't die, that is. The FM radio was even playing one of my favorite country songs, Tim McGraw's "Something Like That."

The song kicks ass, but the best is the piano riffs. I heard one, smiled, and then looked over at Kelly, and she had this innocent look of total calm on her face. I felt proud of myself in a weird way right then – I knew I wasn't betraying the terror I was feeling at that point. I even keyed out the riff across the dashboard as if I were playing the piano as a huge fuckin' column of fire was tearing through the junipers right outside the cab of the engine. I realized I had finally made it.

I took a deep breath and a big swig of warm water from a bottle, then put in a fresh dip and sat back. Over the rattle of the idling diesel engine, the fan of the air conditioner, and the FM radio, we could hear the fire roaring through the canyon. And yes, it did sound like a freight train coming at you. The hotshots' backfire was the first to reach us. It had steamrolled through the deep gulch below us on the right-hand side of the canyon and then rocketed up the small hill.

The flames, thick and explosive, lay across the road and met with the flames now arriving from the left-hand canyon on the west side. When they met, the inferno shot at least 50 feet into the air. It looked just like the conflagrations you see when forest fires explode on the TV news. The main fire, which had started as a backing fire but had been sucked downhill by the backfire, had grown in intensity, and then met up with our safety zone fire. We were in the true eye of a shitstorm and it was the most exciting moment of my life. I must have been calm on the surface, though; Kelly was just kind of smiling and bopping around in the passenger seat, asking me if I knew anybody in town who could give her guitar lessons. "Just keep away from the window for now, we'll talk later," I told her.

As all storms and bad days do, this one eventually passed. Though it seemed like we had been trapped (I won't call it an official "entrapment" because we never deployed our fire shelters) for hours, we were probably passing through the threshold of hell for only about 15 minutes. The fire now found very little to feed on around us, and thus moved on up the hill on the west side of the canyon. I cautiously climbed out from the cab of the engine; the Forest Service foreman and I examined our rigs.

Short of a few bubbles in the decals and some damage to the moldings near the headlights, 312 appeared to be largely unscathed. The same could be said of the Forest Service engine.

"That was as close to the edge as I need to be for awhile," I said to the Forest Service foreman.

"I agree. I guess we just take this as a learning experience."

"That's no shit," I agreed.

It was time to move out from our safety zone and bump up the canyon to see if we could hold this fire in any possible way. There was no time to mess around; we still had a job to do. We backed back down the sidehill and crawled up the blackened section of the canyon where the main fire had jumped the road. Our mission would be to somehow construct and hold an east-west line to prevent the fire from moving farther south.

Later that evening, the Forest Service foreman and I had an audience with the IC to explain our side of the incident. Lacking radio contact, we had not been party to the frantic transmissions between the air attack and the IC as the fire engulfed our little area. It turns out we had been the topic of a rather dramatic situation. Thankfully, there wasn't much finger pointing, and the matter seemed to get more or less pushed under the carpet. This was fine with me; I had for sure learned a damn good lesson from this. In the future, I *would not* get myself into a canyon without at least two routes of escape, I *would not* get myself in a position as a holding crew with the burning crew below me, and I *would not* continue operations or remain in an area that was going to be burned without positive and reliable communications with the incident commander and the burning crew.

There were several other injuries – and a burn investigation – on this fire before it was all over. I'd learned some big lessons on this trip and was glad to get out of there.

With the Wagonbox Fire still ripping, we were de-mobed the very next morning and sent back to our district. We limped out of the long drainage back north, rolling on one flat dual tire and no water in the tank. We had incurred two flat tires in the last 24 hours and were now without a spare. By the time we hit civilization several hours later, I was so fatigued that I was reduced to eating MRE coffee grounds to stay awake and keep the crawling vehicle between the lines. Kelly snored softly in the passenger seat, her head supported by the slack of the seat belt.

The afternoon sun beat down on the farm fields of the high summer, my favorite time of year. As we exited off I-15 that afternoon (after the flat tires were repaired in Pocatello), the traffic was thick with the good people of Idaho out enjoying the glorious effulgence of the July day. I saw families leaving one of the hometown favorite diners with full and happy bellies. I saw bikinis strolling the greenbelt. I saw crowds at the auto wash shining up their rides. I saw families at gas stations arranging water toys in the backs of ski boats, headed up to nearby Blacktail Reservoir for an afternoon of the funnest fun. I felt mildly envious that I wasn't able to do that sort of thing very often, one of the downsides of this job. I still felt tired, but thoughts of a pleasant evening cracking many frosty beers at the Legion Bar in Dubois kept me rolling along.

Blacktail

ONE OF THE COOLEST THINGS about returning from a firefighting detail is pulling into the home station or yard in your muddy, dusty, scratched-up fire engine. As you make that turn into the parking lot, you are aware of, or at least you are imagining, firefighters from other crews and even office people welcoming you home like a bloodied soldier returning from battle. You ceremoniously pull your rig into designated parking area, creakily step down from the cab, and do your best to strut your greasy, dirty self into the dispatch office to turn in your time reports and other paperwork. This is, after all, a government job, and with a government job comes lots of paperwork.

This was the scene on July 11, 1999 in Idaho Falls at the Interagency Fire Center. Kelly Hayes and I had just returned from a fire as part of a two-week work detail with a BLM district south of us. What happened to us on that fire was exciting – but that would be an understatement. I had sweated so much and gotten so dirty that my yellow and green Nomex fire clothes were now black and gray, and stiff enough to nearly stand up on their own. I had perpetual crusty things in the corners of my raw eyes that I had long since quit trying to remove. My feet felt like I had walked barefoot over burning glass shards, and my quads, calves, and back muscles were badly knotted up. Ah, but this is typical stuff on what would turn out to be another non-typical day in the fire world.

My work goals that day were to turn in my reports from the detail, re-stock the fire engine with the supplies necessary for initial attack duty, and make the forty-five-mile drive north back to our duty station in Dubois. I figured that with all these necessary duties, plus a little jawing and bragging, Kelly and I would be back in Dubois with the rest of the station crew sometime around 5:30 that afternoon. If no fires were burning in the district, we would be off duty at 6:00, opening our first beer at about 6:01, and then in freight-train party mode by 7:00. We had worked hard for the last two weeks, and we were all ready to loosen up.

Then I heard the page. "Ben Walters, please report to dispatch. Ben Walters report to dispatch."

This could mean only one thing. Fire.

I interrupted my academic discourse with our warehouse manager Avery, and stepped out of the supply building to hustle over to dispatch. I had only my left foot out the door when I saw the smoke column. Holy shit. There would be no happy hour for me in Dubois today.

Blacktail is the name of the southwest corner of Ririe Reservoir, with its associated boat docks and picnic facilities. In a decent water year, enough fun is stored in the wide canyon that hundreds of boats can get out and have some of the world's finest recreation on water skis or wake-boards or inflatable doughnuts and cigars. I've had my fair share of fun there – I remember getting up on water skis for the first time at the reservoir. I remember getting up on water skis while holding a full beer for the first time there. I first saw Alexis in a bikini there, and rivers of lust had coursed through me. My friendships with summertime and nature and good times with my favorite people still live within my mind in high definition because of Ririe Reservoir, or more specifically, Blacktail. And I'm certainly not the only one who loves Blacktail. On any given summer day, and especially on a day with weather this perfect, there was sure to be hundreds of people frolicking there.

A fire at the Blacktail Recreation Area could be absolutely chaotic and disastrous. Although I had been there many times, I had never thought about a *fire* there before. There is only one way in and one way out of the area, and it's a long, steep switchback road. The road ends in a parking lot that is always jammed with trucks and boats. There is a two- or three-acre picnic area that might be used as a safety zone, but it would be a sketchy proposition.

Surrounding the whole area were steep grass- and sagebrush-covered sidehills that would accelerate any flames from ground zero to thousands of acres of ripe wheatfields on the flats bordering the eastern edge of Idaho Falls itself. Depending on the day, the winds created by the proximity of the lake itself could fan flames into a whirlwind of insanity. On top of all that, you could bet that most folks hanging out there would be perched somewhere along an advanced stage of intoxication by that time in the afternoon; mouthy or belligerent or giddy or just plain stupid.

The BLM office is a block away from the straight-shot road that leads to Blacktail. As I turned right onto this road and headed east, I came to the chilling realization that there had been no other engine crews in the yard, that there were no engine crews in town at all; in fact, all the other engines were either out on other fires or at stations at least 30 minutes away. In short, I was undoubtedly going to be the incident commander on this fire. This was my kickoff at the hometown football game. I was going to be one of the deep men. Kelly Hayes and I, in Engine 312, were headed directly into another shitstorm. An ice ball began to build in my stomach, growing bigger as we raced to the top of the east bench above town and across the flats to Blacktail Canyon. This was the wildland/urban interface fire of my daydreams and nightmares. A fire this close to town would command a very critical public audience, not to mention everyone in the office gathered around the radios in dispatch as I provided the play-by-play.

At the cusp of the canyon I had a first look at my adversary. The flame front was about a quarter-mile wide, burning through the sagebrush and grass. The flames were 10 to 15 feet high in most spots, and would likely reach my position in 30 minutes or so. In the bottom of the canyon people were scurrying around everywhere. From where I stood, they looked like pissed-off ants after you kick the ant pile. No doubt they were panicking, and panicking badly. I stopped at a pullout before the switchbacks began and turned down the cranked FM radio. It was an appropriate fire-me-up song, but it was time for me to move from gung-ho crazy fire-killer to the more cerebral field-general type. I took a deep breath and swallowed hard through a very dry mouth.

"Dispatch, Engine 312." I hoped my voice didn't betray the powerful undertow of panic.

"Engine 312, Dispatch, go ahead." It was dispatcher Dana Bradshaw, calm and sexy and reassuring.

"Okay, we've arrived on-scene at the incident. We're going to call this the Blacktail Fire. I'm going to park Engine 312 at the top of the canyon here, and have Kelly stay with it. I'm going to need the sheriff's department up here immediately to do crowd control. Have them meet up with Kelly at the engine and she'll relay instructions to them from me. In the meantime, I have to hike over a little ways and I'll be able to give you a full size-up then." I was thinking, *Oh God, please don't let me hyperventilate.*

"Copy."

"Engine 312 clear."

When or how I learned it, or whether I just knew it by now, I applied a guiding principle of one of life's hierarchies that day. That is, it's easier to call the shots from up above. Easier to see that forest, that big picture. If I went down that canyon to the boat docks, I would be swarmed by terrified people, hounded that I wasn't spraying water immediately on the fire, and just setting myself (and Kelly) up for failure in more ways than one. Therefore, I decided I would hoof it across the flats over to a good vantage point and call the game from there.

"Kelly, you stay here and flag down anybody trying to go down there and turn 'em around. When the sheriff's deputies get here, tell them to go down to the boat docks and KEEP EVERYONE THERE! I'm going to go a half-mile over to that rim, and I'll be able to talk to you on Tac-4. If for some reason I can't get you on the radio and the fire starts heading this way, just turn the engine around and get the hell out of here back toward Idaho Falls. But I'm pretty sure we'll be okay for a while."

She looked at me with big eyes, now with concern in them, so I reassured her.

"Hey, it's going to be fine, just do what I told you and chill out for a little bit. I'll be back when all the resources and shit start showing up and they start knocking this thing down."

Then I grabbed a warm bottle of water, my handheld radio, and an extra clamshell of AA batteries for it. In the distance I could hear the faint sound of sirens, most likely the sheriff's deputies headed this way.

I wanted them up here for three reasons. First, they could handle any unruly drunks who could get themselves hurt in a situation like this. Second, they could keep people out of the way of the firefighting resources that would soon be here. Third, and most immediately important, I needed them to make sure everyone stayed down at the boat docks. The parking area down there was a relatively safe place. If vehicle after vehicle started coming up the switchback road, there would be a traffic jam, and the fire was headed toward the switchbacks.

Also, technically and legally, firefighters don't do crowd control or evacuate people – even federal firefighters. That legal responsibility falls to the county sheriff.

I jumped across a washout next to where we were parked. When I landed, I heard a sickening crack and felt sharp pain. For about the twentieth time in the past year, I had sprained my ankle, and I sprained it badly. And I had the added pleasure of landing with my right hand in a patch of stinging nettle. Dammit!

Struggling back upright, I climbed the opposite slope and began a max fast limp across the grassy flats. The pain from my ankle was horrendous and the nettle burned the palm of my hand, but the constant surges of adrenaline mostly beat back those annoyances. The field where I walked was agricultural ground, and with each footstep I sank in a few inches. My exertion quickly overmatched my respiratory capacity, and I had to take a breather. The column of smoke kept getting bigger and thicker and blacker. Down below in the canyon, I could hear truck engines revving and more horn honking than I cared for. I knew I'd better push on.

When I had made it about halfway to where I wanted to be, I could see the flames again, and decided to stop and call the size-up to dispatch. Walking to my desired destination was just going to take too long. I wished I'd taken a few more minutes to let my breathing slow down to normal, but the drive and the nerves and the tension I was feeling just wouldn't let me do it.

"Dispatch, Walters," I panted into the mike.

"This is dispatch, go ahead Ben."

"Okay, I have a size-up for the Blacktail Fire when you're ready to copy." My voice had that timbre of nerves that you hear in someone who is not accustomed to giving public speeches but is forced to do so.

"Fire name is Blacktail Fire. Currently, the fire is about 20 acres in size. It's burning in sagebrush, tall grass, and quaking aspen. Fire behavior is running, with flame lengths 10 to 15 feet. Burning on about a 45-degree slope, on an east aspect. Numerous structures, vehicles, and people threatened. Weather is clear, with temperature 94 degrees and winds out of the east/northeast about ten miles per hour. Resources on scene, Engine 312 and two patrol rigs from Bonneville County Sheriff's Department. Here's a list of resources I'm going to need for this fire."

Though I was not conscious of it at the time, I believe that it was in this moment that I realized one of the true tenets of learning. I believe that you have truly learned something when you have gathered enough information from your varied life experiences, processed that information, and turned it around to application, only this time with your stamp on it. True learning can't be just regurgitation of facts, nor can it be completely free-spirit, involving no past experience. I believe that to call it your own, you must apply your knowledge in your own way, but not without incorporating the experience of others.

I planned on throwing everything I could at this fire in terms of suppression resources. Too many times I had witnessed incident commanders screw around ordering this or that crew, or this or that piece of equipment – taking too long, being indecisive. I absolutely despise indecision and lack of vision. The end result is a fire that grows so big that the only thing that stopped it was Mother Nature. *This* was when fires really got expensive. I didn't intend to let this fire do that. I was going to spend the money now, and actually save money in the end. I was going to order up the world to come here as cavalry and kick some serious ass. I was in the public eye, failure was not an option, and this was *my* time to prove myself.

"I'm going to need a heavy airtanker, medium helicopter with at least a 200-gallon bucket, and air attack. For ground equipment I'm going to need a dozer, a water tender, and five engines. For crews, I'm going to need one Type I crew and a Type II hand crew."

"Okay copy." They read the list back to me.

It was easy to type that list of resources, easy to recall the dry facts of what I relayed to our dispatch in spoken English. But it was *not* easy doing it that day. For one, the mixture of nerves and exhaustion thoroughly pervaded my being. And to my chagrin, I realized that somehow in the last 15 or so minutes I had swallowed all the warm water in my bottle, and it was too far now to return to the engine for more. I was having a hard time talking on the radio anyway, but now my tongue would probably swell up as big as a cow's tongue, and the rest of my mouth would feel like I had washed down cotton balls with sand. Lastly, to have ordered the amount and type of resources required to stomp this thing was going to be expensive. Not a few thousand dollars, but easily in excess of a hundred thousand dollars. That would be for this day alone, not figuring the cost if this bastard hit the flats or jumped the canyon. Fire managers are okay with this, as long as you can justify the need. But if not, you are looking at disciplinary action. For an urban-interface situation, I felt I was justified. Now I would need to figure out what to do with all that firefighting firepower. This was the fun part, and this was where I felt confident in my abilities.

I began to settle in, surveying the scene developing below me. The fire itself looked to be straightforward at the moment, but was going to require some work. A flame front about a quarter- mile long did a strange dancehall jig up the hill toward me as I walked along the canyon rim. The first resource to check in was Tanker 00, Ivan from Pocatello Airport, arriving on station over the fire. He was flying one of Aero Union's P3 Orions, and I felt better instantly.

I needed the airpower primarily right then to slow the advance of the flames. I wanted him to open all doors and drop his load of retardant a few yards uphill from the leading edge of the flames and then continue across the sidehill until he hit the switchback road. This would require him to return to the Pocatello tanker base for some reloads, but I figured with an approximate turn-around time of 30 minutes, it would work. The dilemma was my difficulty in explaining to him where I needed him to drop. Our perspectives on the topography were obviously different, and I had never done this before.

"Tanker 00, this is Walters."

"Ahhhh, Walters, Tanker 00." Voice gravelly with feedback, engine noise, and the soothing white noise of tanker pilot coolness.

"I'm going to need you to string this first load on the southern edge and work across the slope to the north. Fuels are heavy, so probably all doors. I'm going to hike down toward where I need it and I'll give you a mirror flash."

In the meantime, I realized I had no actual signal mirror, but I had learned in fire school at some time or other that the lid of a Copenhagen can works well for this, and wouldn't you know it, I had one of those on me. I began the drop in descent and Tanker 00 did the same as he circled to the north over the lake. When I was about 20 feet above the flames – it's never good to be above the fire, but I could contour across the hill to a rocky safety zone if I needed to – I pulled out the Copenhagen can, found the sun's reflection, pointed at my arm, then pointed it at the circling airtanker as I had been taught.

"Okay, Walters, we've got your reflection, we'll make a dry run here and confirm that's where we want it."

A few minutes later the nose and wings of the huge airplane was all I could see as he flew a dry run past my location. Then he circled back north again.

"Walters, Tanker 00, how does that look?" Ivan asked.

"That looks good." I replied.

"Okay we're coming hot."

A few minutes later the nose and wings of the huge airplane was all I could see again, only now it was for real. Strangely, the big plane seemed rather quiet as it soared into the canyon below the rim and only 100 feet above the ground. Then the engines came to life and they're popping and growling and blue smoke and the wings of the big craft see-sawed in the canyon's updrafts. I began to wonder if I was going to die now. Ivan was headed RIGHT AT ME!

Without notice, the modified bomb bay doors opened and out came a cloud of over 2,000 gallons of retardant. The drop was perfect, laid out in a line just ahead of the flames at a perfect width.

Being right in the middle of the drop, I got covered in slurry, which can be dangerous – though a retardant hit can roll an engine, all it did was knock me back a step or two. Then Ivan gunned the engines and climbed out of the canyon and banked back south toward Pocatello.

"Walters, Tanker 00, how'd we do?" he inquired.

"Perfect, just keep stringing it along until you get to that switchback road."

"Copy, see you in thirty or so."

Minutes later the first of my ground cavalry showed up. Excited and ready to rock, they had stopped, as I had instructed earlier, where Kelly was parked with 312. Limping my way on adrenaline alone, I reached the rim of the canyon again and waved the strike team of engines over to my location, where they would stage until the dozer arrived and the airtanker finished his drops. Brad Nash was with Engine 351 from the Pocatello Station 5.

"Brad," I said when he got there, "if you want to take over this fire and I'll go back and grab 312, that's fine with me."

"No way dude, you're doing awesome, just relax and do what you need to do."

"Okay, I'll do it, but do you guys have a bottle of water I could borrow?"

"Well, you can't borrow one, but you can have one."

That bottle of cold water, which had come from a recently iced-down cooler, was one of the best I had ever tasted.

"Can I have one more?" I asked.

Tanker 00, along with his lead plane and air attack and Helicopter 99Romeo and the dozer now were all here; I called the dance from my high point on the canyon rim. Behind me, on the blacktop road, the traffic was snarled as people had driven up from town for a ringside seat. Far below, in the lake, I saw that at least thirty boats were out in the water to claim their 50-yard-line seats. I stood in a patch of rocks and realized that we were kicking ass. I calmed down some.

For the rest of what seemed like my fastest day or my longest dream, I made tactical decisions, filled out paperwork, completed logistical duties, and talked constantly on the radio. I had never felt more in the zone. Ivan had stopped the flames long enough to get the dozer cutting line across the slope. The dozer line had stopped the flames long enough for the engines to get themselves in place for the knockout punches, the hotshot crew cut handline from the bottom of the canyon to the top on the south side of the fire, and the Type II hand crew worked with the helicopter to cool off the hotspots in the trees down near the lake. It all seemed to be going as planned. I called the fire contained at roughly 200 acres at about 10 p.m.

That night we made our fire camp in the now-deserted picnic area near the boat docks. Someone from the office had brought up a hearty supper from Kentucky Fried Chicken, and now the hundred or so firefighters under my command sat under the summer stars and munched chicken legs, buttered biscuits, and coleslaw. I made my way from crew to crew, made sure all was well with everyone, and signed time sheets. I felt I had finally arrived, and I finally breathed normally. I realized I was so tired I had hit the wall, just dead on my feet. The excitement of the Wagonbox Fire and the Blacktail Fire had caught up with me, and I found myself drifting off as I sat on one of the picnic tables. The last things I remember from that night were waves from the lake lapping gently onto the shore and the smell of a fire. My fire. My moment. This may have been my finest moment. I had faced my urban-interface incident command fear – and I had conquered it.

Tuesday, July 13, 1999, 4:00 p.m. – Once again, we have returned to the BLM yard in our even muddier and dustier engine. Though I am tired, I now walk with a new confidence. I have a new spring in my step. I relate the story of the Blacktail Fire to anyone who'll listen, and I thank everyone for their help. I fill out paperwork and help Kelly clean and re-stock the engine. We'll drive back to Dubois soon, back to my favorite stompin' grounds, and I'll go to the bar and enjoy a well-deserved happy hour. Then I'll drink too much, burn down, and try to rise from the ashes tomorrow. Then I'll probably just do it all over again.

In high school I played in one football game that stood out above all the others. Much was expected of me that night, and somehow I delivered. It was hard-fought, but I played my best game ever. That same night (or actually in the early morning hours the next day) I woke up in my linebacker's stance at the foot of my bed, scanning a dream field from left to right, looking for the ball carrier. I was covered in sweat and shivering. When I got hold of myself, realized what was actually happening, I just smiled and crawled back into bed.

In the early morning hours, during my first sleep in a bed in a week, and the first sleep after I had called the Blacktail Fire controlled, I found myself dreaming that the phone was ringing. It was dispatch calling me up at Station 1 to tell me the Blacktail Fire had started up again, outside of the containment lines. I needed to get there immediately, they said. I hung up the phone and scratched my head, trying to decide whether this was a dream or the real thing. It was a lot like the dream about the football game. I was even sweating and shivering. I sat down on the old couch in my underwear to figure it out.

Epilogue

I AM WHO I AM BECAUSE OF THE FIRE CREW. Of course I've had many other influences in life, but none that carried the weight of this particular institution. One of my first mentors and fire heroes told me about the fire season he skipped to go try a more "normal" job. He was okay with it, he said, until he started smelling the forest fire smoke. Then he was not okay anymore, and I don't think he's ever had a different job since going back into the wildland fire business. I felt the same way after I was absent from it about two or three seasons. By then, though, it seemed too late, and I felt too old to go back.

I left the Idaho Falls BLM after I was laid off in December of 1999. I did continue on in fire, but in a more "permanent" setting at the Salt Lake Field Office as an Engine Module Leader. I tried to be more serious at this district; I was always serious on fires when safety mattered, but I love to have fun, so again, I cultivated a class clown image that I never was able to shed. Someday I'll write about some crazy stuff I witnessed, and some bad and good decisions I made there, perhaps in a book called *Tales of Successful Failure*.

After two seasons in Salt Lake, I'd just had enough of missing out on other summer activities, so I completely switched careers and went into secondary education – just because I would get the summers off. But if you use "summers off" as a reason to become a teacher, you won't be satisfied with that career. I did that only long enough to know I do not have the patience to join the ranks of these everyday heroes. I hope to write some stories about those days, too, in another future book.

After my stint as a teacher I went back to fire for one more summer as a fill-in Engine Module Leader with the Salt Lake BLM, but I was out of shape and the heat and the power hiking kicked my ass. Eventually I had to be done ... but damn, I miss it! There will always be an ache there, a longing, and it'll always be the worst in late July and August, when a smoky haze fills the valley and the heat is oppressive and I want to be out there in a long-sleeve yellow shirt sweating with my brothers and sisters. There is just something about fire that gets in your blood.

Acknowledgments

There are people I really need to thank for this project. For the story, I have to surely express my gratitude to the BLM districts at which I worked. For being true friends and for motivating me to do this, I will always be indebted to the Hoffer brothers, Ryan and Kelly. For believing in me and for being patient with me, thanks to my bosses at the BLM, my wonderful family, and my editor, Kelly Andersson. For the book, I must thank family friends Leon Rose and Jeanne Lowney, for taking a first look at early drafts of this and reining me in on my excessive use of four-letter words – though I still had to sneak a few in. To John Maclean I express my gratitude for taking an interest in this story and for putting me in touch with Kelly, who walked me through this entire thing. These two are good people. And to all of you who had a look at the drafts and gave me support, you're awesome.

BEN WALTERS is a reformed party animal, former wildland firefighter, and former schoolteacher who lives in Idaho Falls, Idaho with his awesome and loving wife and children. After bunches of years, bunches of jobs, tons of good times, and a couple of college degrees, he realized it was time to settle down and start putting some of these experiences to paper before the words of his youth slipped away. Look for more of his stories in the future about hunting, fishing, horses, and other things in life important to him. And know that when the August sky is hazy from the fires, he is dreaming about those good old days.